Economic Growth in the Asia Pacific Region

Economic Growth in the Asia Pacific Region

JAMES H. GAPINSKI

St. Martin's Press
New York

338.95
G21e

ISBN 0-312-21619-X

Library of Congress Cataloging-in-Publication Data

Gapinski, James H.
    Economic growth in the Asia Pacific region / by James H. Gapinski.
        p.   cm.
    Includes bibliographical references and index.
    ISBN 0-312-21619-X (cloth)
    1. Asia—Economic conditions.   2. Pacific Area—Economic
conditions.   3. Asia—Economic policy.   4. Pacific Area—Economic
policy.   5. Labor productivity—Asia.   6. Labor productivity—
Pacific Area.   I. Title.
HC412.G34   1999
338.95—dc21   99-20612
                                                                      CIP

Design by Letra Libre, Inc.

First edition: September, 1999
10 9 8 7 6 5 4 3 2 1

To Gerri

My favorite award-winning,
published, professional artist

CONTENTS

TABLES AND FIGURES

TABLES

FIGURES

PREFACE

THIS VOLUME REPRESENTS A NATURAL COMPILATION and extension of my earlier work. It is a compilation because it brings together, ostensibly in an organized manner, material that has been previously communicated through the printed or spoken word. It is an extension because it broadens and deepens that material.

My research interest in the Asia Pacific Region began to take shape sometime before the summer of 1995, but in July and August of that year it became galvanized. Steering activity during that period was a visiting professorship awarded by Curtin University of Technology in Perth, Western Australia. That Perth post enabled me to participate in teaching a course in honors macroeconomics and to interact with faculty members of the School of Economics and Finance. Several of those scholars were actively studying Asia Pacific issues, and contact with them heightened my interest in the Region.

Another boost in interest came during February and March of 1997, when, by virtue of a sabbatical leave from Florida State University, I returned to Curtin for concentrated work on Asia Pacific growth. Insulated from distractions and given the chance to focus on a single subject, the mind began to comprehend growth with surprising clarity. Numerous regressions were run, growth shares were calculated, and economic patterns were tracked at an intense pace through most of that stay. The one major interruption of the visit was itself a learning experience. It took the form of a visit to Andalas University in Padang, situated in West Sumatra of Indonesia. Though short, the trip proved to be highly informative, as it involved interactions with students, faculty, administrators, and civil servants. An unmistakable sense of Indonesia was gained from those sessions and from a partly mandatory stopover in Bali, the advertised vacation paradise of Indonesia.

In June of 1997 a conference on efficiency and productivity growth was hosted by the Institute of Economics of Academia Sinica. Held in Taipei, Taiwan, it introduced me to even more scholars pursuing the same research themes. It also afforded the opportunity to spend a few days in Hong Kong just moments before reversion to China. That experience was a heady one. Festivity was everywhere. Nathan Road was covered with lights and dragons as people sold souvenirs. On the opposite side of Victoria Harbour, Lan Kwai Fong flashed its countdown clock. The bars vibrated with merriment. By contrast, the Governor's Residence, a few short yards from Lan Kwai Fong, remained stoically silent. Only a handful of passersby, myself included, stopped to take pictures. Perhaps the highlight of the Hong Kong expedition was a self-guided tour which started from Victoria Peak on Hong Kong Island, ferried across the Harbour, and then walked up Nathan Road on Kowloon to a point several blocks north of Boundary Street but well into the New Territories. By that tour (or maybe pilgrimage) I was able to retrace in hours the steps taken by history over a span of more than a half century. And in only a few days, history would accelerate backward with the changing of flags.

In September 1997 I went to Kuala Lumpur to participate in a fall meeting of Project LINK, a forecasting group composed of macro modelers from roughly 80 countries. The date of the meeting was especially appropriate because it brought together globally oriented economists at precisely the time when a global issue filled the air. The issue, of course, was the Asian currency crisis, and it claimed a fair amount of the discussion. Also filling the air was the heavy smoke pollution from runaway fires in Indonesia. That smoke likewise draped Singapore, whose proximity to Kuala Lumpur prompted a day trip to the City of the Lion. Without doubt, though, that city-state is the House of Raffles.

The travels to Perth in 1995 and 1997 fueled interest in Asia Pacific growth, and the corollary journeys to Taipei, Hong Kong, Kuala Lumpur, and Singapore sharpened thinking. A third stop at Perth provided the means to try something that was new yet related to the ongoing research program. Through the Institute for Research into International Competitiveness (IRIC), Curtin University awarded me a visiting professorship covering the months of July and August of 1998. The new project was the development of an index of international competitiveness, nicknamed ICOM. From the very outset ICOM revolved around the Asia Pacific Region, and its structure allowed it to track consequences of the Asian currency crisis. That analysis finds its way into Chapter 8.

Books often follow a paper trail, and this one is no exception. A piece in the *Journal of Macroeconomics* started things off. Then came articles prepared for the *Southern Economic Journal,* the collection *Economic Efficiency and Productivity Growth in the Asia Pacific Region,* the *Asia Pacific Journal of Economics and Business,* and *APJEB* again. Each effort played a part in the story, but the most influential for the purpose at hand was the *SEJ* paper and the first *APJEB* contribution. As regards the former I recall notions generated while walking along the beach of St. George Island in the Gulf of Mexico. Similarly, for the latter I imagine reflecting on progress while walking along Scarborough Beach at the Indian Ocean. In a sense, then, this volume's origin runs from sea to sea. It runs even further if presentations and seminars are added to the research mix.

From this historical and geographical record, it should be clear that the volume never would have come into being without the support of many. At Florida State University (FSU), William Laird, serving as chair of the Department of Economics, provided encouragement and resources, financial and otherwise. James Cobbe, his successor, continued the flow of department generosity. At Curtin University, Geoffrey Crockett, who heads the School of Economics and Finance, graciously opened the office door to me. Geoff and Elizabeth, his wife, even went so far as to open the doors of their city home and beach cottage to this American and his family, allowing us to reside at their lodgings while they prepared for and then set out on a sabbatical leave. Like Geoff, Ian Kerr and Harry Bloch of Curtin channeled resources and ideas my way. Another Curtin ally was Peter Kenyon, who kept busy directing IRIC and who offered persuasive rhetoric culminating in the 1998 professorship. Leading three lives as an FSU graduate student, a Curtin faculty member, and a true mate, David Western functioned as a catalyst, triggering action and reaction. It is fair to say that I never would have set foot in Australia without David's persistence 13,000 miles away from Tallahassee. David taught me much. Moreover, he convinced me that it is impossible for an Australian to develop an ulcer. "No worries, mate" is more than an expression.

Without the painstaking efforts by Syafruddin Karimi and Indrawari Dwinanda of Andalas University, the Indonesian connection would not have happened. Likewise, the Taiwan trek, which continued on to Hong Kong, would not have occurred without the tenacity of Cliff Huang, jointly affiliated with Vanderbilt University and Academia Sinica, Tsu-tan Fu of Academia Sinica, and Knox Lovell of the University of Georgia. The Kuala Lumpur and Singapore trips were made possible only by the good graces of Peter Pauly and Erin Foster of LINK. Andrea Mervar, the Croatian representative to LINK, also had a hand in those arrangements. Almost by definition, then, that venture had to work out well.

Building a book and having it transformed into print takes more than thought, an outline, and handscript. It takes word processing, artwork composition, and finally publication. In her usual diligent and efficient style, Karen Wells deciphered my hieroglyphics and transformed them into neat typescript. Peter Krafft earned extra stripes by straightening out my squiggles and converting them into figures with eye appeal. Both Karen and Peter hail from FSU. Representing St. Martin's Press on the publication side of the book was Karen Wolny, the considerate editor whose phone call soon after proposal submission brought a smile to my face and a pen to my hand. Amy Reading energetically served as liaison, and Ruth Mannes carefully supervised production activity.

In the end the family matters most, and thus in the end the family deserves the greatest thanks. Susan made the 1995 Australian adventure enormous fun, and to this day I vividly recall our walk down the lighthouse road in Guilderton by the Crocketts' beach house. Melissa always fills the room and the heart. And Geraldine, whom I met during a bleak winter so many years ago, has made life anything but bleak. She has made it meaningful. To her I dedicate this effort.

PART I

ORIENTATION

CHAPTER 1

CONDITIONS AND PURPOSE

At least I have got a grip of the essential facts of the case. I shall enumerate them to you, for nothing clears up a case so much as stating it to another person, and I can hardly expect your co-operation if I do not show you the position from which we start.

Sherlock Holmes
—A. Conan Doyle, *The Adventure of the Silver Blaze*

IT HAD BEEN A VERY LONG DAY—one of those days when everything seemed to go wrong. The tire went flat, the disk froze, the application failed. Mentally spent and physically drained, the professor left Musgrave Hall and headed to Carfax Center for the usual swim. That workout always invigorated mind and body, and today there was a desperate need for such relief.

Dodging a sudden rainstorm, Professor Terry burst into Carfax and navigated through the crowd to the locker room. To Locker 381 Terry rushed and spun the dial: 34–24–38. Soon the body would be swimming past fatigue, rejuvenating spirit and limb. Then, tossing the new swimsuit on the bench in front of 381, Terry read the words on the label: Made in Hong Kong. Other thoughts sprang to mind: Made in Taiwan, Made in Indonesia, Made in China. Countries in the Asia Pacific Region have grown phenomenally. On that point the professor paused, reflected, and wondered why. Then the doors to the pool flew open.

1.1 THE ASIA PACIFIC REGION

In one way the Asia Pacific Region imagined by Professor Terry could be viewed as a vast expanse defined by the 18 members of the Asia Pacific Economic Cooperation (APEC). More narrowly, though, it can be defined as covering the area lying mainly to the west of the International Date Line and bounded in the south by Australia and New Zealand, in the west by coastal countries of Asia, and in the north by Japan. Under that conception the Region encompasses the four East Asian Tigers of Hong Kong, South Korea, Singapore, and Taiwan; the three Southeast Asian Lions of Indonesia, Malaysia, and Thailand; and the two South Asian Gaurs of Papua New Guinea and the Philippines. These nine nations might be understood as maturing economies. The mature nations in the Region are all members of the Organization for Economic Cooperation and Development (OECD). They are the OECD Elephants, three of which already have been identified: Australia, New Zealand, and Japan. The fourth Elephant, which lies to the east of the Date Line, is the United States. Including the United States in the Region disturbs a reasonably neat rectangular configuration. Nonetheless, U.S. representation coincides with the composition of APEC, and it provides a natural standard for comparison.[1]

The Asia Pacific Region therefore can be seen as 13 nations. Conveniently, it encompasses the Association of South East Asian Nations (ASEAN) as classified by K. C. Ho (1995, pp. 114–15): Indonesia, Malaysia, the Philippines, Thailand, and Singapore. Necessarily it includes the ASEAN 4; namely, ASEAN without Singapore. Likewise, it covers the Pacific Rim states; that is, Hong Kong, Korea, Singapore, Taiwan, Malaysia, and Japan.[2] Of course, excluding China from consideration could be construed as an oversight, especially since that nation falls well within the rectangle. Hence, to the extent that data permit, it too is represented in the Region, bringing to 14 the number of nations being counted. Consonant with the metaphor, China may be called the Panda. A maturing entity, it is charted in Figure 1.1, which maps the Region except for New Zealand and the United States.

Images of the region are vivid, varied, and lasting. Albeit necessarily selective because experiences are necessarily selective, they help to add color and feeling to the inquiry.

Among the most stunning images is the first sight of Hong Kong as the aircraft flies over Victoria Harbour with Kowloon to port and Hong Kong Island to starboard. Almost without warning, an untold number of skyscrapers erupt out of the water to create a City in the Vertical split into two sections by the Harbour, which itself is dotted with an untold number of vessels of all shapes and sizes: liners, transports, and even bulldozer boats for removing debris. Activity is everywhere.

That first impression is reinforced by the perception from ground level. Nathan Road is packed with tourists, shoppers, and business folks, and the walk south toward the hectic Harbour ends in a panorama of buildings streaking upward. Vertical is truly the orientation of this metropolis just as it is for New York City. At the same time, a look across the Harbour to the Island broadly and to the Extension specifically invites recollections of Sydney, with its Darling Harbour and its Opera House. Fittingly, the Extension, the site where this Tiger formally returned to the Land of the Panda, has been referred to as the Opera House with the air let out.[3] Much less operatic is Lan Kwai Fong. That center of the social scene lies at the foot of Victoria Peak and in the neighborhood of what had been the Governor's Residence under British reign. It comes to life when the sun sets and vibrates until dawn in the fashion of the French Quarter. Hong Kong, then, can be regarded as New York, Sydney, and New Orleans rolled up and recast in miniature.

Singapore is the southern sister of Hong Kong. It has many of the same characteristics: an island configuration, intense activity, frenzied crowds, and a sense of the vertical. It too has picturesque stretches such as the banks of the Singapore River around Bridge Road. Indeed, the north bank has much to offer. One prominent landmark is the monument identifying the spot where Thomas

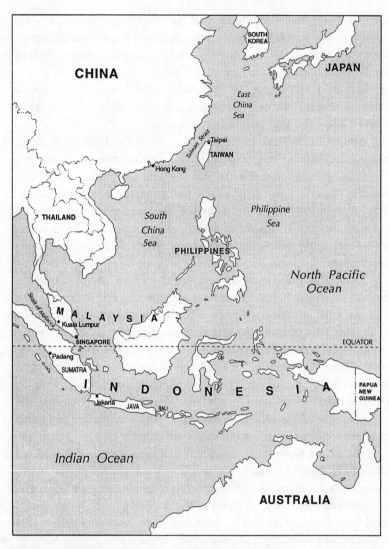

Figure 1.1 A Map of the Asia Pacific Region Excluding New Zealand and the United States

Stamford Raffles landed so many years ago to establish the settlement that grew into the present giant. Nearby can be found Parliament House, the Victoria Theatre, and a grassy expanse called Esplanade Park. The south bank constitutes eatery row with restaurant upon restaurant serving menus for every taste. Yet, like a sister, Singapore differs from Hong Kong. It is more controlled—at least it had been—and Marina Bay lacks the dazzle of Victoria Harbour. Moreover, Raffles is everywhere: from the Raffles Hotel, set in colonial tradition but upgraded to five-star proportions, to Raffles City, an architectural wonder of the shopping world, to Raffles Place, a shopping and financial complex in the middle of downtown. In addition, there is Raffles Avenue. It runs into Raffles Boulevard through, of course, Raffles Link.

If Singapore is Raffles, then Taiwan is Chiang Kai-shek. Against the backdrop of war on the mainland, the People's Republic of China was created in October of 1949, and soon thereafter the Kuomintang government fled to Taiwan. On that island in March of 1950, Chiang Kai-shek became President of the Republic of China (Hsiao and Hsiao, 1996, pp. 224, 226), earning for himself recognition as founding father in much the same way that Raffles did in Singapore. As tribute, the Taipei airport was named after him, and a grand monument in his likeness was created off Jenai Road in the heart of the city. There the president is seated overlooking a huge paved mall with the National Theater housed on the left and the Concert Hall located on the right. The similarity between this memorial and that for Lincoln in Washington, D.C., is rather striking.

Nearby stands the National Museum with its ivory carvings of an intricacy that strains belief. Also nearby are places of worship such as Lung Shan Temple and an edifice of an entirely different sort: the Presidential Office Building. The streets in this central district are jammed with motorbikes, and citizens cover the walkways, which during rainy moments spring into swift rivers of color-splashed umbrellas. Chunghsiao Road, with its access to the train station, extends east from the central district and at Fuhsing Road ushers in an assortment of shops and restaurants that sparkle at night. In Taipei, night has a bright side. But it has a darker side, too, just as the electric Hong Kong has Portland Street with its charred vacant buildings and its characters of dubious intent. Store-front housing, a car parked in a living room, and garbage trucks that summon residents by playing ice-cream tunes are a few of the images of the lesser side of Taipei.

Indonesia tells a similar story from island to island. This archipelago of 13,500 islands at the equator has Jakarta as the capital city. Jakarta itself is situated on Java, positioned roughly at the middle of the chain. To the east of Java is the resort isle of Bali, whose elegant hotels offer relaxation in a tropical paradise from Sanur Beach to Kuta Beach and beyond. Still, for visitors experienced in sea and shore, the Bali scene may be a bit disappointing. The coastline is hardly pristine, and the sidewalks are clogged with vendors insistent on making sales.

West of Java rests Sumatra. On the western edge of that land mass sits the intriguing city of Padang, hardly touristy but at the same time hardly lacking hotel elegance. Adventure in that part of paradise can be discovered behind the wheel as the rules of the road are quite informal. Cars stop at red lights—sometimes. And although vehicles drive British-style on the left, they travel left sometimes. The only firm rule seems to be: "Do what you want—just don't hit anything." Bicycles share the street. Some are rigged with sidecars for transporting light materials that have been carefully crated. They pedal past road repair undertaken with pickaxes and other hand tools rather than with heavy equipment. Similarly, a worker tidying up at day's end uses a broom fashioned from palm branches rather than a mechanical device built from metal. Hotels seem to have two waiters for every guest and three porters for anyone with luggage. Youngsters sit in the airport terminal and sell magazines from their laps; vending machines do not enter the picture. Simply put, activity is labor intensive, but in that respect Padang is representative, not exceptional.

To the immediate north of Indonesia stretches another country split by the sea: Malaysia. Kuala Lumpur, its capital city, has much in common with Hong Kong, Singapore, and Taipei. It is a hub of activity enjoying—or at least experiencing—feverish construction. It also has much in common with the West. Its twin towers might be regarded as the Southeast Asian version of the structures in Chicago and New York. Its Menara, projecting thinly upward, might be likened to the Space Needle in Seattle or the Tower in Sydney. And along Jalan Sultan Ismail, a major thoroughfare, can be found a Hard Rock Cafe playing American pop music and "road runners," a local euphemism, seeking the briefest of dates.

Further south in Kuala Lumpur stands Chinatown, which involves a collection of street markets and restaurants with outdoor seating that spills into the roadway only an arm's length away from vehicular traffic. Kuala Lumpur, though, is also Independence Square, where thousands gather to celebrate Malaysian independence from Britain. It is the National Monument, dedicated to peace among the ASEAN countries. It is the 272 steps of the Batu Caves, and it is the Royal Selangor enterprise, where young workers sit row upon row patiently crafting pewter objects using only basic tools. The labor-intensiveness of Padang can be found in Kuala Lumpur.

Traveling from the maturing countries in the Region to the mature nations can be accomplished in a matter of hours. Hence, in terms of time, the two assemblages are fairly close. In terms of some other characteristics, however, the two are very far apart. One of those wide gulfs concerns pollution. Pollution levels tend to be high in the maturing areas. Reporting on Thailand, Kulick and Wilson (1992, pp. 121–22) note for Bangkok that

> ... lead has been found in umbilical cords of newborn babies. Levels of carbon monoxide, sulphur dioxide and nitrogen monoxide are dangerous. Taxi drivers, street vendors and policemen are at high risk from the dust and toxic gases that periodically droop in thick white clouds over central Bangkok.
>
> The rivers are in a disastrous state. At the mouth of Bangkok's Chao Phraya River the mercury contamination in the sea water is between 7 and 40 times the accepted level, and accumulated heavy metal in fish and shellfish is 10 to 20 times above safety standards. ...
>
> Things are no better in the countryside, where farmers have for decades been applying too much chemical fertilizer and insecticide. Their malignant residue remains in canals, rivers and reservoirs, in fish and in the soil.

Kulick and Wilson hasten to add that such conditions are not peculiar to Thailand (p. 128). Evidence from other maturing communities supports that assertion. There exhausts from automobiles, buses, motorbikes, and other forms of transportation fill the air, creating a haze thick enough to obscure the moon and to cause cyclists and pedestrians to wear masks. The absence of clean water prompts car owners to wash their vehicles with sewer water collected from beneath the city sidewalks by means of a rope and pail. Furthermore, the lack of drinking water forces reliance on bottled water and gives new urgency to the traditional warning for tourists: "Don't drink the water." Of course, exceptions exist. Nonetheless, the rule has broad applicability and holds with enough authority that a traveler, on returning to Perth or Christchurch or Portland, may seek first a drink from a public water fountain. Taken for granted by many if not by most, that simple act would do more than quench. It would signify the arrival in another environment.

1.2 VITAL STATISTICS

Images of the Region give color and feeling to the discussion. Vital statistics give it some precision. That information is presented in Table 1.1.

From the table it is evident that the Region encompasses a variety of government types. For instance, Hong Kong, which until July of 1997 had been a dependent territory of the United Kingdom, now functions as a special administrative region, abbreviated SAR. Korea is a republic. Malaysia and Thailand represent constitutional monarchies whereas Papua New Guinea and New Zealand constitute parliamentary democracies. China stands as a communist state. The degree of liberty associated with those particular expressions of government is quantified in two ways: by a Civil Liberty Index that runs from 1.0 for the highest level of liberty to 7.0 for the lowest level, and by an Equality in Law Index that ranges from 0.0 for least equality under the law to 10.0 for most equality. Consonant with widespread belief, liberty and equality flourish in the mature countries as Australia, Japan, New Zealand, and the United States all

Table 1.1 Vital Statistics for the Asia Pacific Region

Reference	Hong Kong	Korea	Singapore	Taiwan	Indonesia	Malaysia	Thailand	Papua New Guinea	Philippines	China	Australia	Japan	New Zealand	United States
Type	Special Adm. Region	Republic	Republic in Cmnwth.	Multiparty Dem. Reg.	Republic	Const. Monarchy	Const. Monarchy	Parl. Dem.	Republic	Communist State	Fed. Parl. State	Const. Monarchy	Parl. Dem.	Federal Republic
Government														
Civil Liberty Index	2.0	5.0	5.0	4.9	5.3	4.0	4.0	2.0	4.5	na	1.0	1.0	1.0	1.0
Equality in Law Index	7.5	7.5	0.0	5.0	0.0	2.5	2.5	na	2.5	0.0	7.5	7.5	10.0	7.5
Population														
Number, mil	5.5	45.6	2.9	21.5	203.6	19.7	60.3	4.3	73.3	1,203.1	18.3	125.5	3.4	263.8
Area, thou sq km	1.0	98.5	0.6	36.0	1,919.4	329.8	514.0	461.7	300.0	9,597.0	7,686.9	377.8	268.7	9,372.6
Pop. Density, per/sq km	5,329.7	462.6	4,566.3	597.6	106.1	59.8	117.3	9.3	244.2	125.4	2.4	33.2	12.7	28.1
Literacy Rate, pct	77.00	96.00	89.00	86.00	82.00	78.00	93.00	52.00	94.00	78.00	100.00	99.00	99.00	97.00
Infant Mort. Rate, pct	0.58	2.09	0.57	0.56	6.50	2.47	3.57	6.16	4.96	5.21	0.71	0.43	0.86	0.79
Infrastructure														
Major Airports, no.	1	1	3	8	3	3	6	0	2	17	9	6	2	181
Railroads, thou km	0.035	6.8	0.039	4.6	7.0	1.8	3.9	0	0.8	65.8	40.5	27.3	4.7	240.0
Highways, thou km	1.1	63.2	2.9	20.0	119.5	29.0	77.7	19.2	160.7	1,029.0	837.9	1,112.0	92.6	6,243.2
RR Den., km/sq km	0.034	0.069	0.062	0.128	0.004	0.005	0.008	0	0.003	0.007	0.005	0.072	0.018	0.026
Hwy. Den., km/sq km	1.058	0.642	4.555	0.557	0.062	0.088	0.151	0.042	0.536	0.107	0.109	2.943	0.345	0.666
Auto Density, cars/km	231.5	42.7	104.8	149.7	10.9	68.9	9.5	0.9	2.8	1.7	9.2	33.3	16.2	22.9
Vehicle Den., veh/Km	353.6	66.5	149.2	187.2	23.4	82.7	33.9	2.4	8.1	5.8	11.5	53.9	19.5	30.1
Phone Queue, per/phn	1.8	3.4	2.6	2.8	266.8	19.8	81.5	61.4	83.9	60.2	2.1	2.0	1.6	2.1

Notes. Various measures represent the author's own calculations from data in the original sources. *na* means not available.

Sources. Most information derives from the U.S. Central Intelligence Agency (1995). The Civil Liberty Index comes from Barro and Wolf (1989), whereas the Equality in Law Index obtains from Gwartney and Lawson (1997). Vehicular data are given by the *World Almanac and Book of Facts, 1995* and by the United Nations (1996).

post 1.0 for the Liberty Index and high marks for the Equality Index. In fact, on the latter scale New Zealand scores a perfect 10.0. For the maturing areas vibrant freedoms ostensibly can be found in Papua New Guinea and Hong Kong, although it must be stressed that the Hong Kong statistics apply for the period when the British managed affairs. Elsewhere in the maturing community, control is noticeably firmer. To illustrate, Singapore, with respective scores of 5.0 and 0.0, tolerates little. Indonesia may be even stricter, and if media accounts are at all correct, China may be the least permissive society in the Region.

In the other direction, China is the most populous Asia Pacific nation—by far. Its population figure of 1.2 billion individuals is almost 5 times greater than the number for the United States, the second most populous land, and roughly 415 times greater than that for Singapore, the least populated. However, the statistics tell a much different tale when they are adjusted for country area to generate density measures. Now Hong Kong leads the way with 5,329.7 persons per square kilometer, and Singapore moves to second place with 4,566.3. Taken together, the Tigers are the most dense of the country groups as they average 2,739.1 persons per square kilometer. No other group is even close. The three Lions average 94.4; the two Gaurs, 126.8; the Panda, 125.4; and the four Elephants, 19.1. By these figures the Tigers are 143 times more dense than the Elephants. The images of congestion described in the previous section have numerical counterparts.

Literacy can be gauged by the literacy rate, the percent of the population 15 years of age or older that can read and write. Among the mature states the literacy rate is uniformly high, being at or nearly at 100 percent. Of the maturing entities, Korea has the highest rate, 96 percent, but the Philippines and Thailand also top the 90 percent threshold. Singapore comes close with 89 percent. Malaysia, China, and Hong Kong fall a notch or two behind: their rates register 78 percent and 77 percent. The worst record across the Region belongs to Papua New Guinea. At 52 percent, its literacy rate is similar to those of African nations such as Cameroon, Morocco, and Nigeria. Papua New Guinea is also weak in terms of health care. Its infant mortality rate, calculated as the number of deaths for every 1,000 live births and expressed as a percentage, equals 6.16 percent, which is a close second to Indonesia's 6.50 percent. China is third worst with 5.21 percent. At the favorable end of the spectrum are Hong Kong, Singapore, and Taiwan with percentages of 0.58, 0.57, and 0.56 respectively. Their below-unity magnitudes place them on par with the mature societies.

Infrastructure comes next. The abundance of major airports, those with paved runways over 3,047 meters long, depends in part upon country size. The United States has 181; China, 17; and Australia, 9. Small Hong Kong has 1 although even smaller Singapore operates 3. The lengths of railroad track and vehicular highway likewise vary in part with nation size. Adjusting for that factor rearranges the results and places Taiwan first with 0.128 kilometers of track for every square kilometer of area. Singapore takes top honors for highways with a 4.555 posting.

The congestion captured in the earlier images and quantified by population density can be seen again in the vehicle statistics. Across the Tigers on average, there are 132.2 cars for every kilometer of highway. By that ratio each car is "allotted" 7.6 meters—or about eight yards—of road. The Lions are second in auto density averaging 29.7 cars per kilometer. The Elephants are third with 20.4; the Gaurs, fourth with 1.9; and the Panda, last with 1.7. Statistics for total vehicle density follow roughly the same pattern. Plainly, the Tigers are clogged with both people and vehicles. That fact combines with the particularly small land masses for Hong Kong and Singapore to explain why those two powerhouses became vertical: With no room to maneuver sideways except by annexing portions of the sea, they logically expanded upward. The same reasoning explains why Hong Kong and Singapore are almost completely devoid of commercial agriculture: There is virtually no room to grow anything in commercial amounts.

Rounding out infrastructure is communication; specifically, the number of persons per phone. From that account communication for the Tigers can be accomplished about as easily as it can be effected for the Elephants. In Hong Kong, 1.8 people share a phone. In Singapore 2.6 do, and among the four Tigers the average equals 2.7, only slightly higher than the 2.0 average for the Elephants. By contrast, China, Papua New Guinea, Thailand, and the Philippines show poor access to the phone, and Indonesia reports the longest queue for phone service: 266.8 persons. There the Western feature known as Call Waiting translates into the primordial property aptly called People Waiting.

1.3 ECONOMIC FACTS AND FIGURES

Perhaps Professor Terry's impression of Asia Pacifica had been shaped by images of the Tigers and Lions. Perhaps it had been prefaced by statistics on people and places. Or perhaps the impression had been formed around facts of economic performance, which, for some members of the Region, could be called phenomenal or even miraculous.[4] Two popular manifestations of the miracle are the growth rate of output and the growth rate of labor productivity, that productivity being defined as output per worker. Table 1.2 presents those facts for all countries in the Region. Throughout, output is measured as gross domestic product (GDP) expressed in real terms; that is, adjusted for inflation.

Over the thirty-year period from 1961 to 1990, Hong Kong output grew annually at an average rate of 8.85 percent. Growth during the global recession of the early 1980s fell to 5.60 percent but remained commendable nonetheless. The tempo quickened to 7.62 percent in the second half of the 1980s, although it sagged in the early 1990s as Hong Kong exhibited growth-cycle movement. Still, growth hovered at 5 percent annually through 1996. Similar patterns applied to the four Tigers generally. During the 30 years from 1961 to 1990, they averaged growth of 8.75 percent. For the early 1980s they posted 6.19 percent advancing to 9.04 percent in the late 1980s before retrenching to 7.06 percent in the first half of the 1990s. For 1996 their combined rate remained comfortable at 6.13 percent.

The Lions advanced more slowly during the 30 years through 1990, averaging 6.87 percent. Lion growth slower than the Tiger run also characterized both halves of the 1980s, but the ranking reversed thereafter. For example, in the five years from 1991 to 1995,

Table 1.2 Growth Rates for Output and Labor Productivity in the Asia Pacific Region

Country	1961-90	1981-85	1986-90	1991-95	1994	1995	1996
			Output Growth Rates				
Hong Kong	8.85	5.60	7.62	5.52	5.40	4.74	4.73
Korea	8.95	7.92	10.88	7.49	8.58	8.94	7.13
Singapore	8.62	5.88	8.19	8.57	10.54	8.75	6.95
Taiwan	8.59	5.36	9.47	6.64	6.54	6.03	5.70
Indonesia	6.19	7.54	5.52	7.83	7.54	8.21	7.82
Malaysia	7.16	4.34	6.80	8.69	9.24	9.46	8.21
Thailand	7.25	4.61	9.55	8.47	8.74	8.79	6.66
Papua New Guinea	3.12	0.66	0.41	9.63	1.80	na	na
Philippines	4.28	-0.01	5.31	2.21	4.39	4.76	5.48
China	9.09	10.80	7.94	12.02	12.70	10.50	7.64
Australia	3.79	3.09	2.61	2.78	5.60	3.50	4.00
Japan	6.46	3.82	4.81	1.42	0.60	1.40	3.60
New Zealand	2.54	3.15	1.08	1.96	6.40	4.30	2.70
United States	3.28	2.95	3.04	1.88	3.50	2.00	2.40
			Labor Productivity Growth Rates				
Hong Kong	6.03	3.26	6.20	4.01	2.90	3.35	1.29
Korea	6.32	5.50	9.46	4.93	5.55	6.22	2.68
Singapore	5.32	2.66	6.21	5.83	6.96	5.60	4.19
Taiwan	5.87	2.93	7.73	4.86	4.32	4.84	5.45
Indonesia	3.99	5.16	3.09	6.71	3.96	10.56	na
Malaysia	3.95	1.24	3.52	5.48	6.24	6.65	3.74
Thailand	4.53	2.11	7.55	7.36	8.92	7.29	14.26
Papua New Guinea	1.23	-1.32	-1.72	na	na	na	na
Philippines	1.73	-4.08	2.72	-0.44	1.43	2.75	-1.41
China	6.23	7.48	5.32	10.10	10.62	9.01	3.20
Australia	1.52	1.24	0.65	3.80	2.12	2.63	3.68
Japan	5.31	2.92	4.10	0.90	na	1.34	3.15
New Zealand	0.68	1.17	-0.23	-1.11	-4.60	1.09	4.52
United States	1.54	1.63	2.14	0.49	0.52	-1.28	0.44

Notes. Entries refer either to annual percentages or to averages of annual percentages. In a few instances, an average pertains to data available only for a portion of the corresponding period. Output is measured by real GDP. *na* means not available.

Sources. Original data are those reported by the Asian Development Bank in *Key Indicators of Developing Asian and Pacific Countries*, by the International Monetary Fund in *International Financial Statistics Yearbook*, by the OECD in *Main Economic Indicators*, and by Summers and Heston (1993).

the Lions showed 8.33 percent compared to 7.06 percent for the Tigers, and this modest dominance held though 1996, when their joint rate tallied 7.56 percent. The Gaurs, in comparison with the Tigers and Lions, proved to be slow movers. During the 30-year period, they expanded on balance at 3.70 percent, and during the global recession they went almost nowhere. The Philippines even went backward although that Gaur recovered to 5.48 percent by 1996. The Panda, conversely, has been anything but a slow mover. China's pace over the long haul through 1990 registered a shade above 9 percent. It remained torrid during global cooling and heated to almost 13 percent in 1994 before settling down to 7.64 percent in 1996.[5]

Elephants are often associated with sluggishness. True to that interpretation (save possibly for Japan), the OECD Elephants advanced on balance at 4.02 percent from 1961 to 1990. Moreover, their average rates shrank continually from 3.25 percent to 2.13 percent to 2.01 percent over the three half decades beginning with the 1981–85 period. More recently, that mean equaled 3.18 percent in 1996. The United States, in numerous respects a leading world economy, expanded at a rate of 3.28 percent from 1961 to 1990. Its recessions from July 1981 to November 1982 and from July 1990 to March 1991 can be detected in the statistics, which close out at 2.40 percent for 1996. With those numbers serving as guides, the run of the Tigers can be appreciated as phenomenally fast. Their rate of 8.75 percent through 1990 almost triples the U.S. mark, and their 1996 figure of 6.13 percent does about the same. Likewise, the Lions at least double America in those periods.

Since labor productivity growth basically equals output growth minus employment growth, the patterns for output broadly carry over to productivity, albeit with smaller magnitudes. To illustrate, Hong Kong had labor productivity advance over the long period 1961–90 by 6.03 percent annually and saw productivity exhibit growth cycles in the same way that output did. However, productivity completed the record in 1996 with a rate of 1.29 percent. Taken by country group, the maturing nations follow an approximate 6–4–2 sequence in their productivity histories through 1990. That is, the Tigers averaged 5.89 percent in that period while the Lions and Gaurs mustered 4.16 percent and 1.48 percent respectively. For the years beyond 1990, Indonesia and Thailand assume leadership roles among the three groups, and the numbers for the latter nation seemingly echo the sentiment expressed in Kulick and Wilson's *Thailand's Turn* (1992, pp. 1–2). These facts notwithstanding, however, bragging rights to productivity leadership may belong more to China, whose productivity growth in the 1990s registered around 9 percent annually. In sharp contrast, the Elephants generally and the United States particularly have little to brag about. America, for instance, watched productivity expand by 1.54 percent through 1990 and, in its recession half decade 1991–95, witnessed a rate well below 1 percent. By America's standard many of the maturing nations traveled at a fast clip.

Output growth and labor productivity growth are only two measures of economic success. There are others inasmuch as success "trickles down" to many aspects of economic life. One such aspect is unemployment, as a higher output growth rate should correlate with a lower unemployment rate ceteris paribus. That relationship, a transparent variant of Okun's Law (Dornbusch et al., 1998, p. 126), has a theoretical foundation.

A key element in that theory is the real wage Wr, which equals the nominal wage divided by the price level. The nominal wage might be calibrated in ringgits per hour while price may be gauged in ringgits per kilo of rice. Hence, the real wage is essentially the wage denominated in units of output: kilos per hour. As the real wage rises, the cost of employing labor increases, prompting entrepreneurs to employ fewer workers. In other words, labor demand Ld falls. At the same time, the higher real wage induces more individuals into the labor force, and labor supply Ls rises. Figure 1.2 illustrates the situation in its upper panel. Labor demand equals labor supply at Point A, where the real wage equals Wr_A and where employment L equals L_A. Point A identifies labor-market equilibrium.

Unemployment lies beneath the surface of the upper panel. It can be brought into the open by regarding labor demand as having two components: N, the number of individuals already employed, and V, the number of vacant positions that business yet intends to fill. Thus $Ld = N + V$. In like manner, labor supply can be held to have two components: N along with X, the number of individuals still seeking work. Succinctly, $Ls = N + X$. Then

$$Ld \gtrless Ls \qquad (1.1)$$

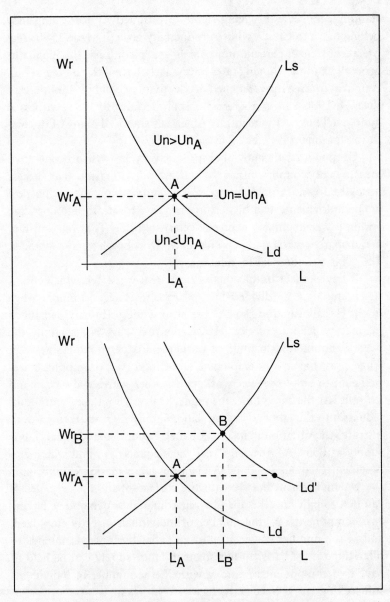

Figure 1.2 Labor-Market Equilibrium and Adjustment

implies

$$V \gtreqless X.$$ (1.2)

Labor-market equilibrium, where $Ld = Ls$, means that $V = X$: the number of vacant slots exactly equals the number of job seekers. Since unemployment rate Un can be considered as seekers divided by the labor force—namely, $Un = X / (N + X)$—it follows that unemployment at Point A is some positive number, say, Un_A. Above Point A, $Ld < Ls$, and consequently $V < X$: applicants outnumber vacancies. Finding employment is harder than at A, and as a result $Un > Un_A$. Conversely, below A, $Ld > Ls$ and $V > X$. Vacancies now outnumber applicants, finding employment is easier than at A, and $Un < Un_A$. In the end, the upper panel can be seen to imply a continuum for the unemployment rate, which declines as the real wage falls.

An increase in the demand for labor, possibly due to an increase in the world's demand for the product made by labor, shifts the demand curve rightward to Ld' in the lower panel of Figure 1.2. At the original wage Wr_A, labor demand now exceeds labor supply, and vacancies now exceed applicants. Hence the unemployment rate falls, at least initially. Thrown into disequilibrium, the market begins adjusting toward the new equilibrium, Point B. In the process the real wage rises to Wr_B. Moreover, employment rises to L_B. But since output varies directly with labor quantity, additional labor means additional output. Thus reduced unemployment rates associate with increased output levels and, by extension, with increased output growth rates.

Unemployment rates for the Asia Pacific nations appear in Table 1.3. There several features stand out, the first being the usually low values for the rates in the maturing lands. Judged against the United States experience, those rates are truly low. In the half decade 1976–80, the United States had an unemployment rate of 6.8 percent, but Hong Kong showed 3.9 percent; Taiwan, 1.5 percent; and Thailand, 0.9 percent. Similarly, for the period from 1986 to 1990, the U.S. rate of 5.9 percent was easily bettered by the Hong

Table 1.3 Unemployment and Inflation Rates in the Asia Pacific Region

Country	1976-80	1981-85	1986-90	1991-95	1994	1995	1996
			Unemployment Rates				
Hong Kong	3.9	3.8	1.7	2.2	1.9	3.2	2.8
Korea	4.0	4.2	2.9	2.3	2.4	2.0	2.0
Singapore	3.8	3.1	3.7	2.5	2.6	2.7	3.0
Taiwan	1.5	2.3	1.9	1.6	1.6	1.8	2.6
Indonesia	2.4	2.4	2.6	3.9	4.4	7.2	na
Malaysia	3.8	5.4	6.9	3.3	2.9	2.8	3.0
Thailand	0.9	2.5	3.2	1.6	1.3	1.1	2.0
Papua New Guinea	na	na	na	na	na	na	na
Philippines	4.5	6.0	8.1	8.7	8.4	8.4	7.4
China	5.2	2.6	1.8	2.6	2.8	2.9	3.0
Australia	5.8	8.1	7.3	9.9	9.8	8.5	8.6
Japan	2.1	2.5	2.5	2.6	2.9	3.1	3.4
New Zealand	1.7	4.4	5.7	8.9	8.2	6.3	6.1
United States	6.8	8.3	5.9	6.5	6.1	5.6	5.4
			Inflation Rates				
Hong Kong	10.2	7.9	8.4	7.3	6.9	2.4	5.4
Korea	21.0	7.7	6.3	6.4	5.5	5.4	3.6
Singapore	4.5	2.9	3.1	3.4	4.6	2.6	2.1
Taiwan	8.9	3.8	2.4	3.0	1.9	1.9	3.0
Indonesia	20.0	11.3	8.4	10.5	7.8	9.4	8.4
Malaysia	9.7	2.6	1.6	4.0	5.1	5.0	4.3
Thailand	8.4	6.3	4.8	4.6	4.3	4.7	4.8
Papua New Guinea	13.4	3.2	10.2	4.2	na	na	na
Philippines	7.5	21.2	8.4	9.7	10.0	7.5	8.9
China	na	3.7	7.2	12.3	19.5	13.0	8.3
Australia	10.1	8.3	7.0	1.8	1.1	2.8	2.0
Japan	5.3	2.1	1.5	0.9	0.2	-0.6	-0.5
New Zealand	14.5	10.5	9.2	2.8	0.5	1.6	1.9
United States	7.8	5.8	3.8	2.8	2.2	2.5	2.0

Notes. Entries are either percentages or averages of percentages, although on occasion an average reflects data available only for a portion of the relevant period. Values for inflation are based on the implicit price deflator for GDP and have an annual orientation. *na* indicates not available.

Sources. Besides the references by the Asian Development Bank, the International Monetary Fund, and the OECD listed in Table 1.2, data authorities here consist of the *China Statistical Yearbook* by the People's Republic of China, the *Statistical Yearbook of the Republic of China* by the Republic of China, and the *Yearbook of Labour Statistics* by the International Labour Organization.

Kong, Taiwan, and Thailand percentages of 1.7, 1.9, and 3.2 respectively. This circumstance carried over through 1996, when the U.S. reading of 5.4 percent was plainly inferior to the percentage sequence for the trio: 2.8, 2.6, and 2.0. The consistently low unemployment rates for many of the maturing countries lend numerical support to the assertion by Clark and Kim (1995b, p. 6) and others that critical labor shortages existed in the Region.

A second feature embedded in Table 1.3 concerns the ranking of unemployment rates within the maturing community. For the most part, the Tigers as a group outperform the Lions, which in turn outperform the Gaurs. For the half decade 1981–85, the Tigers have an average unemployment rate of 3.35 percent compared to 3.43 percent for the Lions and to 6.00 percent for the Gaurs, represented by the Philippines. Analogously, the half decade 1986–90 lists the respective percentages as 2.55, 4.23, and 8.10, and in 1995 the series is 2.43, 3.70, and 8.40. As regards unemployment, the Tigers score impressively, whereas the Gaurs score poorly. The Panda, although never registering the lowest unemployment rate, nonetheless always does well on that count after 1980.

Feature 3 is the negative relationship between unemployment on the one hand and output growth on the other. By Table 1.2 Singapore shows a rise in output growth from 5.88 percent to 8.57 percent between the two half decades 1981–85 and 1991–95. Correspondingly, its unemployment rate in Table 1.3 falls from 3.1 percent to 2.5 percent. Taiwan's output growth expands from 5.36 percent to 6.64 percent as its unemployment rate declines from 2.3 percent to 1.6 percent. For Malaysia the output figure changes from 4.34 to 8.69 as the unemployment counterpart changes from 5.4 to 3.3. Thailand reports much the same: 4.61 to 8.47 versus 2.5 to 1.6. Exceptions to the rule can be found, of course, but they might be thought to associate with violations of the ceteris paribus proviso on which the rule is premised.

The demand shock depicted in Figure 1.2 precipitated a decrease in unemployment and an increase in output growth. It also set into motion a boost in the real wage. Evidence supporting that theoretical response can be deduced by combining information on wages in manufacturing with accounts of the implicit price deflator for GDP. Conducting that exercise for Hong Kong shows that the real wage, indexed at unity for 1985, rises from 0.597 in 1976 to 1.308 in 1994. Labor, being short in supply, becomes more expensive by virtue of market forces. Likewise, over that period Korea observes the real wage climb from 0.591 to 2.158; Singapore, from 0.606 to 1.540; and Taiwan, from 0.554 to 1.889.

Theory and empirical evidence join forces in describing economic performance in the Asia Pacific Region.[6]

Yet another way to view economic performance is through the eyes of the Phillips curve. Introduced by A. W. Phillips (1958) and enhanced over time to reflect the changing current of mainstream reasoning, it relates the inflation rate, surveyed in Table 1.3, to the unemployment rate in a trade-off—or inverse—fashion. It also allows for factors that affect the location of the trade-off. In mathematical terms it can be written as

$$\hat{p} = g(Un) + \hat{p}^e - \hat{y}, \tag{1.3}$$

where p denotes product price, p^e signifies expected price, and y represents labor productivity. The circumflex ($\wedge$) indicates a proportionate growth rate. Function g manifests the trade-off whereas $\hat{p}^e$ and $\hat{y}$ act as shift factors. By imposing linearity on g for convenience, equation (1.3) becomes

$$Un = v - \rho(\hat{p} - \hat{p}^e) - \omega\hat{y} \tag{1.4}$$

the v, p, and ω being positive constants.

Expression (1.4) maintains that the unemployment rate declines as unanticipated inflation rises. It also declines as labor productivity growth quickens. This message, which can be likened to the lesson learned from the lower half of Figure 1.2, means that under ceteris paribus circumstances higher productivity growth should shift the Phillips curve *leftward*. According to Table 1.2, each of the four Tigers experiences a sizable increase in productivity growth between the half decades 1981–85 and 1986–90. Thus if ceteris paribus holds even approximately, then the Phillips curve for each Tiger should shift leftward at some point during the 1980s. Figure 1.3 confirms such responses for Korea and Taiwan, while Figure 6.1 in Chapter 6 substantiates the cases for the city economies of Hong Kong and Singapore.[7]

Leftward Phillips shifts constitute good news because they imply either lower unemployment at the same inflation rate or lower

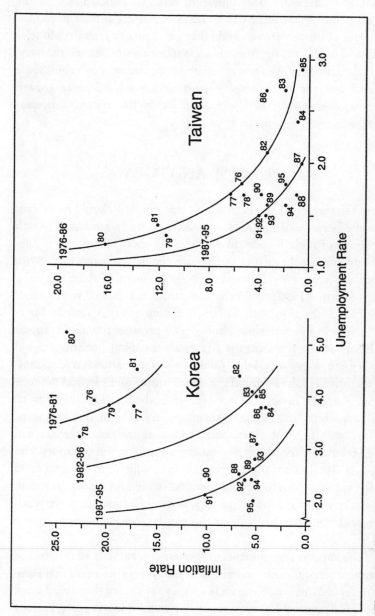

Figure 1.3 Phillips Curves for Korea and Taiwan

inflation at the same unemployment rate. This good news for the Tigers coincides with the cheery news contained in their phenomenal rates of output growth and labor productivity growth. Miracles trickle down, causing miraculous apparitions all along the way. Miracles, though, need not occur uniformly. Almost as proof, some countries in the Asia Pacific Region have exhibited fierce growth whereas others have not been as lucky. In this regard, Professor Terry was right to wonder why.

1.4 PURPOSE AND FORMAT

From the thrust of the discussion to this point, it should be evident that the purpose of the work at hand is to study economic growth in the Asia Pacific Region. In doing so the endeavor appeals to theory and empirical evidence to examine the determinants of growth. From the efforts by Denison (1967), Levine and Renelt (1992), Sala-i-Martin (1997), and others, it recognizes that there are many possible causes of growth. In fact, it champions that view at different points in the exposition, but overall presents economic growth as being driven primarily by five factors: capital quantity, capital quality, labor quantity, labor quality, and international trade. Capital quantity revolves around gross investment and physical depreciation. Capital quality centers on embodied technical progress. Labor quantity means employment, whereas labor quality means education, a form of disembodied technical progress. International trade refers to exports or to openness, a combination of exports and imports. Total factor productivity growth, which can be interpreted as the amount of output growth not accounted for by the growth in capital quantity and labor quantity, becomes a function of the qualities and trade. Accordingly, it too can be considered as a growth driver.

The various determinants may operate separately or jointly. For instance, foreign trade may result in technology transfers that stimulate capital quality. In the same way, expansion of the capital stock through domestic initiatives might lower production costs, thereby stimulating trade. Labor quality improvements through education might foster technological breakthroughs that enhance capital quality. Yet, regardless of whether or how the various components interact among themselves, they all come together to explain growth. That explanation, in turn, provides a natural framework for studying major issues that bear on Asia Pacific growth in the future. One of those issues is Hong Kong's reversion to China, while another is the Asian currency crisis, which hit immediately after Hong Kong was returned. Policy implications likewise are natural corollaries of the growth explanation.

Since this volume deals with growth, it reviews celebrated growth theories and their extensions. It then presents a theory appropriate for the Asia Pacific Region. Those tasks fall on the shoulders of Chapter 3, the first component of Part II. Steady growth and convergence—that is, productivity catch-up—also become the responsibility of that chapter. In the same way that Chapter 3 focuses on theoretical propositions, Chapter 4 concentrates on empirical evidence. It treats the development of the data file used to explore growth determinants. To bring both depth and breadth to the exercise, that file is built to cover 120 countries. For each a set of capital stocks is constructed, and the underlying procedure is described. Afterward, Chapter 4 examines economic profiles for the individual Asia Pacific countries and for country groups composed from all 120 nations in the file. It finishes by bringing empirical life to the convergence issue. Chapter 5 pulls together the theoretical precepts and empirical evidence to quantify the contribution to growth from each of the five primary determinants. In the process it answers Professor Terry's question, "Why phenomenal growth?" Given its content, that chapter can be regarded as the principal component of the volume. Its vehicle is regression analysis, which leads to a quantification of growth shares for each of the individual Asia Pacific countries and for each of the country groups that span the globe. Chapter 5 also seeks to resolve the controversy swirling around the importance of total factor productivity to economic growth.

Part III consists of special studies. Chapter 6 offers a detailed account of the two city-states in the Region: Hong Kong and Singapore. Since those two Tigers are included in the discussion of the Region throughout Part II, Chapter 6 involves some overlap. Actually, that overlap is intentional to make the inquiry fairly self-contained and easily applicable to earlier treatments of those economies. Chapter 7 takes up the thorny question of how Hong Kong may fare under China. At the heart of that research is a reversion matrix that, based on the regression work in Chapter 5, quantifies the growth consequences of numerous scenarios possible under China rule. Chapter 8 looks at the growth consequences of the Asian currency crisis that, once started, seemed to have a domino effect. Again, the regression work of Chapter 5 comes into play.

Much lies ahead. However, before the narrative leaps into theory, practice, and implications, there may be some merit in reviewing a few matters of historical significance. That endeavor occupies the next chapter, which concludes Part I.

CHAPTER 2

HISTORICAL MUSINGS

" . . . Now, Watson, I want you to do something for me."

"I am here to be used, Holmes."

"Well, then, spend the next twenty-four hours in an intensive study of Chinese pottery."

. . . Certainly I should not like now to pose as an authority upon ceramics. And yet all that evening, and all that night with a short interval for rest, and all next morning, I was sucking in knowledge and committing names to memory. There I learned of the hall-marks of the great artist-decorators, of the mystery of cyclical dates, the marks of the Hung-wu and the beauties of the Yung-lo, the writings of Tang-ying, and the glories of the primitive period of the Sung and the Yuan. I was charged with all this information when I called upon Holmes next evening.

Sherlock Holmes and John H. Watson
—A. Conan Doyle, *The Adventure of the Illustrious Client*

IMAGES OF THE ASIA PACIFIC REGION offered in the previous chapter bring color and feeling to the discussion. Vital statistics add precision. Further texture can be obtained from an historical review of events that swept across the Region. For manageability these musings must be sharply focused. Section 2.1 looks at China and its involvement with Japan. China's move toward a market economy opens the inquiry in Section 2.2, which goes on to cover the Tiananmen Square Massacre and its aftermath. Taiwan, the island that became a safe haven for the Republic of China, constitutes the subject of Section 2.3, while Korea, also steeped in Chinese tradition, occupies Section 2.4. Thoughts connecting the historical accounts to the main theme of the volume shape Section 2.5.

2.1 THE PANDA AND AN ELEPHANT

China, the Panda, dates back to an age long before Christ, and its evolution into the twentieth century can be seen as a steady progression of a dynastic sequence.[1] The Xia Dynasty, ruling from 2205 BC to 1766 BC, gave way to the Shang Dynasty, which yielded to the Zhou and then to the Qin. After the Qin appeared the Han, which carried the dynastic tradition into the Anno Domini period. Later history marks the Song Dynasty from 960 to 1279 followed by the Yuan and the Ming. The last dynasty, which brought vestiges of the past into modern times, was the Qing, also known as the Manchu. As the chronology in Table 2.1 indicates, it ruled from 1644 to 1912.

The dynastic chain made enormous contributions in philosophy and culture. Confucius thinking, anchored by the philosopher's beliefs in benevolence and harmony, attracted disciples who further developed that line of reasoning. Similarly, poetry blossomed, painting flourished, and pottery—as Dr. Watson learned at Holmes's urging—thrived. Yet over such glories and achievements hung wars and rebellions. For instance, the Opium Wars culminating in 1842 and 1860 found China defeated by the United Kingdom, and the First Sino-Japanese War of 1894–95 left it beaten by Japan. The opium conflicts revolved around Hong Kong, and the Japanese situation spun around Korea. At home the Boxer Rebellion reared its head.

Military setbacks at foreign hands do little to foster affection and admiration for outsiders, and after the loss to Japan, the Chinese mood regarding foreigners was hardly a happy one. Indicative of that sentiment was the slogan adopted by a secret sect known as

Table 2.1 Chronology of Events in China

Date or Period	Event
2205 BC	Xia Dynasty begins reign.
1644 AD	Qing, or Manchu, Dynasty assumes the throne but ends all dynastic rule in 1912.
1842	First Opium War with the United Kingdom ceases with the British as victor.
1860	Second Opium War with the United Kingdom concludes with Britain again being victorious.
1894-95	First Sino-Japanese War leaves China defeated by Japan.
June 20, 1900	Manchu government declares war on foreign nations in the Boxer Rebellion, at whose conclusion the foreign contingent prevails.
1901	Boxer Protocol brings the Boxer Rebellion to a formal close.
October 10, 1911	Wuchang Uprising ignites the revolution that gives birth to the Republic of China.
January 1, 1912	Sun Yat-sen becomes provisional president and accordingly the first president of the Republic of China.
February 12, 1912	Emperor Hsuan T'ung abdicates the throne, terminating the reign of the Manchu Dynasty.
March 10, 1912	Yuan Shih-k'ai is officially installed as provisional president, filling the post vacated by Sun Yat-sen consonant with an earlier understanding.
May 5, 1921	Sun Yat-sen reclaims the position of provisional president.
July 1, 1921	Chinese Communist Party (CCP) formally comes into being at proceedings attended by Mao Tse-tung.
January 1924	First Kuomintang (KMT) Congress meets and ushers in the Kuomintang-Communist alliance.
June 5, 1926	Chiang Kai-shek accepts the post of commander-in-chief of the government military following Sun Yat-sen's death in March 1925.

April 12, 1927	KMT troops stage an attack in Shanghai and eliminate hundreds of Communists and several Communist leaders, bringing the KMT-CCP coalition to a bloody end.
October 1928	Chiang Kai-shek has undisputed control of the KMT.
September 1931	Japan initiates military action enabling it to occupy Manchuria.
1934	Amau Declaration gives Japan protectorate status over China.
1935	Foreign Minister Hirota Koko of Japan enunciates his Three Principles, which in part call for a military agreement with the Chinese government directed against the Communists.
December 12, 1936	Chiang Kai-shek is arrested in Sian by officials who believe, in direct opposition to Chiang's own inclination, that the government should direct its attention against the Japanese rather than the Communists.
December 25, 1936	Chiang is released, and the bandit suppression raids against the Communists stop.
December 28, 1936	Japanese army issues an anti-Communist statement indicating that it is prepared to devise whatever measures are necessary to keep peace in East Asia.
February 10, 1937	Communists propose to recognize the KMT as the civil and military authority provided that the civil war ceases and that attention is aimed at foreign aggressors.
July 7, 1937	Lukouchiao, or Marco Polo Bridge, Incident marks the start of the Second Sino-Japanese War.
September 22, 1937	Mao Tse-tung publicly proclaims a united front composed of the KMT and the Communists.
December 13, 1937	Nanking, the capital city, falls to the Japanese, initiating the six-week Rape of Nanking.
December 7, 1941	Japan attacks the United States at Pearl Harbor, and on the next day China formally declares war against Japan.

December 1, 1943	Cairo Declaration, signed by Chiang Kai-shek, President Franklin Roosevelt of the United States, and Prime Minister Winston Churchill of the United Kingdom, asserts that Japan must return Manchuria, Taiwan, and the Pescadores to China.
April 1944	Japan launches and then successfully conducts Operation Ichi-Go to control the north-south railway in China and to destroy air bases.
February 1945	U.S. president Roosevelt and Soviet leader Stalin conclude the Yalta Pact, which specifies the terms under which the Soviet Union would enter the war against Japan.
August 14, 1945	Japan surrenders unconditionally to the Allied forces, thereby ending World War II, and China signs a Sino-Soviet treaty reflecting the provisions of the Yalta Pact.
January 13, 1946	Agreement on the cessation of civil war between the Nationalists (KMT) and the Chinese Communists becomes effective, but hostilities continue nonetheless.
June 7, 1946	A truce in civil-war fighting takes effect for a ten-day period but is extended through June 30.
July 1946	Civil war resumes in China.
November 7, 1948	Battle of the Hwai-Hai commences and over a two-month period inflicts heavy losses on the Nationalists.
January 21, 1949	Chiang Kai-shek retires from the presidency.
October 1, 1949	Mao Tse-tung announces the establishment of the People's Republic of China (PRC), and Beijing becomes the capital city.
December 9, 1949	KMT Nationalists flee China for Taipei, and Chiang Kai-shek, following the next day, soon declares himself president of the Republic of China on Taiwan.
1966	Mao Tse-tung initiates the Cultural Revolution intended to overhaul Chinese politics and practice.
Fall 1971	PRC takes the China seat from Taiwan in the United Nations.

February 1972	U.S. president Richard Nixon visits Beijing and signs the Shanghai Communiqué, which includes a statement articulating the U.S. position on the relationship between Taiwan and mainland China.
September 9, 1976	Mao Tse-tung dies, and with his death the Cultural Revolution comes to a halt.
October 10, 1976	Hua Guofeng is announced as the Party chairman and successor to Mao.
July 1977	Hua is confirmed as Party chairman, and Deng Xiaoping is installed as number three in the Party on his way to becoming China's next paramount leader.
1978	Economic reform is launched.
July 1, 1979	The United States extends diplomatic relations to the PRC and simultaneously severs those with the Republic of China on Taiwan; soon thereafter Deng Xiaoping meets with U.S. president Jimmy Carter in Washington.
May 1984	Economic reform expands to cover prices as the dual price system is established, its strictures later being relaxed.
June 4, 1989	Tiananmen Square Massacre starts in the early morning hours and leaves dead hundreds, perhaps thousands, of democracy-seeking demonstrators.
February 1997	Deng Xiaoping dies, leaving Jiang Zemin in charge.
July 1, 1997	Hong Kong reverts back to China.
October 1997	Chinese president Jiang Zemin visits U.S. president Bill Clinton in Washington.
June 1998	President Clinton visits President Zemin in Beijing, and the two leaders publicly exchange views on the Tiananmen incident.

the Boxers. As Clubb (1978, p. 24) writes, that motto boldly proclaimed, "Support the Manchus, annihilate the foreigners." It left nothing to the imagination. Leading the Manchus at that time was the Empress Dowager Tz'u Hsi, who herself was not fond of foreigners. On her instruction government forces were combined with the Boxer rebels, and on June 20, 1900, a declaration of war against foreign powers was issued. That move proved to be a colossal blunder because it pitted government troops and the Boxers, who believed that magic made them invincible in battle, against no fewer than eight nations including the Japanese. The international contingent dispatched the matter and on August 14, 1900, took the capital. The Boxer Protocol of 1901 brought a formal end to the Boxer Rebellion. An important provision of the decree was the granting of the right of foreign military personnel to be stationed in the country. That right extended to the Japanese.

Events led many to conclude that the Manchu dynasty was no longer able to run China effectively. Reforms were needed, and the old guard was not equal to the challenge. Logically, then, ousting the Manchus became a mission for some, and the mission took wing on October 10, 1911, when military insurgents bolted and gained control of Wuchang, a city in central China. In rapid succession provinces declared independence from the Manchus, and negotiations commenced to bring the revolution to a close. The settlement, which brought down the curtain on thousands of years of dynastic rule, gave birth to the Republic of China. On January 1, 1912, Sun Yat-sen, a well-known personage with revolutionist leanings, assumed the post of the provisional president of China, thus becoming the first president of the Republic of China. However, Sun would hold the position only briefly. After the Chinese throne was officially abdicated on February 12, he stepped aside for Yuan Shih-k'ai, who was sworn in as president on March 10, 1912. Yuan's ascent to power involved a fair amount of plot and intrigue. Natural ascent and a bit more plot and intrigue would have Sun Yat-sen return to the office of the provisional president on May 5, 1921. But another event of perhaps much greater significance would occur in that same year and would dramatically affect the course of Chinese history up to the present day.

While the military and political maneuverings were taking place, intellectual discontent swept over a community of sophists. Chinese thinking had become stuck in a mire of inflexibility and superstition, and scholars sought to strike out in new directions. They challenged Confucianism and entertained discussions on democracy and communism. Beijing University distinguished itself as a center for such expanded reasoning of the New Culture movement. At that institution the chief librarian championed the concept of communism, and his assistant, Mao Tse-tung, evidently was not unsympathetic to the recitations. Communism in China was an idea seeking implementation.

In 1920 the catalyst arrived in the person of a representative from the Communist International (Comintern), which had been created by Lenin during 1919. Now backed by money and organization, the idea of communism assumed concrete form in Shanghai on July 1, 1921, for it was there and then that the Chinese Communist Party (CCP) officially came into being. Significantly, in attendance at the proceedings was Mao Tse-tung.

Although the ultimate aim of the CCP was to overthrow the government, immediate problems, notably warlordism, took precedence. An expedient for solving those concerns was an alliance with the Nationalist government, the Kuomintang (KMT). In January of 1924 the First Kuomintang Congress endorsed consultation with the CCP on domestic matters and denounced warlordism. Concomitantly, Communists were allowed to have membership in the KMT, and Mao became a figure in the KMT Central Committee. To Soled (1995, p. 44), the political alliance was a marriage of convenience. Marriages of that sort often end in divorce, and the divorce between the KMT and the CCP would be more than bitter—it would be bloody.

Sun Yat-sen died in 1925, and during the next year an enterprising individual named Chiang Kai-shek accepted the post of commander-in-chief. By his orders KMT military personnel attacked radicals in Shanghai on April 12, 1927, and in the process killed hundreds of Communists including several Communist leaders. This massacre of April 12 marked the end of the KMT-CCP alliance and moved the KMT-CCP confrontation to the battlefield in civil war. Chiang himself went on to run the KMT. By October 1928 he was serving, in the words of Clubb (1978, pp. 149–50), "as chairman of the State Council and ex officio President of the National Government, chairman of the Standing Committee of the KMT Central Executive Committee, and commander-in-chief of the Nationalist armies."

As the decade of the 1930s unfolded, America sank into the Great Depression, and economists began to rethink the doctrine of laissez faire as the guide to economic policy. In regard to China, Japan was thinking about a military policy that hardly could be viewed as laissez faire. In September of 1931 Japan triggered an incident that enabled its forces to occupy Manchuria. Moreover, the Amau Declaration of 1934 gave it protectorate status over China. The next year Hirota Koko, the Japanese foreign minister, issued his Three Principles that, among other things, called for an end to anti-Japanese sentiment in China and, perhaps more ominously, for a Sino-Japanese military agreement directed against the Chinese Communists. Following the anti-Communist theme, the Japanese army on December 28, 1936, offered the Nationalists aid in their crusade against the Communists but quickly added that it would devise whatever measures deemed necessary to preserve peace in East Asia. Japan was flexing its military muscle in China, and the Communists were an obvious target.

Meanwhile, Chiang Kai-shek seemed to be less concerned about the Japanese than about the Communists. As Soled (1995, p. 45) writes, Chiang regarded both the Japanese and the Communists as diseases, but the former was one of the skin whereas the latter was one of the heart. This attitude led to a bizarre happening that preceded and prompted the Japanese offer in December. Eager to pursue a sixth bandit suppression raid against the Communists, Chiang traveled to Sian to advise the local leaders that the attack was to begin soon. The authorities, however, were of a mind that action should be directed at Japan and that the civil war should be stopped. To emphasize their point, they arrested Chiang. Nanking, the capital city, was stunned by that act of December 12 just as Washington would be shocked by news that the American president had been arrested in one of the 50 states because of views that differed from those of the sitting governor. Negotiations proceeded in earnest, and even Chiang's wife participated. Then on Christmas Day Chiang was released. Soon after this Sian incident, a shift in policy became evident: The sixth bandit suppression raid never took place, and truce seemed to settle over the civil war. To impart some formality to the accomplished fact, the Communists, who had much to lose if they were obliged to fight both the Nationalists *and* the Japanese sent a telegram to Nanking on February 10, 1937, indicating that they were prepared to recognize the Nationalists as the civil and military authority provided that the civil war ceased and that energies were channeled against foreign aggressors. Seven months later, in September 1937, Mao Tse-tung publicly announced the united front between the Kuomintang and the Communists. United they would stand—or so the adage goes.

With Japan spoiling for a fight to build empire, any excuse would suffice. On July 7, 1937, Japanese troops stationed in the vicinity of Beijing learned that one of their number was missing and went to search in an area patrolled by a Chinese garrison. After an exchange of words, the Japanese opened fire, and the Chinese replied in kind. This Lukouchiao—or Marco Polo Bridge—Incident marked the start of the Second Sino-Japanese War, during which Japan scored victory upon victory. Nanking tumbled on December 1937 precipitating the so-called Rape whereby, in the estimation of R. T. Phillips (1996, p. 127), tens of thousands of Chinese noncombatants suffered humiliation and death. That lawlessness lasted for six weeks. Canton toppled in October of 1938, but soon thereafter the Japanese war machine paused in China, leaving the Nationalists holed up in their new capital city of Chungking. There Chiang Kai-shek waited for the arrival of a third combatant to tip the scale against Japan.

Chiang's wait came to a sudden end on December 7, 1941, when Japan bombed and strafed the United States into the Pacific Theater of World War II. Immediately China declared war on Japan, although, as the Americans were about to discover, Chiang was reluctant to engage the enemy. Apparently Chiang was protecting his military apparatus for a possible resumption of the civil war once the global conflict terminated. And posturing itself for the resolution of that wider calamity, China, through the Generalissimo, signed the Cairo Declaration of 1943. American president Franklin Roosevelt and British prime minister Winston Churchill also penned that December promise to return to China territories stolen by Japan. But with hostilities still raging against Japan on the mainland and beyond, the Cairo promise represented a rain check for another day.

In April of 1944 the Elephant sleeping in the land of the Panda awoke to launch Operation Ichi-Go, aimed at controlling the north-south railway and heaping destruction on air bases. By September 1944 its mission had been accomplished. Nevertheless, time was running out for the Japanese. In February 1945 President Roosevelt and Soviet boss Joseph Stalin concluded the Yalta Pact, which specified terms under which the Soviet Union would enter the war against Japan. Those terms involved the transfer of some Chinese territory to the Soviet Union, and they became the subject of a Sino-Soviet treaty that was signed within moments of Japan's surrender on August 14, 1945. The global war had been decided, and the Japanese were the enemy no longer. To the Chinese Nationalists, the enemy would be the Communists—again.

Following Japan's concession, Chiang Kai-shek invited Mao Tse-tung, the head of the Communists, to visit Chungking to discuss matters. Mao accepted. After various rounds of discussion nurtured by American general George C. Marshall, who had been appointed by President Harry Truman to seek the unification of China by peaceful means, an agreement ending all civil war activities in China was reached and became effective on January 13, 1946. Battlefield skirmishes flared nonetheless. In due course Chiang, now head-quartered in Nanking, agreed to a ten-day truce commencing June 7, 1946. The truce was later extended to month's end, but peaceful resolution of differences between the Nationalists and the Communists could not be achieved. The Marshall mission had failed, and the civil war resumed the very next month.

Initially the Nationalists claimed impressive victories; yet in taking town after town they stretched their forces thin. Around April 1947 the tide of battle began to turn, and in November 1948 the Nationalist forces, under the direction of Chiang himself albeit from

Nanking, suffered a huge defeat in what Clubb (1978, p. 290) calls a battle of annihilation. This Battle of the Hwai-Hai started November 7, 1948, lasted two months, and cost Chiang 550,000 men. Accordingly, little remained of the Nationalist military machine as 1949 dawned. On January 21, 1949, Chiang retired as president and watched as the Communists, victors of the civil war, assumed control of China on October 1, 1949. On that date Mao announced the establishment of the People's Republic of China (PRC), and Beijing became the capital city. Two months later, in December 1949, Chiang Kai-shek and the Nationalist government fled to Taiwan, relocating the Republic of China there.

Mao Tse-tung ran mainland China as paramount leader for about a quarter of a century after creation of the PRC. During that time he instigated much and accomplished much. For instance, in 1966 he initiated the Cultural Revolution, which sought to overhaul Chinese politics and practice. In the fall of 1971 he witnessed the PRC take the China seat in the United Nations from Taiwan and the Republic of China. During February of 1972 he received U.S. president Richard Nixon in Beijing, thereby renewing relations that had broken off between the two countries. Besides restoring contact, the summit produced the Shanghai Communiqué, wherein the United States addressed the tension between Taiwan and mainland China by acknowledging "that all Chinese on either side of the Taiwan Strait maintain there is but one China and that Taiwan is a part of China. The United States Government does not challenge that position. It reaffirms its interest in a peaceful settlement of the Taiwan question by the Chinese themselves" (Soled, 1995, p. 362). Soon after the summit, China, true to its metaphorical image, sent two pandas to the National Zoo in Washington as a token of friendship. A few years later, though, the ailing and aged Mao died. With his death on September 9, 1976, the Cultural Revolution came to a close.

Taking up the reins from Mao was Hua Guofeng. Hua, however, proved to be something of a political way station en route to Deng Xiaoping, the next paramount. On January 1, 1979, the United States implemented diplomatic relations with the PRC and simultaneously severed those with the Republic of China on Taiwan. In that same month Deng visited Washington to meet with President Jimmy Carter and in the process gave a personal touch to the formalities. Meanwhile, on the mainland, China was undertaking economic reforms to move its system toward markets.

2.2 ECONOMIC REFORM, TIANANMEN, AND AFTERWARD

Under Mao the economic system of the People's Republic of China had a command structure rather than a market format.[2] Agriculture was collectivized and commune based, business enterprises were state owned, prices were controlled through a detailed planning mechanism, and foreign trade was designed merely to supplement domestic output by filling in holes left by Chinese producers.

A feature permeating this system was the soft budget constraint. Western firms operate by weighing revenues against costs. Failure to account for those conflicting forces may result in losses and, ultimately, in bankruptcy. A budget constraint that is hard—namely, that truly binds—motivates businesses to manage their affairs carefully, perhaps optimally, and creates incentives all the way down the line. By contrast, a soft budget constraint has little bite. Enterprises, as Gapinski (1993, p. 36) remarks, have license to operate without looking over their accounting shoulders. Those that incur losses receive bailouts in one form or another, and bankruptcy poses no real deterrent to mismanagement since financial rescue is merely an arm's length away. Evidence by Hay et al. (1994, pp. 330–35) provides a clue about the degree of softness in the Chinese constraint. Those scholars confirm the existence of long-term loss makers in China and estimate that, for the period 1984–87, government subsidies accounted for 15 percent of the funds going to the troubled entities. In comparison, firms profitable during those years had only 1 percent of their funds provided through government subsidy. Looked at another way, the bulk of government subsidies in that period went to only a handful of outfits suffering losses.

It may be instructive to recognize that budget softness, while a characteristic of the Chinese economic system, was hardly unique to

China; rather it was symptomatic of socialistic systems generally. The Yugoslavia that existed prior to the devastating breakup in 1991 illustrates. There Agrokomerc, a food processor employing about 13,500 workers in the small Bosnian town of Velika Kladuša, issued promissory notes totaling approximately 300 million U.S. dollars in a single year. The notes, whose issuance received the blessing of local politicians, were used to invest in infrastructure, to restore an old castle, to install cable television, and the like. By stretching its budget constraint through the bulk issuance of credit, Agrokomerc was able to stretch cable to its door (Gapinski et al., 1989, p. 42). In like vein, Kornai (1986, pp. 18–19) reports that about 10 percent of Yugoslav firms under study operated at a financial loss. From that standpoint Yugoslavia and China had something in common.

Soft budgets can be interpreted as being detrimental to economic incentives and performance, and concomitantly economic reform may be understood as an attempt to impart hardness to budgets. In China that reform began during 1978, as Table 2.1 shows. Agriculture was decollectivized, and the commune approach to farming was scrapped and replaced by a household responsibility system, which gave households a say in the production and marketing decisions of farm goods. Away from the countryside, state-owned enterprises too gained greater autonomy and control over production activity.

In May of 1984 reform spread to prices. Economic theory holds that prices set by fiat misallocate scarce resources and create distortions between demands and supplies. Depending upon the particular levels at which prices are set, shortages or surpluses appear, and those imbalances can be persistent. Economic fact indicates that fiat prices also can be a nightmare to manage. Riskin (1987, p. 348) talks about a 1983 realignment of textile prices in China. More specifically, the price of cotton was raised while that of synthetics was lowered, but the maneuver took more than six months to complete and required a "staff" of roughly 10,000 people. Similarly Rockwood (1979, p. 173) speaks about fiat pricing in the United States during World War II and estimates that the effort and its corollaries invoked the services of about 200,000 persons. In theory and in fact, pricing by decree typically represents bad economics. By the same token, good economics, in theory and in fact, usually rests with market pricing.

Because Chinese authorities believed the prevailing price system to be greatly distorted, they elected to move from fiat to markets gradually and in May 1984 formally adopted a dual price system. By that system, according to Hay et al. (1994, p. 8),

> outputs and inputs of each enterprise were to be divided into two parts, i.e., planned and non-planned. Mandatory prices set by the State would apply to planned outputs and inputs while non-planned output could be sold to the market at prices with an upper limit not higher than 20% above the mandatory prices.

Relaxation of strictures occurred in October 1984 and February 1985. Actually reform went beyond the prices of commodities; it went all the way to credit to include the charging of interest on investment loans.

As regards international trade, China opened the door to the outside world about the same time that it was implementing economic reforms on the home front. By Riskin's (1987, p. 317) tabulations, China's merchandise trade soared in 1978 and again in 1980. Foreign trade now meant more than just filling in the output blanks; it became a vehicle for technology transfers and a factor in economic growth. Manifestations of China's open door policy were the special economic zones and the financial incentives that they held for foreign investors.

In undertaking a transition from an economic system driven by decree to one more attuned to markets, China granted to individuals new autonomy to make economic decisions. That autonomy, however, presumed a basic freedom of action to make decisions. Consequently, the move toward markets may have inspired a move toward democracy; at least it may have inspired the thought of democracy. Contact with outside influences through the increased openness of trade may have deepened such inspirations. In any event, students and sympathizers gathered at Tiananmen Square in central Beijing to seek democracy and increased freedoms. Their demonstration was soon crushed, however. During the early morning hours of June 4, 1989, tanks rolled in, shots rang out, and hundreds—possibly thousands—fell dead in a massive display of military might. News correspondent Harrison Salisbury, reflecting upon his eyewitness experience of the Tiananmen Massacre, offered this recollection (Salisbury, 1989, p. 52):

> I tune in BBC. Some professor is talking about the concept of time, chaos, and the universe. Perhaps the universe is contracting and not expanding. Time may be running backward. A good thought for the day. Indeed, it seems to be running backward before my eyes. These are scenes that come right out of the Boxer Rebellion. . . .

Salisbury (1989, p. 62) then added:

> It is a nutty situation. But fatal. As I said in the TV bite, we are at the end of the Deng era, the end of the era of innovation, creativity, and liberalization.

Hay et al. (1994, p. 3) concur by suggesting that the massacre ended a decade of economic reform in China.

World reaction to Tiananmen was swift. The United Nations drafted a resolution deploring the incident, the United States imposed economic and military sanctions on China, and the World Bank suspended review of Chinese loan requests. Outrage had the backing of economics. Before long, however, outrage mellowed. As Soled (1995, pp. 117, 196) reports, the practice of business-as-usual resumed, and economic reforms continued. And surely the death of Deng in February of 1997 and the passing of leadership to Jiang Zemin put a fresh face on matters. Nonetheless, the cloud of Tiananmen hung over Victoria Harbour on July 1, 1997, when Hong Kong reverted to China. It hung over Jiang's state visit to America in October of that year, and it hung over President Clinton's trip to China in June of 1998. It continues to hang over Taiwan.

2.3 THE TAIWAN TIGER

The flight of Chiang Kai-shek to Taiwan gave the Nationalist government a platform from which to press for recovery of the mainland. At the same time, it meant that Taiwan—also known as Ilha Formosa, the Portuguese term for "Beautiful Island"—again had a new wave of inhabitants.[3]

From 1624 to 1661 the Dutch ran the island as a colony. Then, as Table 2.2 chronicles, a Fukienese general named Koxinya took control and governed until 1683, when Ilha Formosa fell to the Manchu Dynasty of China. China ruled over that land for two centuries until the First Sino-Japanese War, which China lost. It lost the island as well. On April 7, 1895, by the Treaty of Shimonoseki, Taiwan and the neighboring Pescadores were ceded to Japan. A month later, on May 29, the Japanese set foot on Taiwan soil only to be greeted by violent resistance that, all told, cost more than 10,000 Taiwanese their lives.

Unquestionably, some locals despised their Japanese captors; others resented being treated as colonial subjects. Yet through the years conditions improved as gains from imperial influence began to manifest themselves. In particular, the Japanese maintained law and order, bolstered education, promoted property rights, and developed infrastructure, thereby creating a good climate for investment. As a result, economic prosperity rose to new heights, and the quality of life advanced to the point at which conditions were better on Taiwan than on the mainland. As Gold (1986, p. 47) notes, "China had lurched from crisis to crisis while Taiwan experienced fifty years of stable economic and social development under repressive Japanese imperial rule." In the face of improved economic and social circumstances, it may have been difficult for the locals to hate the occupiers continuously. Instead, ambivalence prevailed.

Fifty years of Japanese control over Taiwan came to an abrupt end in August of 1945 with Japan's defeat in World War II. When news of Japan's surrender hit Taiwan, ambivalence turned into euphoria as the citizenry anticipated rescue and deliverance. Expectations ran high—too high.

Table 2.2 Chronology of Events in Taiwan

Date or Period	Event
1624 onward	Dutch rule "Ilha Formosa" as a colony.
1661	Fukienese general Koxinya takes control of the island.
1683	Taiwan passes into the hands of the Manchu Dynasty, which governs it for two centuries.
April 7, 1895	Treaty of Shimonoseki concluding the First Sino-Japanese War cedes Taiwan and the neighboring Pescadores to Japan.
May 29, 1895	Japanese establish themselves on Taiwan, now a colony of Japan.
December 1, 1943	Cairo Declaration calls for a return to China of territory, Taiwan included, stolen by Japan.
August 14, 1945	Japan surrenders unconditionally to the Allied forces, thus bringing World War II to a close.
October 25, 1945	Japan formally surrenders Taiwan to China.
February 27, 1947	Altercation occurs in Taipei leaving one person dead.
February 28, 1947	Demonstrators confront the government in Taipei, triggering the 2-28 Incident, which costs thousands of lives.
December 9, 1949	KMT Nationalists flee mainland China for Taipei, and Chiang Kai-shek arrives the next day, announcing Taipei as the temporary capital of China.
March 1950	Chiang declares himself president of the Republic of China (ROC) on Taiwan.
June 25, 1950	Korean War commences, and the United States dispatches the Seventh Fleet into the Taiwan Strait to protect its interests in the area.

Fall 1971	Taiwan withdraws from the United Nations before the General Assembly of that body votes to assign the China seat to the People's Republic of China (PRC).
January 1, 1979	America establishes diplomatic relations with the People's Republic of China, severing formal ties with Taiwan.
1998	Political discussion distinguishes between groups favoring independence for Taiwan and those seeking unification with China.

On October 25, 1945, Japan formally surrendered Taiwan to China consonant with the Cairo Declaration. Soon after that historic return, however, it became evident that the Nationalists were more conqueror than liberator. Taiwan was being conquered again, this time by its own Chinese. Gripped by a brutal civil war with the Communists on the mainland, the Nationalists drained Taiwan's resources and directed them to that cause. In the process the order and success that Taiwan had experienced at Japanese hands eroded. According to Hsiao and Hsiao (1996, pp. 219, 223), production in 1946 stood at only a third of the level registered at the high-water mark of 1940. Equally bad was inflation, which in 1946 topped 300 percent. Unemployment hovered at 15 percent, food shortages appeared, and crime and disorder reclaimed the streets. Expectations of all-things-made-good were hardly being met under the Nationalists. Frustration breeds aggression, and by early 1947 conditions on Taiwan reached combustible proportions. Any spark could ignite an explosive response. On Thursday, February 27, 1947, an altercation occurred in downtown Taipei near the river. It was the spark.

Reacting to a report that smuggled cigarettes were being sold at a tea store on what is now called Yenping North Road, agents from the Taipei City Monopoly Bureau confronted a widow named Lin Chiang-mai and insisted that she hand over the suspected merchandise. A scuffle broke out, and one of the agents struck Lin on the head with a pistol. Blood flowed and screams erupted. Then, in an attempt to flee the scene, one of the agents discharged his weapon, killing a bystander named Ch'en Wen-hsi. Although they managed to escape, the officials left behind their vehicle, which was burned by the crowd that had gathered. The next day, February 28, a mob of hundreds swarmed around the Taipei Provincial Administrative Executive Office, headquarters of the government, seeking satisfaction for the previous day's deed. At that point the situation went from bad to worse as shots were fired, killing two more people and injuring others.

Violence persisted for days. Mainlanders were beaten and killed, and chaos ruled. Informed of these happenings, President Chiang Kai-shek decided from his continental post to send the Twenty-first Division to restore order on Taiwan. Troops arrived on March 9, 1947, and over subsequent weeks killed thousands of Taiwanese. As Lai et al. (1991, p. 155) observe, estimates of the lives lost range anywhere from 1,000 to 100,000. Kerr (1965, p. 310), in his own thoughts on the 2–28 Incident, puts the figure between 10,000 and 20,000. To some experts there may have been method to the madness behind the killings. Gold (1985, p. 51), for instance, feels that the Nationalists systematically struck at students, editors, and anyone else who might be regarded as critical of the government. Yet one may believe otherwise and see the victims as randomly selected targets of opportunity. That interpretation fits the comment offered by Lai et al. (1991, p. 156). In their words, "the tactic of shooting indiscriminately at people and houses had long been used by KMT troops and warlord armies on the Mainland when putting down opposition." Witnesses of the Tiananmen Square Massacre might concur.

Meanwhile, the civil war back home was not going well for the Nationalists. In January of 1949 Chiang Kai-shek suffered a critical setback at the Battle of the Hwai-Hai. October of that year saw the Communists under Mao Tse-tung establish the People's Republic of China (PRC), thereby making Taiwan a de facto independent country. Shaken, the KMT Nationalists headed to Taipei on December 9, 1949, and Chiang flew in the next day proclaiming Taipei to be the temporary capital of China. A few months later, in March of 1950, Chiang declared himself president of the Republic of China (ROC) on Taiwan. Restoring Nationalist control of the mainland was a principal objective of the transplanted government.

About this time, the United States, which had been supportive of Chiang's campaign against the Communists, lost patience and sought to sever its connection with the Generalissimo. On December 23, 1949, the U.S. Secretary of State asserted that Taiwan was China's responsibility, and on January 5, 1950, President Harry Truman articulated a hands-off policy toward the island. Significantly, the secretary of state added that Taiwan and Korea both fell beyond America's line of interest. Taking the United States at its official word, the Communists marched into South Korea, triggering the Korean War. The date was June 25, 1950, and only moments later the United States reversed itself. Suddenly Taiwan became strategically important to America in its efforts to contain communism, and to protect both the island and American interests, the Seventh Fleet was deployed into the Taiwan Strait. By this odd twist, Chiang, in Kerr's (1965, p. 396) view, was saved by Mao.

As the years passed it became increasingly clear that the KMT government would not be returning to mainland China. In 1964 the PRC tested an atomic bomb, thereby exploding the dream that the Nationalists might reclaim the homeland by military action. Furthermore, one by one Western nations began to establish diplomatic ties with Beijing. As Gold (1985, pp. 93, 142) writes, such recognition necessarily meant breaking relations with Taiwan and the ROC since a country can maintain full relations with only one government of China. Acknowledging the PRC translated into denying the ROC in the "either-or" decision. Momentum continued to build against Taiwan, prompting the ROC to withdraw from the United Nations during the fall of 1971 just before the General Assembly voted to assign the China seat to the PRC. Chiang lived long enough to see that setback but not long enough to observe what may have been the heaviest blow to the island. On January 1, 1979, the United States established diplomatic relations with the PRC, cutting formal ties with Taiwan.

Diplomatic events intensified doubts about the prospects for Taiwan to continue as a de facto independent society. Nonetheless, today sentiment for independence can be found both within the KMT and within the opposition group known as the Democratic Progressive Party. Other organizations such as World United

Formosans likewise champion independence. Those forces aim to establish Taiwan as a sovereign nation and to secure admission into the United Nations. Public opinion on the matter, at least according to statistics reported by Leng (1996, p. 50), has become increasingly favorable among the Taiwanese. By the same token, it is possible to find expressions of support for unification with China. A circle within the KMT has endorsed it. Furthermore, trade between the two lands has been eased, travel across the strait has been relaxed, and communications have been improved. Indeed, each side has much to offer the other: Taiwan possesses a powerful production engine and all the thrust that accompanies modern technology; China possesses a huge market and abundant natural resources. Under such circumstances, as Hwang (1991, p. 43) contends, the governments across the channel simply cannot ignore the pressure for unification. Actually, the arguments regarding this Taiwan Question run parallel to those raised in relation to the 1997 reversion of Hong Kong to China. Consequently the degree of success or failure surrounding that enterprise has obvious implications for the Taiwan situation. The Hong Kong Question bears on the Taiwan Question, and the answer to the former may decide the response to the latter.

2.4 A SECOND TIGER: KOREA

The Cairo Declaration provided not only for Taiwan; it also provided for Korea by asserting that "in due course Korea shall become free and independent." Surely the spirit of the words, if not the words themselves, led many Koreans to believe that independence would take hold soon after Japan's defeat in World War II. What actually happened was something much different. As Sohn et al. (1982, p. 329) remark, "liberation did not bring that independence for which the Koreans had fought so hard, but the inception of ideological conflict in a partitioned nation."

During its very early years, Korea was steeped in Chinese tradition.[4] As the chronology summarized in Table 2.3 indicates, Yi T'aejo assumed the throne in 1392 and built a government structure

Table 2.3 Chronology of Events in Korea

Date or Period	Event
1392 onward	Yi T'aejo assumes the Korean throne and builds a government structure reflecting Chinese tradition.
1592	Imjin War begins when the Japanese leader Hideyoshi Toyotomi invades Korea.
May 1875	Korean forces stationed on Kangwha Island fire upon a Japanese naval vessel.
1876	Treaty following the Kangwha incident allows the Japanese to settle in various Korean port areas.
February 1894	Tonghak rebellion starts in Chŏlla province.
July 1894	First Sino-Japanese War begins as Japan launches an unprovoked strike against Chinese forces at Asan Bay near Seoul.
April 7, 1895	Treaty of Shimonoseki ends the First Sino-Japanese War and secures Japan's hold on Korea.
Early 1900s	Righteous Armies of Korea volunteers conduct guerrilla raids against the Japanese on the peninsula.
August 29, 1910	Japan annexes Korea, which becomes a Japanese colony.
March 1, 1919	March First Movement erupts, leaving more than 7,500 participants dead.
December 1, 1943	Cairo Declaration asserts that "in due course Korea shall become free and independent."
August 14, 1945	Japan surrenders unconditionally to the Allies, thereby ending World War II.
August-September 1945	Korea is split at the 38th parallel with the north being occupied by the Soviet Union and the south by the United States.

November 14, 1947	United Nations passes resolutions calling for the independence of Korea and for free and independent elections.
May 1948	Elections are held only in the south because of Soviet opposition to balloting in the north.
May 31, 1948	Newly formed government meets and in the course of the session christens the Republic of Korea (ROK).
July 20, 1948	Syngman Rhee is elected president consonant with the new constitution.
August 15, 1948	Republic of Korea becomes independent.
September 1948	In the north the Democratic People's Republic of Korea (DPRK) emerges and claims authority over the entire peninsula.
December 1948	United Nations recognizes the Republic of Korea as the only legitimate authority on the peninsula.
June 25, 1950	Korean War breaks out as North Koreans attack south across the 38th parallel.
September 1950	General Douglas MacArthur leads United Nations forces through Inch'ŏn in a counterattack against the North Koreans.
April 11, 1951	MacArthur is relieved of his command and is replaced by General Matthew Ridgeway.
July 27, 1953	Armistice is signed, ending the Korean War.
April 26, 1960	Syngman Rhee resigns as president of South Korea.
May 16, 1961	Major General Park Chung Hee stages a coup and later becomes president by election.
October 26, 1979	President Park is assassinated.
December 12, 1979	Major General Chun Doo Huan gains power by coup and later becomes president by election.
February 25, 1988	Roh Tae Woo becomes president.

| 1993 | Kim Young Sam takes over as president. |
| 1998 | Kim Dae Joong enters the president's office for a term scheduled to run into the next millennium and likely to involve discussion about unification of the South and North. |

that reflected Chinese influence. Apart from intermittent raids on Korea by Japanese pirates, life on the peninsula evolved more or less smoothly for about two centuries. Then, as the sixteenth century drew to a close, hostilities erupted. A Japanese leader named Hideyoshi Toyotomi had designs on China and insisted that Korea grant him passage into China. Being sympathetic to China, Korea refused, and in 1592 the Imjin War broke out. Together Korean and Chinese forces repulsed the Japanese attackers. Japan was down and out—temporarily. It would reassert itself later.

The month of May 1875 heard Korean guns fire upon a Japanese naval vessel at Kangwha Island, and in the aftermath Japan extracted a treaty giving it a right to settle its own people in various Korean port areas. The resulting interplay of peoples did not work out for the best. Hoare and Pares (1988, p. 46) report that "the more efficient Japanese destroyed both the Korean fishing industry and the small-scale coastal trade. The export of rice . . . caused domestic hardship." Furthermore, local artisans were put out of work. The Koreans were distraught, and they directed their discontent at the Japanese through the Tonghak movement.

Tonghak, or Eastern Learning, commanded the status of a religion and became the rallying point for peasantry in the crusade to rid Korea of foreigners in general and the Japanese in particular. During the month of February 1894, rebellion erupted in the southwest province of Chŏlla and spread northward toward Seoul gaining strength along the way. Feeling threatened, the Korean government turned to China—not Japan—for assistance. China responded by sending a force of ships and personnel into Asan Bay on the peninsula's western coast. Although not invited, Japan deployed its own assemblage of boats and troops to Inch'ŏn just north of the bay. Meanwhile, the Korean government announced that it had been able to deal with the crisis on its own and that outside help was not needed. The die had been cast, however. Seizing the chance to end Chinese influence over Korea, Japan made a preemptive strike against the Chinese force at the bay. That action of July 1894 triggered the First Sino-Japanese War. As regards Korea, the consequent Treaty of Shimonoseki of 1895 secured Japan's hold on the peninsula.

As they did earlier through the Tonghak rebellion, the Koreans balked at Japanese control. In the dawning of the new century, they struck out through Righteous Armies of volunteers, who, by one estimate, numbered 70,000 in 1908. For their part, however, the Japanese soon tired of dissident activity and moved to annex Korea. Annexation was proclaimed on August 29, 1910, and as of that moment Korea was formally given up to Japan. Speaking emotionally, Lee (1984, p. 313) laments, "thus the Korean nation, against the will of its entire people, was handed over to the harsh colonial rule of Japan by a coterie of traitors."

Korea, like Taiwan, was now a Japanese colony. And like Taiwan, Korea did receive some benefits from Japanese control. For instance, steps were taken to improve health, transportation, and even the arts. Still, in the eyes of the Koreans, the negatives associated with Japanese domination greatly outweighed any positives that might be found, and again protest was ready to ignite. The funeral of former King Kojong in Seoul provided the opportunity.

Scheduled for March 3, 1919, the funeral rites would attract a large number of mourners from all across the country. Sensing that prospect, 33 Koreans met at the T'aehwagwan Restaurant in Seoul on March 1, promulgated a Declaration of Independence, and proclaimed Korea to be an independent nation. The March First Movement enveloped the entire country and incited two million people to cheer for independence. The Japanese response was predictable. The military rolled in and rolled over the demonstrators. The record tabulated by Sohn et al. (1982, p. 262) for that March shows 7,509 participants killed, another 15,950 injured, and still another 46,306 jailed. Two schools were destroyed along with 47 churches and 715 houses. But beneath the statistics lie atrocities such as the beating and stabbing death of a teenager named Yu Kwan-sun and the death by fire of an entire village (Sohn et al., 1982, p. 265). March 1, 1919, in Korea has a tragic and ominous similarity with February 28, 1947, in Taiwan and with June 4, 1989, in China.

Against this backdrop of turmoil and tribulation, it is easy to understand why Koreans were encouraged by the Cairo Declaration of 1943 and elated by the unconditional surrender of Japan in August of 1945. Surely, independence was on its way—or so they thought. What arrived instead were occupation forces from the United States and the Soviet Union and a line of demarcation splitting the country in two. That line was the 38th parallel. The Soviet Union, given its geographical presence at the northern tip of the peninsula, took control of the land area north of the parallel. The United States controlled the south, which included Seoul, the capital; Inch'ŏn the neighboring port city famed from the 1894 war; and Pusan, a port city on the southeast coast. Thus divided, Korea was anything but "free and independent."

In an attempt to resolve the Korean situation, the United Nations on November 14, 1947, passed resolutions calling for the independence of Korea, for the withdrawal of the occupying forces, and for free and independent elections. Elections proceeded in May of 1948, but because of Soviet objections to the idea, they were held only in the south. On May 31 the new government body met for the first time. It christened the Republic of Korea (ROK), and on August 15, 1948—three years after Japan's surrender—the ROK became independent. Disturbed by this chain of events, the Soviets and the North Koreans created the Democratic People's Republic of Korea (DPRK) and maintained that it had authority over the entire peninsula. Nonetheless, in December of 1948, the United Nations again spoke, this time to recognize the ROK, not the DPRK, as the only valid government of Korea. In short order, the United States and 50 other nations followed the UN action and officially recognized the ROK.

Leading the ROK at this time was Syngman Rhee, who came to the presidency already well established. After the collapse of the March First Movement, the Korean exile community in Shanghai created the Provisional Government of the Republic of Korea and announced Korea's independence. Rhee headed that group, and now he headed the ROK on Korean soil. Hardened by past battles, he soon would have to react to new ones.

When the United States drew a line in the sand leaving Taiwan outside its field of interest, it also left Korea outside. That move invited in the Communists, and in they came. On June 25, 1950, the North Koreans attacked across the 38th parallel and, with their superior military apparatus, drove the Rhee government from Seoul ultimately to Pusan. There the ROK waited with its back to the sea and with nowhere to go. Its fortunes changed, however, as rescue arrived in the person of General Douglas MacArthur, who landed a force at Inch'ŏn and soon had the North Koreans on the run. Fighting advanced north all the way to the Yalu River, riling the Chinese into joining the conflict. The front then shifted south, eventually settling at the 38th parallel. On July 27, 1953, armistice was signed and the parallel was replaced by a demilitarized zone (DMZ) straddling the line. A career casualty of the Korean War was MacArthur, whose zeal in pursuing the Communists despite orders resulted in his dismissal. His replacement, General Matthew Ridgeway, assumed command in April of 1951.

Following armistice, political activity in South Korea revolved around Rhee, who kept office through the presidential election of 1960. Election improprieties, however, blemished his victory and provoked a massive protest in Seoul on April 19, 1960. Police responded to that disturbance by killing a hundred demonstrators. Representing an iceberg of deeper opposition, the protest was followed on April 26 by Rhee's resignation. Nonetheless, the government that replaced him did not last long, for on May 16, 1961, Major General Park Chung Hee staged a coup and shortly thereafter ascended, by election, to the presidency. Subsequent constitutional changes enabled Park to succeed himself indefinitely. Park ruled with an iron hand, much to the dissatisfaction of the populace, and in August of 1974 an attempt was made on his life, only to take that of his wife instead. A few years later another attempt proved successful: a bullet hit its mark and Park was killed. The date was October 26, 1979.

History then repeated itself. Just as Park's immediate predecessor did not last long in office, neither did his immediate successor; on December 12, 1979, Major General Chun Doo Hwan assumed power by coup. Chun, like Park, went on to become president, relinquishing the post to Roh Tae Woo in 1988. Roh took the ROK into the new decade and managed the country until 1993, when Kim Young Sam took charge. Year 1998 found Kim Dae Joong in the president's seat, which he is scheduled to occupy into the next millennium.

Running through the life and times of Korea since the close of World War II has been the unification issue. Unification caught the attention of the United Nations soon after the country split at the parallel, it formed a battle cry of both the North and the South during the War, and it became a subject of political discussion by various representations of the ROK government. Hoare and Pares (1988, p. 222) see it as a particularly important matter, and Kim (1995, pp. 220, 236) sees it as an occurrence likely to happen if only as a response to the desires of the Korean people. In any event, unification is a major concern that connects three of the four Tigers: Korea, Taiwan, and Hong Kong.

2.5 BACK TO THE THEMATIC QUESTION

The historical musings in this chapter strove to provide a flavor of the past that shaped countries in the Asia Pacific Region. That past, whose account begins long before the time of Christ, saw the collapse of the dynastic system. It witnessed the Sino-Japanese wars, the creation of the People's Republic of China on the mainland, and the sudden departure of the Republic of China to Taiwan. It observed World War II, economic reforms, Tiananmen, the reversion of Hong Kong, and President Clinton's summit in Beijing. History watched Taiwan withdraw from the United Nations. It recorded the Korean War and the division of a country at the 38th parallel. It also chronicled uprisings, rebellions, revolutions, assassinations, coups, and elections.

The past of the Region has been tumultuous. In fact, it has been tumultuous to the point at which some interpreters of events may feel that the economic miracle relates less to high growth rates and more to the sheer ability to achieve any growth at all. Such insight gives extra weight to the question "why." To that thematic question the volume now turns.

PART II

THEORY, FACTS, AND EXPLANATION

CHAPTER 3

MODELING GROWTH

"You have a theory?"
"Yes, a provisional one. But I shall be surprised if it does not turn out to be correct."

Sherlock Holmes
—A. Conan Doyle, *The Adventure of the Yellow Face*

THE THEORY OF ECONOMIC GROWTH is delineated by models that offer different, albeit related, explanations of the growth process. Typically, those models may be distinguished by the characteristics that they envision for the production function. To illustrate, the model by Harrod (1939) presumes that the production function restricts input use to a fixed proportion. By contrast, the neoclassical model by Solow (1956) allows variable factor proportions. A third approach, pursued by Phelps (1963) and others, blends variable proportions with fixed proportions by hypothesizing that proportions remain variable as physical capital is being built but become absolutely fixed when capital has been constructed. Capital is putty ex ante but clay ex post. Cambridge theorists such as Kaldor (1961) provide yet another view by dismissing the production function altogether; somewhat ironically, however, it returns by the back door.

Adding texture to those differences are the conceptions about *shifts* in the function. Shifts, popularly called technical progress, can be neutral or nonneutral, and alternative taxonomies apply in that context. Shifts also can be disembodied or embodied as well as exogenous or endogenous. Endogeneity, in turn, may be imparted in various ways.

Combining the characterizations of factor substitutability with those of technical progress creates a large assortment of growth paradigms. This chapter considers a few models to convey the breadth of growth theory, stressing, of course, the system taken to be appropriate for the study of Asia Pacific growth. First, though, it sets aside Section 3.1 to elaborate on the three dimensions of progress. Section 3.2 examines the celebrated beginnings of modern growth theory and contrasts the model of Harrod with the neoclassical interpretation of Solow. Section 3.3 summarizes extensions of growth theory and observes that "new growth" is really not new. Section 3.4 turns squarely to the model postulated to explain Asia Pacific growth. Of necessity, that discussion is rather detailed. Section 3.5 moves on to describe the model's steady growth solution, which repeats a fairly standard property that steady equilibrium growth occurs at Harrod's natural rate. Section 3.6 completes the theoretical treatment by addressing the analytics of convergence. A point of interest there is the distinction between steady growth convergence and country-to-country convergence.

3.1 DIMENSIONS OF PROGRESS

Technical progress may be imagined to have three dimensions: bias, mechanism, and responsiveness.[1] Bias asks whether progress is neutral or nonneutral in relation to the distribution of income. Progress is neutral if it leaves the distribution unchanged and nonneutral if it changes the distribution. Perhaps more conveniently, the dichotomy can be framed in terms of the production function. Hicks neutrality, for example, refers to progress that leaves the marginal rate of technical substitution unaltered at a given capital-labor ratio. Likewise, Harrod neutrality is progress that does not alter the capital-output ratio at a constant marginal product of capital, and by analogy

Solow neutrality does not alter the labor-output ratio at a constant marginal product of labor (Hamberg, 1971, pp. 148–49).

The connections among these three brands of neutrality can be seen by writing the production function as

$$Y_t = G(B_t K_t, C_t L_t), \tag{3.1}$$

whose Y_t, K_t, and L_t denote the quantities respectively of output, capital, and labor at time t. Multiplicative element B_t is a function of time, which serves to indicate the "level" of technology. Augmenting the capital input, B_t can be understood to measure capital quality, and hence $B_t K_t$ can be perceived as efficient capital or as capital in efficiency units. Similar logic applies to augmentation factor C_t. It captures labor quality and combines with labor quantity to yield efficient labor $C_t L_t$. To go one step further, technology indices B_t and C_t can be posited to increase at the constant exponential rates b and c thereby making $B_t = e^{bt}$ and $C_t = e^{ct}$ in arithmetic notation.[2] Rate b may be called the rate of capital-augmenting technical progress whereas c represents the rate of labor-augmenting progress. As regards function G, it reflects constant returns to scale along with the usual derivative properties.

In this setup Hicks neutrality means that the augmentation factors expand at the same rate; namely, $b = c > 0$. By implication, expression (3.1) collapses to $e^{bt} G(K_t, L_t)$, where the technology index e^{bt} becomes a multiplicative factor of the full G function. Under Harrod neutrality only the labor input is augmented; that is, $c > b = 0$. The reverse situation applies under Solow neutrality, which augments only the capital input: $b > c = 0$. All three neutralities, although separate and distinct, come together under the umbrella of the Cobb-Douglas function since, for any technology index D_t,

$$D_t K_t^\alpha L_t^{1-\alpha} = K_t^\alpha \left(D_t^{1/(1-\alpha)} L_t \right)^{1-\alpha} = \left(D_t^{1/\alpha} K_t \right)^\alpha L_t^{1-\alpha}, \tag{3.2}$$

where the positive exponents α and $1-\alpha$ are serially the output elasticities with respect to capital and labor. Here Hicks neutrality appears first, followed in order by Harrod neutrality and Solow neutrality.

Mechanism, the second dimension of progress, looks at the way that progress enters the production process. As in the case of bias, there is a dichotomy, although now it contrasts disembodiment with embodiment. Disembodiment refers to technical advances that work their way into the production system without requiring the acquisition of new capital goods. At bottom, they are organizational in nature. Relocating a desk closer to a computer or repositioning a communications bay from starboard to port exemplify advances of the disembodied sort. And since they occur independently of capital, all machines regardless of age share equally in them. Capital is homogeneous with respect to progress.

Embodied progress is the exact opposite: technical advances enter the production system only on the back of new capital. To take advantage of the latest computer technology, a business must acquire a new personal computer rather than roll its 30-year-old mainframe across the hall. In like fashion, to capture the latest improvements in avionics and fuel savings, an airline must fly new aircraft rather than rearrange seats in yesterday's propeller fleet. New capital is the vehicle of progress. In that circumstance capital must be distinguished by vintage—by date of construction—because it contains or embodies the technology extant at the time when it was built. For the same reason, capital cannot share in subsequent technical advances, and consequently it is heterogeneous with respect to progress.[3] As a corollary point, the production function may be thought of as being defined at the vintage level, with each layer of capital having its own function. Aggregate output, then, derives from a set of vintage production functions.

Responsiveness, the third dimension of progress, asks whether progress responds to economic conditions and involves a dichotomy of its own: exogeneity versus endogeneity. Exogenous progress occurs independently of economic events. It follows a fixed course as it holds to, say, a given type of neutrality and a given rate of motion. Endogenous progress, by comparison, moves with events. Its bias may change and its rate may drift due to variations in input costs, factor shares, or education levels. Exogeneity has merit in its simplicity and in its representation of the average characteristics of progress. Endogeneity has merit in treating the evolution of technology as a natural outcome of economic processes.

In modeling technical progress it is possible to draw rather freely from the three dimensions. For instance, progress can be Hicks neutral, disembodied, and exogenous or Harrod neutral, embodied, and endogenous. Moreover, disembodiment can occur alongside embodiment. A common combination in the growth literature matches Harrod neutrality with disembodiment and exogeneity. In fact, the models portrayed in the next section adopt that match-up. The Asia Pacific model offered in Section 3.4 has neutrality, embodiment together with disembodiment, and exogeneity. By relying on the Cobb-Douglas function, its postulate of neutrality encompasses the renderings by Hicks, Harrod, and Solow.

3.2 CELEBRATED BEGINNINGS

Modern growth theory, it may be argued, began to take formal shape soon after the publication of *The General Theory of Employment, Interest, and Money* by John Maynard Keynes (1936). For macroeconomic equilibrium to occur, saving must equal investment. But could equilibrium be maintained through time if saving depended upon the *level* of income when investment depended upon the *change* in income? The answer to this question involving a basic antinomy is affirmative provided that income grows. Harrod (1939) explains.[4]

Saving relates to income in a proportional manner. That is,

$$S_t = sY_t, \tag{3.3}$$

where S_t and Y_t denote net saving and net income at time t and where the constant saving coefficient s lies between zero and unity. Investment observes the simple accelerator, whose origin dates back at least to the turn of the century (Gapinski, 1997a, p. 4), and therefore

$$I_t = v\frac{dY_t}{dt}. \tag{3.4}$$

I_t is net investment at t while the acceleration coefficient v is a positive constant. In equilibrium

$$I_t = S_t, \tag{3.5}$$

or, from equations (3.3) and (3.4),

$$\frac{\left(\dfrac{dY_t}{dt}\right)}{Y_t} = \frac{s}{v}. \tag{3.6}$$

After integration, condition (3.6) becomes

$$Y_t = Y_0 e^{(s/v)t}, \tag{3.7}$$

Y_o denoting the output level in the initial period, time zero.

Equation (3.7) is instructive. It says that for equilibrium to be maintained through time under the basic antinomy, output must grow at the rate s/v. Necessarily, then, s/v is the equilibrium growth rate, but Harrod prefers to call it the warranted rate because the equilibrium path is unstable: a departure from the path causes a perpetual movement away from it.

This knife-edge property of the equilibrium path can be seen by comparing the warranted growth rate against the actual rate, written as s/v_R to put it on the same footing as its equilibrium counterpart. Symbol v_R may be interpreted as the realized acceleration coefficient, whereas v indicates the planned measure. When the actual rate exceeds the equilibrium rate, $s/v_R > s/v$ implying that $v_R < v$. Investment falls behind desired levels, orders mount, and growth quickens, driving the actual rate further from equilibrium. In the opposite case in which the actual rate falls below equilibrium, $s/v_R < s/v$, implying $v_R > v$. Now there is too much capital, cutbacks occur, and actual growth fades cumulatively away from equilibrium.

One of the building blocks of Harrod's reasoning is the warranted growth rate. Another is the natural growth rate, defined as the maximum rate allowed by increased labor supply and by technical progress. Labor growth proceeds at a rate n, and progress, which manifests Harrod neutrality, disembodiment, and exogeneity, occurs at a rate c, making the natural rate $n + c$. Being a maximum, the natural rate constitutes a limiting value for a sustained actual growth rate. Consequently, when the warranted rate lies below the natural, the actual rate, unimpeded by the natural, may drift above the warranted, triggering inflationary conditions known as secular exhilaration. Conversely, when the warranted rate surpasses the natural rate, the actual rate, blocked by the natural, cannot reach equilibrium, prompting the depressionary tendencies of secular stagnation.

Secular turmoil can be avoided if the warranted and natural rates coincide. Yet coincidence happens only by accident because the warranted rate, with its s and v, and the natural rate, with its n and c, are largely fixed. There is no automatic adjustment mechanism available to bring the rates together. Of particular importance is the rigidity of v, which can be seen from equation (3.4) as the capital-output ratio K_t / Y_t. A fixed capital-output ratio, however, means that fixed factor proportions K_t / L_t characterize the production structure. Hence, it is fixed proportions that prevent the warranted rate sY_t / K_t from adjusting to the natural rate $n + c$ in Harrod's paradigm.[5]

Assumptions are fundamental to theory. They reduce a complicated reality to a manageable level from which lessons can be learned and insights can be gained. Often assumptions entail no loss of generality, and the conclusions that they facilitate in the narrow context carry forward into the broad circumstance. Sometimes, though, an assumption is critical to the extent that it decides the conclusion. One such assumption is Harrod's presumption of fixed factor proportions. In the words of Solow (1956, p. 65), "All theory depends on assumptions which are not quite true. . . . When the results of a theory seem to flow specifically from a special crucial assumption, then if the assumption is dubious, the results are suspect." In the long-run setting of economic growth, Solow continues, variability rather than fixity of proportions should be the rule. From that reasoning comes the neoclassical growth model (Solow, 1956).

The production function behind that model may be written as

$$Y_t = G\left(K_t, C_t L_t\right). \tag{3.8}$$

Technology index C_t expresses Harrod-neutral exogenous disembodiment and evolves exponentially at the rate c from an initial level C_o; mathematically, $C_t = C_o\, e^{ct}$ in keeping with the earlier treatment. Also as before, function G, besides having the usual derivative properties, exhibits constant returns to scale. Consequently, expression (3.8) can be reexpressed in intensive form without time subscripts as

$$q = g(x), \tag{3.9}$$

whose $q = Y/(CL)$ and $x = K/(CL)$. For the g function, $g\ (0) = 0$, $g\ (\infty) = \infty$, $g' > 0$, and $g'' < 0$, the prime and double prime marks signifying the first and second derivatives respectively. In addition, the Inada boundary conditions hold; namely, $g'\ (0) = \infty$ and $g'\ (\infty) = 0$.

Saving is proportional to income consonant with hypothesis (3.3), and equilibrium means the equality of investment and saving consonant with condition (3.5). Therefore, it follows that equilibrium may be stated as

$$\frac{\dot{K}}{K} = \frac{sY}{K}, \tag{3.10}$$

where the dot abbreviates the time derivative. That is, $\dot{K} = dK/dt$, which is net investment I.

Equation (3.10) describes equilibrium in terms of a growth rate, and plainly its sY/K is Harrod's warranted rate. For equilibrium growth to occur at a *steady* rate, a customary theme of growth discourse, Y/K must be constant over time. But from schedule (3.8), $Y/K = G\ (1,\ CL/K)$. Constancy of Y/K thus reduces to the constancy of CL/K. Technology index C advances at the rate c, and, as in the

Harrodian framework, labor L expands at the rate n. Hence CL/K and Y/K are constant when

$$K = K_0 e^{(n+c)t}. \qquad (3.11)$$

Correspondingly,

$$Y = Y_0 e^{(n+c)t}. \qquad (3.12)$$

Steady equilibrium growth finds capital and output growing at Harrod's natural rate. Furthermore, in steady growth the warranted rate equals the natural rate. Equation (3.10), with $\dot{K}/K = n + c$ from result (3.11), verifies the point.

There is more to the story. Not only does the warranted rate equal the natural rate in steady growth, but it also exhibits an inherent tendency to adjust to the natural rate. Confirmation of this stability comes from $\dot{x}$.

Converting x into log form and taking time derivatives leaves $\dot{x}/x = \dot{K}/K - (n + c)$. Substituting sY/K for $\dot{K}/K$ from equality (3.10) leaves $\dot{x}/x = sg/x - (n + c)$, sg/x being a restatement of the warranted rate. Thus

$$\dot{x} = sg - (n + c)x. \qquad (3.13)$$

From Figure 3.1, whose top half sketches separately the two components of $\dot{x}$ and whose bottom half maps $\dot{x}$ itself, it is evident that $\dot{x}$ becomes zero at x^*. There, $sg/x = n + c$ as the warranted rate equals the natural rate. For an x greater than x^*, $sg/x < n + c$ as the warranted rate drops below the natural. Simultaneously, though, $\dot{x} < 0$, causing x to decline to x^* and the warranted rate to rise to the natural. By contrast, when x falls short of x^*, the warranted rate outstrips the natural. In that situation $\dot{x} > 0$, causing x to rise to x^* and the warranted rate to decline to the natural.

In the neoclassical model steady equilibrium growth occurs at the natural rate. Any departure of the warranted rate from the natural rate triggers an automatic adjustment mechanism that drives the warranted back to the natural. That mechanism is the variabil-

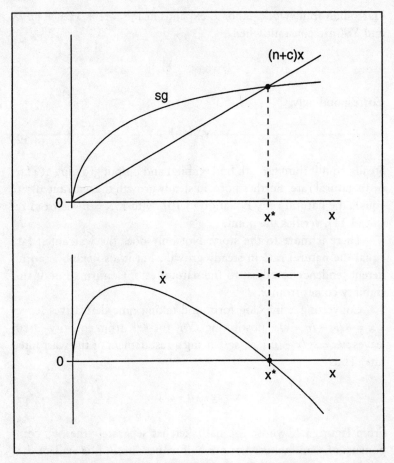

Figure 3.1 Neoclassical Growth Existence and Stability

ity of factor proportions—the x. Under variable proportions economic growth is hardly Harrodian.

3.3 EXTENSIONS

Fixed proportions of the Harrod system and variable proportions of the neoclassical paradigm come together in the putty-clay model.[6]

Traceable to Johansen (1959, p. 158) and Salter (1960, p. 17) and compellingly presented by Phelps (1963, p. 265), the idea behind the synthesis is that capital leads two lives: one during design and another during operation. On the drawing board capital can be molded and remolded across various designs, each of which specifies the labor input needed to run a machine and the output level resulting from that combination. Since designs relate inputs to output, they can be represented by an ex ante, or blueprint, production function that exhibits variable proportions. Nonetheless, once a design is chosen and built, capital loses its putty nature and becomes hard-baked clay. Its operation, therefore, is governed by an ex post production function that imposes fixed proportions. During the planning stage business slides along smooth ex ante isoquants searching for an optimal design. Upon making its selection and bringing the new capital on line, it finds itself relegated to the right angles of the ex post isoquants.

Given clay ex post, business has no ability to retrofit existing capital in response to changing economic conditions generally or to rising wages specifically. A cockpit designed for a crew of three cannot be reconfigured to be handled by a "crew" of one. Likewise, an oil tanker cannot be reconstructed to eliminate all hands except the captain. As a result, rising wages can eat into quasi rent, the difference between revenue and labor cost, and can lead to a situation in which the operation of a machine would bring about a negative rent. To avoid such a loss, business would retire the machine as obsolete. It follows that entrepreneurs must anticipate the future in making current input decisions to avoid a mistake that would hasten obsolescence. Expectations of price, cost, and the like become an essential part of the decision process.

Neither complication besets the neoclassical model. There factor proportions are always variable, and capital can be understood as putty-putty: putty during design and putty during operation. Optimization rules often insist upon the equality of the marginal product of labor and the real wage, and since the average product of labor exceeds the marginal product, quasi rent remains positive throughout the physical life of capital. Obsolescence never poses a threat. Moreover, because cockpits and tankers can be instantly and repeatedly retooled, the future can be dealt with when it arrives. The future is later. Current input decisions need not revolve around expectations.

Putty-clay provides a synthesis of the celebrated beginnings. Kaldor (1961, pp. 207–09), representing the Cambridge school, provides the antithesis by rejecting altogether the concept of the production function. A motivating force behind this departure from convention is embodiment. Under embodiment, says Kaldor, movements along a production function due to increases in capital quantity cannot be disentangled from shifts in the function due to the accompanying improvements in capital quality. A formulation presumably immune to such confusion is the technical progress function, which specifies that the growth in labor productivity depends positively upon the growth in the factor proportion. Positive first and negative second derivatives summarize the belief that investment opportunities favorable to output are captured in accordance with a systematic plan that dictates pursuing first investment opportunities that raise output most. The function also has a positive intercept to reflect society's dynamism or creative spirit and willingness to accept new ideas.

Rejecting the production function means throwing marginal productivity theory out with the bathwater. Marginal productivity theory explains the distribution of income by equating the marginal products of capital and labor with the respective input prices. But with no production function linking inputs to output, there can be no marginal products and no marginal productivity theory. A replacement theory fashioned by Kaldor (1956, p. 95) postulates a saving schedule that distinguishes between the saving from profits on the one hand and from wages on the other. The corresponding saving coefficients differ, the former exceeding the latter, and consequently total saving depends upon the distribution of income. In this way, too, the Cambridge growth paradigm stands apart form the celebrated beginnings, whose proportional saving function (3.3) makes no reference to distribution.

By an ironic twist of logic, Kaldorian thinking, in fact, does not make a clean break from neoclassical wisdom. The technical progress function, Kaldor's answer to the production function, can be written in linear form as $\dot{y}/y = \sigma + \rho\,\dot{x}/x$, where y denotes Y/L and where x now notates K/L, time subscripts being suppressed. Constants σ and ρ are positive, and ρ lies below unity. Integrating this expression and taking antilogs soon yields a Cobb-Douglas much like the formulas in statement (3.2). With this result, Cambridge theory, to paraphrase Hicks (1937, p. 153) from another forum, takes a big step back to neoclassical orthodoxy.

Embodiment need not invalidate the production function. The Kaldorian irony suggests that the function may continue to hold under that brand of progress, and Solow (1960, pp. 90–93), as usual, presents a pioneering effort substantiating validity. To accommodate embodiment Solow posits production to take place at the vintage level and sums across vintages to arrive at aggregate measures. Aggregation proceeds with apparent ease in the assumed Cobb-Douglas framework. However, a later inquiry by Fisher (1965, pp. 264–74) stresses that aggregation is anything but easy. A proviso underlying the procedure asserts that labor must be rearranged until the marginal product of labor is equal across vintages. This equi-marginal-product rule makes sense on economic grounds because business, seeking an optimum labor allocation, strives to equate labor's marginal product to the real wage. Under the rule, it applies the practice on a vintage-by-vintage basis. Moreover, the rule assures that aggregate output attains a maximum in keeping with the belief that a production function is a boundary surface.

Yet despite its economic sense, the equi-marginal-product rule does require that factor proportions remain variable ex post. And there is more. All embodiment progress must be capital altering; that is, embodiment must reveal itself only as a monotonic transformation of capital. In addition, the vintage production functions must exhibit capital-generalized constant returns (CGCR): they must show constant returns to scale in labor and a monotonic function of capital. Clearly, capital alteration and CGCR go hand in hand. A special case of these companion conditions is capital augmentation within a constant returns specification, the precise pairing stipulated by Solow (1960, p. 91). Aggregation, then, imposes severe restrictions on the structure of production. It is not easy. Appendix A confirms just how difficult it is.

Embodiment constitutes an important extension of the technical progress hypothesis inherited from the celebrated beginnings. Another extension of a similar caliber is endogeneity, commonly associated with the "new growth" theorists. "No economist, so far as I know, has ever been willing to make a serious defense of the proposition that technological change is literally a function of elapsed calendar time," intones Romer (1994, p. 12). That proposition, a defining characteristic of "old growth," may be represented in the arithmetic of equation (3.8) as $\hat{C} = c$, where the circumflex ($\wedge$) indicates the growth rate $\dot{C}/C$. Progress is exogenous, as it remains unresponsive to economic events. The new growth theorists reach beyond exogeneity and basically tie the rate of progress $\hat{C}$ to some decision variable. For instance, Lucas (1988, pp. 17–19) imagines $\hat{C}$ to be proportionally dependent upon the time devoted to human capital creation. Similarly, Romer (1990, p. S83), building on earlier work (Romer, 1986, p. 1003), takes $\hat{C}$ to be proportionally determined by the amount of human capital employed in research. So premised, the logic soon leads to the conclusion that output and machinery grow at the rate of progress (Romer, 1990, p. S92). Human capital, also interpreted as education and labor quality, is seen by the new growth theorists as a crucial driver of growth. Human capital matters importantly for growth.[7]

It may be worth noting, however, that new growth is not without its critics. A skeptical Solow (1994, p. 378) feels that "the new-growth-theory treatment of endogenous technical progress is pretty crude. It certainly doesn't come close to describing what happens in economic research and there is no reason to suppose it is much better on technological research." Pasinetti (1994, p. 356), of Cambridge persuasion, has doubts as well, and Nordhaus (1994, p. 373), looking at both the old and the new, summarizes their dialogue as a dispute. Evidently, not everyone is convinced.

Another point worth noting is that new growth is really not new: Intense work making progress endogenous in growth models debuted decades before contemporary thinking made print. Anchoring that work is the innovation possibility function of Kennedy (1964, pp. 543–45). Also called the invention possibility frontier, it describes the boundary line along which business picks and chooses the preferred type of progress; more precisely, the type of bias. According to Amano (1967, pp. 3–4) the optimal type might be the one that maximizes the rate of increase in profit or, equivalently, that maximizes $\hat{T}$, the rate of output growth due to technical progress. From expression (3.1), $\hat{T}$, which stands for $Y^{-1} \partial G/\partial t$, becomes

$$\hat{T} = \alpha\hat{B} + (1 - \alpha)\hat{C}. \tag{3.14}$$

Here α and $1\text{-}\alpha$ denote the shares of output going to capital and labor respectively; they are variables in the present setting. $\hat{T}$ obviously depends upon the growth in capital quality and labor quality and for that reason might be considered as anticipating the discussion of total factor productivity growth presented in the next section and beyond.

The invention possibility frontier may be written as

$$\hat{B} = H(\hat{C}). \tag{3.15}$$

Because of resource constraints, business can select faster capital augmentation only by accepting slower labor augmentation. In mathematical language, the first derivative of H is negative. The second derivative is negative too, as resource shortages place caps on the augmentation rates. Figure 3.2 sketches the frontier. Point P_1 identifies Harrod neutrality. Point P_2 represents Solow neutrality; Point P_3, where $\hat{B} = \hat{C}$, marks Hicks neutrality.

Maximizing $\hat{T}$ in equation (3.14) subject to frontier (3.15) locates the optimum technology configuration at point P_4, where $dH/d\hat{C} = -(1 - \alpha)/\alpha$. Entrepreneurs, intending to optimize, choose the brand of progress that augments capital at the rate $\hat{B}_{p4}$ and labor at the rate $\hat{C}_{p4}$. For the long-run situation, however, Amano (1967, pp. 7–10, 15–16) establishes that the income shares evolve in a way that moves the optimum point from P_4 to P_1. Endogenous progress becomes Harrod neutral in steady growth, and consequently steady growth occurs at Harrod's natural rate.[8] This result duplicates the conclusion reached under exogenous progress and

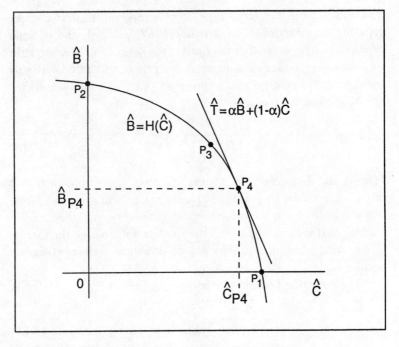

Figure 3.2 Endogenous Rates of Factor Augmentation

suggests that exogeneity may be a reasonable presumption for the long-run circumstance.

Running throughout the extensions of the celebrated beginnings is the property that steady equilibrium growth occurs at the natural rate. The Asia Pacific model to be formulated in the next sections shares that feature. Moreover, it agrees with the neoclassicals in rejecting the claim of perpetually fixed proportions for the long run. Instead, it accepts variable proportions, but it does not go so far as to embrace the putty-clay axiom that variability applies only ex ante. Putty also applies ex post. The model does go far enough to embrace embodiment as a critical part of technology and as an integral part of technology transfers. Production happens by the Cobb-Douglas. That specification, together with embodiment that is exclusively capital-augmenting, satisfy the Fisher conditions and thereby enable aggregation across vintages. Furthermore, the combination of the Cobb-Douglas and embodiment give at least a nod to Kaldor's Cambridge. Disembodiment too enters the system as labor quality improvements through education occur over time and invigorate labor units equally regardless of their age. It *is* possible to teach old dogs new tricks. By showcasing education the model manifests a kinship with the new growth philosophy, but it stops short of making progress endogenous through human capital or through other mechanisms. Progress remains exogenous. On that score comfort can be taken from Amano and others that such a tack causes no loss of generality in the steady state.

The Asia Pacific model nestles nicely within the tradition of growth theory. It draws from the precedents to capture features, such as embodiment and human capital, that add intellectual richness to the inquiry. At the same time, it sets aside properties, such as putty-clay and endogeneity, that would greatly encumber the clarity of exposition. In the end it offers insights of its own. To avoid confusion the notation is defined anew and is then maintained throughout most of the volume.

3.4 AN ASIA PACIFIC MODEL

Even a casual tour of the workplace reveals that today's machinery has features and capabilities not found in yesterday's tools. Capital goods are heterogeneous, and they are heterogeneous because they embody the technology extant at the time of their construction. Consequently, capital must be distinguished by vintage. Moreover, each vintage of capital combines with labor to generate output by a production function that is Cobb-Douglas in form:

$$Y_{vt} = \zeta \left(e^{\mu v} K_{vt} \right)^{\alpha} \left(E_t^{\theta} L_{vt} \right)^{1-\alpha}. \tag{3.16}$$

Symbol Y_{vt} denotes the quantity of output produced from vintage v capital at time t, K_{vt} represents the quantity of vintage v capital surviving at time t, and L_{vt} signifies the quantity of labor employed on vintage v at t. Output and labor are homogeneous over the heterogeneous vintages, and the vintage index satisfies the condition $v \leq t$.

Parameter μ is the rate of embodied technical progress. Augmentation factor $e^{\mu v}$ constitutes a capital quality index reflecting the level of embodiment, and therefore improvements in capital quality stem from embodied progress. Augmentation factor E_t^{θ} measures labor quality. It obviously bases quality on E_t, the stock of general knowledge possessed by labor at t, but it adds the refinement that what governs production is the degree to which knowledge improves performance on the shop floor. Knowledge elasticity θ allows for that performance bias. Because knowledge applies equally to all laborers regardless of the vintage on which they work, it applies equally to all vintages as well. Therefore, the rate of change in the labor quality index can be understood as the rate of disembodied technical progress. Expressed mathematically without subscript, the disembodiment rate is $\theta \hat{E}$, where $\hat{E}$ stands for $\dot{E}/E$, $\dot{E}$ being the time derivative dE/dt. Plainly, the production process involves both embodied progress and disembodied progress. Perhaps just as plainly, its parameters satisfy the restrictions $\zeta > 0$, $1 > \alpha > 0$, $\mu \geq 0$, and $1 \geq \theta \geq 0$.

Labor is assigned to capital by the equi-marginal-product rule, and therefore its marginal product is uniform across vintages. Such assignment maximizes aggregate output Y_t, which sums the outputs from all vintages in existence; specifically, vintages t back through $t-T$, T being the age of the oldest vintage. Formally,

$$Y_t = \int_{t-T}^{t} Y_{vt} dv. \tag{3.17}$$

Similarly, aggregate labor L_t sums labor units over vintages t through $t-T$:

$$L_t = \int_{t-T}^{t} L_{vt} dv. \tag{3.18}$$

The summation arithmetic, as Appendix A confirms, eventually yields the aggregate production function

$$Y_t = \zeta J_t^\alpha \left(E_t^\theta L_t\right)^{1-\alpha},$$

(3.19)

where the aggregate stock of efficient capital is

$$J_t = \int_{t-T}^t e^{\mu v} K_{vt} dv.$$

(3.20)

As regards J_t, heterogeneous vintage stocks are weighted by the capital-quality index to create a homogeneous measure that can be summed.

Capital deteriorates at the exponential rate δ, with $\delta \geq 0$. Hence, $K_{vt} = I_v e^{-\delta(t-v)}$, I_v representing gross investment at time v. It then follows that

$$J_t = \int_{t-T}^t e^{\mu v} I_v e^{-\delta(t-v)} dv.$$

(3.21)

The aggregate stock of efficient capital depends upon the level of gross investment and upon the rates of embodiment and depreciation. Its average age A_t can be taken as

$$A_t = \frac{H_t}{J_t},$$

(3.22)

$$H_t = \int_{t-T}^t \left(t - v\right) e^{\mu v} I_v e^{-\delta(t-v)} dv.$$

(3.23)

Magnitude H_t adjusts the age t-v of vintage v at time t by the efficient amount of that vintage and, through summation, determines the aggregate age of capital. Normalizing by J_t then yields the average age.

What about growth? In customary fashion output growth $\hat{Y}$ can be shown from equation (3.19) to be

$$\hat{Y} = \hat{\zeta} + \left(1 - \alpha\right)\theta\hat{E} + \alpha\hat{J} + \left(1 - \alpha\right)\hat{L}.$$

(3.24)

Output growth is a weighted combination of input growth. Growth in ζ is included to allow for factors besides capital and labor that may drive economic activity. One of those factors is international trade. Dornbusch (1993, pp. 87–88) observes that foreign trade improves resource allocation, and Western (1996b, p. 6) focuses the logic squarely on the Asian experience. Trade improves allocative efficiency. A parallel to this reasoning can be found in the rationale used to justify the inclusion of real money balances in the production function. Sinai and Stokes (1972, p. 290) point out that in a money economy, productive efficiency may increase as capital and labor are released from special tasks required in a barter economy. Likewise, allocative efficiency may increase as Asian entrepreneurs, influenced by incentives from participation in the global community, release capital and labor from some pursuits and reallocate them to others. By this view output could expand even if there were no increases in the quantities and qualities of capital and labor. Equation (3.24) admits that possibility. Of course, considerations in addition to trade might move ζ, but for now

$$\hat{\zeta} = \zeta_F F, \tag{3.25}$$

variable F measuring foreign trade. By hypothesis, $\zeta_F > 0$.[9]

Labor productivity growth follows quickly from output growth. Labor productivity is Y_t/L_t, which may be symbolized as y_t. As a result, labor productivity growth $\hat{y}$ becomes

$$\hat{y} = \hat{\zeta} + (1 - \alpha)\theta\hat{E} + \alpha\hat{j} \tag{3.26}$$

from equation (3.24). Symbol $\hat{j}$ notates the growth of j_t, which designates capital intensity J_t/L_t. Thus labor productivity growth depends upon the rate of "structural change," the rate of disembodiment, and the rate of capital deepening.

Growth shares identify the contributions that the separate determinants make to growth. With respect to output growth, those shares come straightforwardly from equations (3.24) and (3.25):

$$1 = \left(1-\alpha\right)\hat{L}/\hat{Y} + \left(1-\alpha\right)\theta\hat{E}/\hat{Y} + \alpha\hat{J}_K/\hat{Y} + \alpha\hat{J}_\mu/\hat{Y} + \zeta_F F/\hat{Y}. \quad (3.27)$$

Here the growth of efficient capital $\hat{J}$ is imagined to be split into two components that reflect efficient growth from quantity $\hat{J}_K$ and efficient growth from quality $\hat{J}_\mu$. Succinctly,

$$\hat{J} = \hat{J}_K + \hat{J}_\mu. \quad (3.28)$$

Given this decomposition, equation (3.27) identifies the contributions to output growth due to labor quantity, labor quality, capital quantity, capital quality, and foreign trade respectively.

In the same manner, the shares for labor productivity growth appear from equations (3.24), (3.25), and (3.28) as

$$1 = \left(1-\alpha\right)\theta\hat{E}/\hat{z} + \alpha\hat{J}_K/\hat{z} + \alpha\hat{J}_\mu/\hat{z} + \zeta_F F/\hat{z}, \quad (3.29)$$

where $\hat{z}$ indicates weighted labor productivity growth $\hat{Y} - (1-\alpha)\hat{L}$.[10] Equation (3.29) divides labor productivity growth into contributions from labor quality, capital quantity, capital quality, and trade respectively.

Total factor productivity growth refers to the amount of output growth not accounted for by the growth in capital and labor quantities. This interpretation means that by definition

$$T\hat{F}P = \hat{Y} - \alpha\hat{J}_K - \left(1-\alpha\right)\hat{L}, \quad (3.30)$$

$T\hat{F}P$ signifying the growth rate of total factor productivity TFP. But from statements (3.24), (3.25), and (3.28)

$$T\hat{F}P = \left(1-\alpha\right)\theta\hat{E} + \alpha\hat{J}_\mu + \zeta_F F: \quad (3.31)$$

total factor productivity growth depends upon the growth in labor and capital qualities, as the previous section suggested, and upon foreign trade. This interpretation is consistent with the views of

Griliches (1967, p. 316), Chen (1977, pp. 122, 127), Swee and Low (1996, p. 4), and Li (1997, p. 1093). It is also consistent with the remarks by Krugman (1994, p. 78) and Young (1995, p. 642). Furthermore, from expressions (3.24), (3.25), (3.28), and (3.31) or from definition (3.30),

$$\hat{Y} = \alpha \hat{j}_K + (1-\alpha)\hat{L} + T\hat{F}P, \tag{3.32}$$

$$1 = \left[\alpha \hat{j}_K + (1-\alpha)\hat{L}\right] / \hat{Y} + T\hat{F}P / \hat{Y}. \tag{3.33}$$

Output growth varies with the growth in quantities and in TFP. Necessarily, then, it is fully explained by the corresponding shares.

A similar rule holds for labor productivity growth. Through equation (3.32)

$$1 = \alpha \hat{j}_K / \hat{z} + T\hat{F}P / \hat{z}: \tag{3.34}$$

labor productivity growth is completely explained by the shares from capital quantity and TFP.

3.5 STEADY GROWTH

The process of economic growth can have two different representations. One rendering is a period-by-period account that may reveal considerable variation through time. Output growth might range widely from half decade to half decade, and labor productivity growth might swing markedly as well. Such lively patterns reflect the vigor of daily changes in economic conditions. A second rendering pertains to the long haul. It abstracts from temporary variations in conditions and concerns itself with an economy's long-run growth state. That state can be thought to entail steady equilibrium growth, which proves to be a special solution to the model discussed in the previous section.

Deriving that solution begins by imagining that knowledge E_t grows at the rate ξ from an initial level E_o at time zero:

$$E_t = E_0 e^{\xi t}. \tag{3.35}$$

Labor quantity L_t expands at the rate η by

$$L_t = L_0 e^{\eta t}. \tag{3.36}$$

Moreover, structural change occurs at the rate τ:

$$\hat{\zeta} = \tau. \tag{3.37}$$

Appropriately, $\xi > 0$, $\eta > 0$, and $\tau > 0$. Saving S_t is proportionally tied to output Y_t by a saving coefficient s that satisfies the restriction $1 > s > 0$. Thus, in equilibrium,

$$I_t = sY_t \tag{3.38}$$

From these four postulates output growth in schedule (3.24) becomes, *sans* time subscripts,

$$\hat{Y} = \tau + (1-\alpha)\theta\xi + (1-\alpha)\eta + \alpha(s\lambda/\pi - \delta) \tag{3.39}$$

after it is recognized from Appendix B that formulation (3.21) makes

$$\hat{J} = s\lambda/\pi - \delta. \tag{3.40}$$

The λ, which equals $1-(I_{-T}/I)e^{-(\mu+\delta)T}$, is constant, since investment, by equation (3.38), grows at output's constant rate ϕ in a steady growth setting. The adjusted capital-output ratio π equals $\bar{J}/Y$, with $\bar{J} = e^{-\mu t}J$. As equation (3.39) discloses, π is the key to steady equilibrium growth because $\hat{Y}$ becomes constant only when π becomes constant. Therefore, a critical question is, "When does π become constant?"

The answer lies in $\hat{\pi}$, which, after substitutions from expressions (3.39) and (3.40), yields

$$\dot{\pi} = (1 - \alpha)s\lambda - \Lambda\pi, \tag{3.41}$$

where $\Lambda = \tau + \mu + (1 - \alpha)\delta + (1 - \alpha)\theta\xi + (1 - \alpha)\eta$. Expression (3.41) implies that π becomes constant—that is, $\dot{\pi} = 0$—when $\pi = \pi^*$,

$$\pi^* = (1 - \alpha)s\lambda / \Lambda. \tag{3.42}$$

Figure 3.3 illustrates. Its upper panel shows that $(1 - \alpha)s\lambda = \Lambda\pi$ when $\pi = \pi^*$, and its lower panel confirms that $\dot{\pi} = 0$ at the π^* mark.

But the lower diagram also confirms stability. If π exceeds π^*, it falls to π^*, and if π locates below π^*, it rises to π^*. Steady equilibrium growth exists, and it is stable. This property clearly resembles the neoclassical feature depicted in the bottom half of Figure 3.1. And, like the circumstances in the neoclassical paradigm specifically and in the folklore generally, steady equilibrium growth occurs at the natural rate. That is, when condition (3.42) holds, output growth in schedule (3.39) reduces to the constant

$$\hat{Y}^* = \eta + \theta\xi + (\tau + \alpha\mu) / (1 - \alpha). \tag{3.43}$$

Steady growth proceeds at the rate $\phi = \eta + \theta\xi + (\tau + \alpha\mu)/(1 - \alpha)$. Rate ϕ, however, serves to combine the growth rates of labor, disembodied and embodied technology, and allocative efficiency, and in that way it represents an enhanced version of Harrod's natural rate. The matching rate of labor productivity growth is

$$\hat{y}^* = \theta\xi + (\tau + \alpha\mu) / (1 - \alpha). \tag{3.44}$$

As for the age of capital A, it becomes a constant in steady growth. More to the point, from definition (3.22) and (3.23), A reduces to

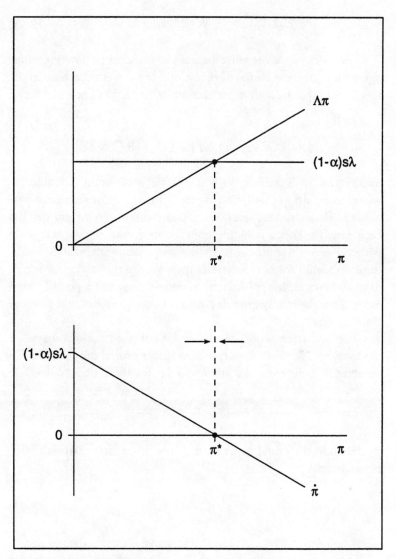

Figure 3.3 Asia Pacific Growth Existence and Stability

$$A = 1 / (\phi + \mu + \delta). \tag{3.45}$$

This expression makes sense because it associates a lower average age with a greater volume of recent, quality-corrected capital in the total stock; that is, with faster accumulation, embodiment, or decay.

3.6 TOWARD STEADY GROWTH

Steady growth is unlikely to be the initial state of an economy because, as equation (3.42) and Figure 3.3 manifest, it requires a particular balance of resources. Only one capital-output ratio permits such growth, and it is highly improbable for an economy to start with the exact resource composition required by that ratio. Fortuitous accidents are as rare here as they were in the celebrated beginning by Harrod. More likely, an economy begins at a point located away from the steady growth position but approaches that position through time.

The approach sequence can be described in various ways, an obvious measure for the purpose being the capital-output ratio. To demonstrate, differential equation (3.41) for π can be solved as

$$\pi = \left(\pi_0 - \pi^*\right)e^{-\Lambda t} + \pi^*, \tag{3.46}$$

π_o denoting the initial value of π. A few steps later relation (3.46) converts into

$$t_\varepsilon = -\Lambda^{-1} ln\, \varepsilon, \tag{3.47}$$

whose $\varepsilon = (\pi - \pi^*)/(\pi_0 - \pi^*)$. In this format ε indicates the fraction of initial capital-output discrepancy that must be eliminated before the economy can arrive at steady growth. For example, $\varepsilon = 0.20$ means that 20 percent of the initial gap remains to be closed, its $t_{0.20}$ giving the time elapsed in bringing the economy to that 20 percent mark. An ε of unity implies that $\pi = \pi_o$ and that 100 percent of the adjustment process remains. Appropriately, elapsed time is zero. By contrast, an ε of zero says that $\pi = \pi^*$ and that zero percent adjustment lies ahead: the process is complete. In that case elapsed time is infinite.

Another way to describe the approach sequence is through the growth in labor productivity. Using the $\hat{Y}$ expression (3.39) to elaborate the magnitude $(\hat{Y} - \eta) - (\hat{Y}^* - \eta)$ results in

$$\hat{y} - \hat{y}^* = -\alpha s \lambda \left(\pi \pi^* \right)^{-1} \left(\pi - \pi^* \right), \tag{3.48}$$

which can be reworked into

$$\hat{y} - \hat{y}^* = s \lambda e^{\mu t} \left(M - M^* \right), \tag{3.49}$$

$$\hat{y} - \hat{y}^* = -\alpha s \lambda \zeta^{1/\alpha} \left[E^{\theta} / \left(y y^* \right) \right]^{(1-\alpha)/\alpha} e^{\mu t} \left[y^{(1-\alpha)/\alpha} - \left(y^* \right)^{(1-\alpha)/\alpha} \right]. \tag{3.50}$$

The M represents the marginal product of efficient capital $\alpha Y/J$, M^* designates its steady growth value, and y^* symbolizes the level of labor productivity in steady growth. These three companion equations assert that labor productivity advances faster when the capital-output ratio is lower, when the marginal product of efficient capital is higher, or when the labor productivity level is lower than the relevant steady growth benchmark.

Figure 3.4 sketches the dynamics behind relation (3.50). For convenience it focuses on logarithms and correspondingly tracks steady growth labor productivity as $ln \, y^* = ln \, y_0^* + \hat{y}^* \, t$. Country A begins at time zero with a productivity level below the steady growth norm. Yet its growth rate—the slope of the "A" line—exceeds $\hat{y}^*$, enabling adjustment to steady growth. Country A exhibits steady growth convergence, its labor productivity level gravitating to the steady growth level. Gauging that movement is t_ε which can be interpreted as convergence time: the time needed for the convergence process to reach a point at which only 100ε percent adjustment remains. In like manner, Country B, identical to A in all respects except for a lower initial productivity level, also shows steady growth convergence. Along the way, Country B, exhibiting

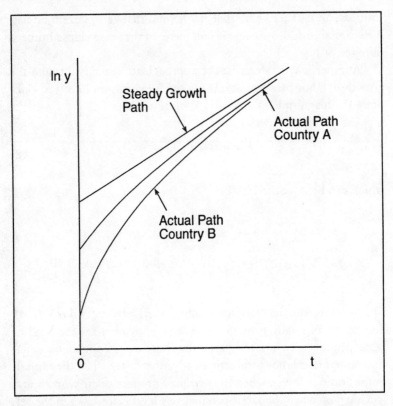

Figure 3.4 Steady Growth Convergence and Country-to-Country Convergence

by statement (3.50) faster initial growth than does A, catches up to A. There exists country-to-country convergence, whereby a nation having an initial labor productivity level less than that of another nation grows faster in productivity and catches up to the leader's level. Thus, steady growth convergence and country-to-country convergence can amount to much the same thing.

But not always. Country-to-country convergence presumes that nations have identical underlying conditions or different conditions that on balance operate as identical. That presumption may be hard to satisfy in practice. To Solow (1994, p. 376), "convergence of growth rates makes sense if you believe that the same technology is effectively available everywhere. That is far from obvious to me." To Barro (1994, p. 1), the "convergence property seems to apply empirically for economies that have similar underlying struc- tures ... but not for a heterogeneous collection of countries.... One reason for the failure of convergence in this broad context is that countries are effectively heading toward different long-run tar- gets for per capita income." Figure 3.5 illustrates. Countries A and B both evidence steady growth convergence. Moreover, Country B,

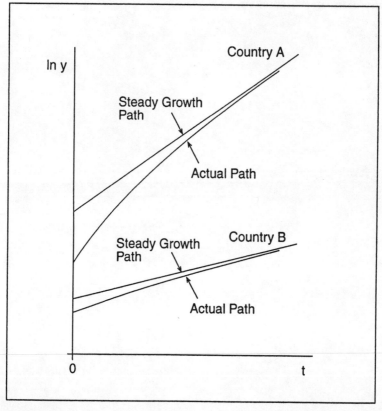

Figure 3.5 Steady Growth Convergence and Country-to-Country Divergence

possessing the lower initial productivity level, might be thought to grow faster than A and to converge to A in country-to-country fashion. Instead, it diverges, as its actual productivity path drifts away from that for A. The nations diverge simply because they are moving toward different targets.

Steady growth convergence can suggest country-to-country convergence although it need not. Similarly, expression (3.50) and its companions (3.48) and (3.49) may provide instructive descriptions of intercountry convergence provided that their ceteris paribus conditions are met; in other words, provided that the sovereignties are fairly homogeneous in economic structure. These lessons shall be useful in later discussions.

CHAPTER 4

ECONOMIC PROFILES

And now, Watson, we shall order breakfast, and afterwards I shall walk down to Doctors' Commons, where I hope to get some data which may help us in this matter.

Sherlock Holmes
—A. Conan Doyle, *The Adventure of the Speckled Band*

GIVING PRACTICAL SUBSTANCE to the theoretical structure requires data, the preparation of which is described in Section 4.1. From those data the economic profiles of the Asia Pacific countries can be sketched, and they form the subject of Section 4.2. Afterward, Section 4.3 broadens the inquiry by presenting economic profiles for country groups that embrace 120 nations worldwide. Implications for convergence and divergence can be found in the behavior patterns of the countries and groups, and that topic drives Section 4.4.

4.1 A DATA FILE

At the center of the data file lies an amazingly extensive, phenomenally rich body of information known as the Penn World Table Mark 5.5 (PWT) prepared by Summers and Heston (1993). This collection, which represents a revision of earlier endeavors (Sum-

mers and Heston, 1988, 1991), covers 150 countries annually over
the 41-year period 1950–90, although details are not available for
all countries in all years. Still, PWT, with its cross-section and time-
series dimensions, is impressive. Focusing on national accounts, it
contains series on gross domestic product (GDP), the components of
GDP, and the corresponding prices. Real series are expressed in
1985 international dollars, rendering them comparable across countries. PWT also has information on population and derivable information on labor. However, it does not have data on capital stocks.[1]

Although the present inquiry is concerned with Asia Pacific
countries, there is merit in building into the file all the data-
abundant countries found in PWT. The later regression analysis
would benefit from the extra degrees of freedom, and comparative
analysis would be strengthened through the greater variety of characteristics afforded by the wider coverage. Hence, the first step in
handling PWT is to determine how many countries have long
enough time series to permit retention. The frequency distribution
of the data suggests that countries be retained if their observation
count equals 27 or more. Under that criterion 28 nations including
China are set aside. However, that cut leaves only two states to represent Eastern Europe. Inasmuch as such representation seems to be
rather thin, they too are jettisoned, leaving a sample of 120 nations.
Those survivors, besides maintaining their separate identities for individual study, are consolidated into ten country groups based on
geographic location and on taxonomies offered by the Organization
for Economic Cooperation and Development (OECD) in *Main Economic Indicators,* the World Bank (1993, p. xvi), and Dosi et al.
(1994, p. 162). The ten groups and their memberships are presented
in Table 4.1. That broadened setting envisions the Gaurs to encompass countries beyond Papua New Guinea and the Philippines. It
likewise imagines the Elephants to cover nations beyond Australia,
Japan, New Zealand, and the United States. Country codes from
PWT and partition codes, to be explained shortly, also appear in
Table 4.1.

As regards the data proper, output Y is taken from PWT as
real GDP expressed in billions of 1985 dollars. Labor quantity L,
in millions of workers, also comes from PWT. Labor quality E is

Table 4.1 Directory of Countries

Country Name	Ctry. Code	Part. Code
East Asian Tigers		
Hong Kong	88	1
Korea (South)	96	1
Singapore	108	1
Taiwan	111	1
Southeast Asian Lions		
Indonesia	90	3
Malaysia	99	1
Thailand	112	3
South Asian Gaurs		
Bangladesh	85	3
Fiji	144	3
India	89	3
Myanmar	101	3
Nepal	102	3
Pakistan	104	3
Papua New Guinea	146	3
Philippines	105	3
Sri Lanka	109	3
Latin Rim Bulls		
Argentina	72	2
Brazil	74	2
Mexico	64	2
Venezuela	83	2
Latin American Tapirs		
Bolivia	73	2
Chile	75	2
Colombia	76	2
Costa Rica	55	2
Ecuador	77	2
El Salvador	58	2
Guatemala	60	2
Guyana	78	2
Honduras	62	2
Nicaragua	65	2
Panama	66	2
Paraguay	79	2
Peru	80	2
Suriname	81	2
Uruguay	82	2
Caribbean Iguanas		
Barbados	52	2
Dominican Republic	57	2
Haiti	61	3
Jamaica	63	3
Puerto Rico	67	3
Trinidad and Tobago	70	3
Middle Eastern Camels		
Cyprus	118	3
Iran	91	3
Iraq	92	3
Israel	93	3
Jordan	95	3
Syria	110	3
Turkey	139	3
Perimeter African Rhinos		
Algeria	1	2
Egypt	14	2
Malta	130	2
Morocco	30	2
South Africa	41	2
Tunisia	46	2
Sub-Saharan Hippos		
Angola	2	3
Benin	3	3
Botswana	4	3
Burkina Faso	5	3
Burundi	6	3
Cameroon	7	3
Cape Verde	8	3
Central African Rep.	9	3
Chad	10	3
Comoros	11	3
Congo	12	3
Ethiopia	15	3
Gabon	16	3
Gambia	17	3
Ghana	18	3
Guinea	19	3
Guinea-Bissau	20	3
Ivory Coast	21	3
Kenya	22	3
Lesotho	23	3
Liberia	24	3
Madagascar	25	3
Malawi	26	3
Mali	27	3
Mauritania	28	3
Mauritius	29	3
Mozambique	31	3
Namibia	32	3
Niger	33	3
Nigeria	34	3
Reunion	35	3
Rwanda	36	3
Senegal	37	3
Seychelles	38	3
Sierra Leone	39	3
Somalia	40	3
Swaziland	43	3
Tanzania	44	3
Togo	45	3
Uganda	47	3
Zaire	48	3
Zambia	49	3
Zimbabwe	50	3
OECD Elephants		
Australia	143	1
Austria	115	1
Belgium	116	1
Canada	54	1
Denmark	120	1
Finland	121	1
France	122	1
Germany (West)	123	1
Greece	124	1
Iceland	126	1
Ireland	127	1
Italy	128	1
Japan	94	1
Luxembourg	129	1
Netherlands	131	1
New Zealand	145	1
Norway	132	1
Portugal	134	1
Spain	136	1
Sweden	137	1
Switzerland	138	1
United Kingdom	140	1
United States	71	1

measured as the average years of schooling. This annual series is derived from the Barro and Lee (1993) decade and half-decade benchmarks by means of linear interpolation and extrapolation. For each PWT nation that Barro and Lee do not study, E is created from the schooling averages for countries having like characteristics. For instance, a Sub-Saharan country missed by Barro and Lee has its E values determined by interpolating and extrapolating the averages applicable to all the Sub-Saharan nations that Barro and Lee do study.

Capital stock J is constructed in keeping with the discrete-time variant of specification (3.21). The requisite gross investment I is the PWT series expressed in billions of 1985 dollars. This measure is backcasted far enough to enable the generation of a capital stock value for 1950 under the assumption that the maximum life of capital T is 39 years and, equivalently, that the number of vintages in service is 40. Prior to backcasting, however, the I series for each country is converted into logs and checked for stationarity using an augmented Dickey-Fuller test involving two-period lags of first differences. Where investment proves to be stationary, it is projected backward as an AR(2) process in log levels and transformed into antilogs. Where it proves to be nonstationary, it is backcasted as an AR(2) process in first-differenced logs, which eventually are converted into investment levels.

Aggregating the extended investment series I into a capital stock series J by the discrete version of formulation (3.21) requires values for the embodiment rate μ and the depreciation rate δ. Although the true values are unknown, reasonable assignments might be made by following guidelines from several sources. Sato (1966, p. 265) suggests that $0 \leq \mu \leq 0.06$ and that $\delta = 0.08$. Lewis and Seidman (1991, p. 473) propose $0 \leq \mu \leq 0.05$ while Chang (1993, p. 256) tries $\mu = 0.03$ and $\delta = 0.05$. Barro and Sala-i-Martin (1992, p. 226) and Conlisk (1993, p. 266) also use $\delta = 0.05$. These estimates set the tone for the assignments, but as they apply to countries of the OECD sort, they do not have general applicability.

To deal with the situation, the 120 countries are divided into three partitions based on real GDP per capita. Partition 1 consists of those country groups whose 1980 real GDP per capita exceeds

5,900 dollars. Partition 2 includes those with per capita incomes between 5,900 and 2,500 dollars, while Partition 3 involves those with
incomes below 2,500 dollars. Thus, the East Asian Tigers and the
OECD Elephants fill out Partition 1 as Table 4.1 observes. The
Latin Rim Bulls, the Latin American Tapirs, the Caribbean Iguanas,
the Middle Eastern Camels, and the Perimeter African Rhinos are
placed in Partition 2. The Southeast Asian Lions, the South Asian
Gaurs, and the Sub-Saharan Hippos are placed in Partition 3.[2]

For Partition 1 countries it is presumed that embodiment doubled quality-corrected capital over the 50 years from 1901, the beginning of the extended investment series, to 1950, the start of PWT.
That is, for Partition 1, $e^{\mu t} = 2$ when $t = 50$. For Partitions 2 and 3,
quality doubling took progressively longer: 60 and 90 years respec-
tively. Thus, the corresponding μ vector $\underline{\mu}$ becomes $\mu_1 = 0.0139$, μ_2
$= 0.0116$, and $\mu_3 = 0.0077$, subscripts indicating the partition num-
ber. Such a descending sequence is not without precedent. For example, Solow (1988, p. 315) and Wolff (1991, pp. 567, 572–74)
hold that embodiment rates are likely to be lower when investment
is less, and real investment does decline across partitions: from 68.3
billion dollars for Partition 1, to 7.3 billion for Partition 2, to 3.7
billion for Partition 3—or, relative to real GDP, from 27.7 percent
to 17.6 percent to 12.5 percent.

Quality doubling provides one set of μ values. With the inten-
tion of bracketing the unknown true set, six other quality multiples
are permitted: 1, 4, 6, 10, 14, and 18. The unit case, where $e^{\mu t} = 1$
when $t = 50, 60,$ and 90, implies that $\mu_1 = \mu_2 = \mu_3 = 0$, making capital technologically homogeneous in each partition. Figure 4.1 reports the seven sets of μ values. The first entry in each set belongs
to μ_1; the last entry, to μ_3. Clearly, the μ_1 assignments fit the guidelines from the precedents.

The δ assignments are decided under the presumption that advanced countries are less inclined to retain old capital than are developing nations. In other words, advanced societies retire capital
more quickly, leading to the assignment rule $\delta_1 > \delta_2 > \delta_3$, where
again the subscripts indicate the partition number. As an illustra-
tion, Partition 1 is imagined to keep 35 percent of capital in service
only through age 19; arithmetically, $e^{-\delta(t-v)} = 0.35$ for age $t - v$ of 19.

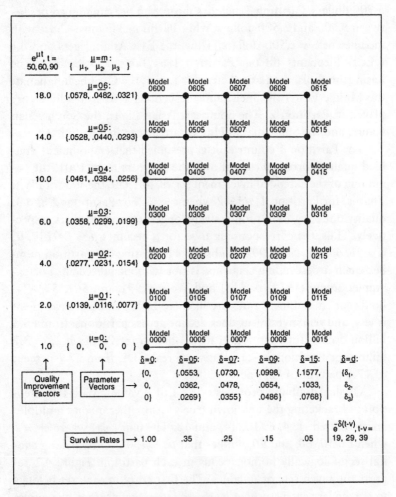

Figure 4.1 The Capital Grid with Identifiers

Partitions 2 and 3 retain old capital more willingly and keep 35 percent through ages 29 and 39 respectively: $e^{-\delta(t-v)} = 0.35$ for a $t - v$ of 29 and 39 respectively. As a result, $\delta_1 = 0.0553$, $\delta_2 = 0.0362$, and $\delta_3 = 0.0269$. To help bracket the unknown true set of δ values, other survival rates are considered besides 35 percent; namely, 25 percent,

15 percent, and 5 percent. Included as well is 100 percent survival through the maximum life of capital. That conception of one-horse-shay capital has $\delta_1 = \delta_2 = \delta_3 = 0$. Figure 4.1 lists the five δ vectors $\underline{\delta}$. The first entry again refers to the Partition 1 rate, which, like μ_1, fits the precedents. The last entry is the Partition 3 rate.

Together the seven μ vectors and the five δ vectors generate 35 capital types whose serial numbers contain four digits, the first two reflecting the $\underline{\mu}$ designation $\underline{m}$ formed from a stylized version of μ_1 and the second two reflecting the $\underline{\delta}$ designation $\underline{d}$ created from a stylized δ_1. Figure 4.1 has all of those particulars as well. It may be prudent to emphasize the summary in Figure 4.1 by reiterating that each capital model, quantified in billions of 1985 international dollars, applies to all 120 countries, and that each country matches up with all 35 capital models. In short, the capital grid is quite large. From a practical standpoint, however, it may be too large: It may needlessly encumber the subsequent arithmetic. Consequently, the capital models carried further into the inquiry are the nine types J_i indicated on the diagonals in Figure 4.2. There J_1 signifies homogeneous shays while J_5, occupying the middle slot, represents median capital. The sharper focus of Figure 4.2 involves no sacrifice of content.

With the nine J_i series in hand, it becomes merely a matter of additional calculation to measure, in years, the capital ages A_i from ratio (3.22) and the discrete version of equation (3.23). That age calculation proceeds for 1985, the base period of PWT. Gratifyingly, the results support the plausibility of the μ and δ assignments for Partition 1, which steers the assignments for Partitions 2 and 3. In the particular case of the United States, the nine ages A_i have a mean value of 7.5 years. Based on a standard test of means, this value is not statistically different from the estimate of 8.1 years reported by the U.S. Department of Commerce (1993, p. 213) for the age of the net capital stock in American industries. Nor is it statistically different from the estimate of nine years offered by Bahk and Gort (1993, p. 574) for the life of plants in the United States. In a sense, the capital diagonals of Figure 4.2 generate an age distribution for U.S. capital that is centered roughly at the values reported by the Department of Commerce and by Bahk and Gort.

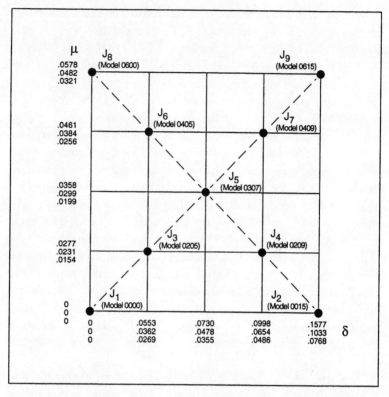

Figure 4.2 The Capital Diagonals with Identifiers

A parallel conclusion comes from the work of Maddison (1987, p. 664). Maddison reports the average age of the gross nonresidential fixed capital stock for six countries: France, Germany, Japan, the Netherlands, the United Kingdom, and the United States. For 1984 the mean age across countries equals 12.4 years, and for all three years studied (1950, 1973, and 1984) it equals 12.2 years. Ages A_1 and A_8, drawn in reference to the capital diagonals consonant with the specification of the Maddison stock data in gross terms, yield a six-country average age of 11.9 years. By the test of means, this estimate too is not statistically different from either Maddison number.

At the risk of anticipating discussion in the next section, two other results on plausibility might be mentioned. Both involve the average capital-output ratio $k_{12}{}^a$ for capital types J_1 and J_2, which, being technologically homogeneous, permit comparisons with empirical postings elsewhere. To illustrate, $k_{12}{}^a$ for Germany equals 3.4, which resembles the 4.2 value determined empirically by Siebert (1992, pp. 52–53). Moreover, $k_{12}{}^a$ for all Partition 2 countries equals 2.3 and almost repeats the 2.1 estimate documented by Gapinski et al. (1989, pp. 266, 274) for the former Yugoslavia. That country easily can be regarded as having Partition 2 characteristics.

From these considerations it seems fair to say that the empirical evidence substantiates the plausibility of the μ and δ assignments. By implication that evidence also can be said to substantiate the method for constructing the capital stock series.

Rounding out the immediate data file are series relating to saving and international trade. All come from PWT. The saving rate s quantifies real saving as a fraction of real GDP. It is obtained by the usual income-account identity that postulates saving as output net of personal and government consumption. Real exports are taken as a fraction X of real GDP, whereas real openness U sums exports and imports and expresses the result as a fraction of GDP. By including imports it constitutes the more encompassing gauge of trade. Other variables in the data file can be treated in the appropriate contexts later.

4.2 ASIA PACIFIC PROFILES

From the data file come economic statistics for the countries individually and in groups. Those for the 13 countries of main interest appear in Table 4.2.

One property to catch the eye there concerns the great size differences among nations. Papua New Guinea is the smallest with an output level Y of 4.5 billion dollars. By contrast, the United States, whose output level of 3,125.5 billion is almost 700 times the Papua New Guinea level, is largest. Great differences in size persist even within categories. For instance, within the Tiger family, output

Table 4.2 Economic Statistics by Country

Country	Y billion dollars	L million workers	E years	J_l billion dollars	J_m billion dollars	y dollars per worker	k_l decimal	k_m decimal	M_l decimal	M_m decimal	y_o dollars per worker
Hong Kong	35.5	2.7	6.16	98.3	1,824.3	11,896	2.81	40.25	0.099	0.052	4,105
Korea	100.2	13.1	6.12	273.5	6,152.5	6,934	2.25	42.33	0.139	0.064	2,244
Singapore	13.5	1.0	3.96	49.6	1,141.0	12,422	2.92	59.06	0.120	0.050	5,171
Taiwan	69.7	6.6	5.40	198.7	4,265.5	9,634	2.45	44.31	0.124	0.057	2,339
Indonesia	156.6	51.5	2.74	321.6	1,537.3	2,829	1.59	7.04	0.097	0.049	1,605
Malaysia	39.6	4.7	4.13	123.1	2,580.7	7,719	2.68	47.88	0.113	0.054	3,461
Thailand	83.7	21.2	4.10	205.2	826.1	3,670	2.24	8.31	0.054	0.030	1,582
Papua New Guinea	4.5	1.4	1.23	18.2	56.0	3,157	3.98	11.82	0.030	0.020	2,074
Philippines	69.3	16.1	5.44	188.1	692.1	4,187	2.52	8.78	0.049	0.029	1,768
Australia	163.2	6.2	9.86	1,034.9	13,259.1	25,959	6.26	71.83	0.044	0.030	16,296
Japan	1,003.3	68.9	7.59	5,026.5	90,739.5	14,101	4.43	72.91	0.070	0.033	2,707
New Zealand	30.4	1.2	7.50	199.4	2,264.2	24,539	6.49	68.52	0.043	0.032	17,294
United States	3,125.5	99.4	10.74	17,720.1	204,102.0	30,991	5.67	58.99	0.049	0.036	20,152

Country	$100\,\dot{Y}$ percent	$100\,\dot{L}$ percent	$100\,\dot{E}$ percent	$100\,\dot{J}_l$ percent	$100\,\dot{J}_m$ percent	$100\,\dot{y}$ percent	$100\,\dot{j}_l$ percent	$100\,\dot{j}_m$ percent	$100\,U$ percent	$100\,X$ percent	$100\,s$ percent
Hong Kong	8.85	2.82	1.58	8.22	11.81	6.03	5.40	8.99	188.39	95.49	24.79
Korea	8.95	2.63	3.47	12.93	17.04	6.32	10.30	14.41	53.22	25.33	22.80
Singapore	8.62	3.30	2.02	15.13	18.15	5.32	11.83	14.84	307.41	149.78	25.98
Taiwan	8.59	2.73	2.91	11.80	15.23	5.87	9.08	12.50	76.45	38.69	25.94
Indonesia	6.19	2.20	4.73	13.46	15.35	3.99	11.25	13.15	37.52	22.03	24.91
Malaysia	7.16	3.21	3.32	10.61	14.05	3.95	7.40	10.84	95.00	49.15	28.41
Thailand	7.25	2.72	2.11	9.44	11.43	4.53	6.71	8.71	46.66	21.89	16.39
Papua New Guinea	3.12	1.89	2.04	3.80	5.70	1.23	1.91	3.81	78.47	34.87	9.22
Philippines	4.28	2.55	2.06	6.71	8.44	1.73	4.16	5.89	44.16	21.63	15.35
Australia	3.79	2.27	0.51	4.18	7.53	1.52	1.91	5.26	31.61	14.51	28.24
Japan	6.46	1.15	0.89	10.29	12.87	5.31	9.14	11.72	22.08	10.04	35.05
New Zealand	2.54	1.85	1.08	3.00	6.49	0.68	1.14	4.64	54.05	25.59	24.17
United States	3.28	1.74	1.00	3.04	6.62	1.54	1.30	4.88	14.92	6.76	22.57

Notes. Entries are averages of annual values that cover the 30 years from 1961 to 1990. Those for the marginal products M_l and M_m use estimates for the capital output-elasticity α obtained by the method described in Chapter 5. All currency magnitudes are expressed in real terms.

ranges from a low of 13.5 billion for Singapore to a high of 100.2 billion for Korea. Similarly, the Lions have output stretch from 39.6 billion for Malaysia to 156.6 billion for Indonesia. The four Elephants—the mature nations of Australia, Japan, New Zealand, and the United States—also exhibit huge variations in heft. Such variations carry over to the capital stock measures, as the homogeneous-shay series J_1 and the mean series J_m, which represents the average across all nine capital types, demonstrate.

Another property to stand out from the profiles regards labor productivity y. Productivity for the four Tigers and for Malaysia ranks considerably above the levels for Indonesia, Thailand, and the two Gaurs of Papua New Guinea and the Philippines. A similar situation holds for initial labor productivity y_o. Consequently, it is fair to say that living standards, whether judged from the early years or from more recent experience, are hardly uniform across the nine maturing countries.[3] What is uniform about those living standards is that they all fall substantially below the U.S. benchmark.

The discrepancy in labor productivity of the maturing countries relative to that for the United States is duplicated to some extent by the capital-output ratios and the marginal products of capital. The k_1 in Table 4.2 refers to the uncorrected capital-output ratio for J_1 capital; namely, $k_1 = J_1/Y$. Its k_m counterpart refers to the uncorrected capital-output ratios averaged across all nine capital types. Marginal products of capital, the M_1 and M_m, carry analogous interpretations. As the table shows, the nine maturing economies in the Asia Pacific region have capital-output ratios that typically fall below the U.S. mark and marginal products that typically rise above the U.S. norm. Thus, in keeping with equations (3.48), (3.49), and (3.50), some sort of catch-up with the United States is suggested.

Column $100 \hat{y}$ of Table 4.2, where—as elsewhere—a circumflex ($\hat{}$) indicates a growth rate in proportionate terms, bolsters the suggestion but advises that catch-up may operate in varying degrees. Labor productivity for the Tigers grows at rates that easily surpass 5 percent and that locate well above the U.S. rate of 1.54 percent. Indonesia and Malaysia, too, have productivity rates exceeding the U.S. target, but their numbers drop a shade below the Tiger postings. Apparently, then, the Tigers and the two Lions exhibit convergence to the United States, but for the Tigers, convergence is more aggressive.

On the other side of the ledger, the two Gaurs have productivity growth rates that are about the same as the U.S. rate or that actually dip below it. Those nations may not be converging; in fact, they may be diverging—falling behind. An explanation for their nonconformist pattern is found in the saving coefficient. Clearly, the saving coefficients for the two Gaurs are far beneath the one for the United States. Hence, from equation (3.42) those nations may have a sustained growth path that differs from the U.S. path, and they may not be moving to that reference. Additional evidence regarding nonconvergence comes from the marginal products M_1 and M_m, which for the Gaurs are seen to be at or below the U.S. norm. Equation (3.49) interprets the situation as Gaur growth that perpetuates or widens the differential productivity levels already extant.

Thailand, the third Lion, leaves mixed impressions. Its capital-output ratios remain below the U.S. threshold, and in accord with equation (3.48), its productivity growth does top the U.S. figure. Yet its saving coefficient—like those for the Gaurs—is much less than the U.S. coefficient, and its average marginal product of capital M_m is also less than the target. By that evidence, convergence is not anticipated. Unscrambling the mixed images of Thailand and checking the conclusions for the other maturing economies may require an analytical approach that is more sensitive to productivity movements than are sweeping thirty-year averages. That alternative procedure is discussed later.

The lower portion of Table 4.2 contains much information besides facts of productivity growth. Importantly, it presents information that, by equation (3.26), relates to the determinants of that growth. The ζ component of $\hat{y}$, as equation (3.25) reminds, reflects foreign trade, which is quantified from PWT by real exports $100\,X$ and real openness $100\,U$. Both series exhibit the same fundamental patterns across countries. By either criterion Singapore ranks first in trade; Hong Kong places second; Malaysia, third; and the United States, a distant last.

Education growth, the second determinant listed in equation (3.26), occurs slowly on balance. The maximum for $100 \hat{E}$ registers only 4.73 percent in the case of Indonesia, whereas the minimum of 0.51 percent applies to Australia. These lethargic statistics give a quantitative feel to the comment by Barro (1994, p. 11) that expanding the education base of a country is difficult business.

Capital deepening, which completes the causal forces itemized in formula (3.26), varies widely across nations. The capital deepening series $100 \hat{j}_1$ for J_1 capital posts a high of 11.83 percent for fast-moving Singapore and a low of 1.14 percent for listless New Zealand. Analogously, series $100 \hat{j}_m$, which averages the deepening rates over capital types, peaks at 14.84 percent for Singapore and bottoms out at 4.64 percent for New Zealand and 3.81 percent for sluggish Papua New Guinea. These matchups between the $\hat{j}$ cause and the $\hat{y}$ effect are telling.

Figure 4.3 illustrates those matchups for all 13 countries, which are identified by letter codes. Without loss of generality, it uses $\hat{j}_m$ in the comparisons. The resulting configuration between $100 \hat{y}$ and $100 \hat{j}_m$ is obviously jagged, but it nevertheless exhibits an unmistakable positive slope in agreement with equation (3.26). Figure 4.3 also presents the configurations for $100 \hat{y}$ and $100 \hat{E}$ and for $100 \hat{y}$ and $100 U$, the more inclusive trade variable being chosen also without loss of generality. Both of those configurations show great volatility at low levels of the causal agents, but they still support, albeit vaguely, the positive relationships called for by schedule (3.26).

Capital is one of the major themes running through Table 4.2 and Figure 4.3. That theme is pursued a bit further in Table 4.3, which reports the age of capital and the proximity of actual capital to an optimal stock.

The A_1 indicates in years the age of J_1 capital, whereas A_m shows the average age across the nine machine types. Since the average age reflects, consonant with equation (3.45), the "rejuvenating" effects of embodiment and deterioration in the aging process, while the measure for homogeneous shays does not, it yields the lower estimates. Given the rapid capital expansion in Singapore, it assumes the lowest value there; that is, Singapore has the youngest average capital stock. Korea ranks second; Malaysia, third; and Indonesia, fourth. In fact,

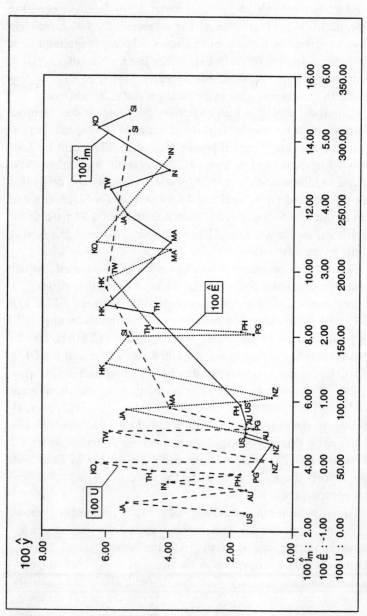

Figure 4.3 Labor Productivity Growth and Its Determinants by Country

Table 4.3 Additional Characteristics of Capital by Country

Country	Age A$_1$	Age A$_m$	Proximity Marginal Product of Capital M$_m$	Proximity Real Rate of Interest r	Proximity Sign of M$_m$ – r
Hong Kong	10.15	5.30	0.050	−0.021	+
Korea	7.70	4.54	0.041	0.041	0
Singapore	7.31	4.42	0.031	0.022	+
Taiwan	8.50	5.07	0.041	0.028	+
Indonesia	6.73	4.86	0.026	−0.003	+
Malaysia	8.32	4.58	0.039	0.005	+
Thailand	10.19	7.17	0.023	0.058	-
Papua New Guinea	14.81	10.21	0.016	0.029	-
Philippines	11.32	7.78	0.022	−0.003	+
Australia	14.50	7.15	0.028	0.032	-
Japan	10.64	6.09	0.026	0.032	-
New Zealand	15.83	7.63	0.029	0.024	+
United States	15.72	7.49	0.034	0.034	0

Notes. Entries for the marginal products are averages calculated across all nine capital types over the 15-year period 1976–90. The real interest rate is the difference between the nominal rate and the inflation rate. Its numbers, expressed as decimals rather than as percentages, are also computed as averages over the period 1976–90.

Sources. Data on marginal products are the ones already described. Those on the nominal rates of interest for all countries except Hong Kong, Singapore, and Taiwan come from the *International Financial Statistics Yearbook* of the International Monetary Fund. For Hong Kong and Singapore they stem from *Key Indicators of Developing Asian and Pacific Countries* prepared by the Asian Development Bank, while for Taiwan they result from the *Statistical Yearbook of the Republic of China* compiled by the Republic of China. Inflation rates based on the GDP deflator are given by the Fund in its *Yearbook* except for the case of Taiwan, whose numbers are provided by the Republic of China in the *Statistical Yearbook*. Estimates to interpolate missing values have various origins.

young capital is the rule across the four Tigers and three Lions. Only Thailand breaks the pattern. At the opposite end of the scale, the oldest capital belongs to the Philippines and Papua New Guinea, whose average ages place them twelfth and thirteenth respectively. Among the four Elephants, Japan possesses the youngest machinery. Having suffered massive destruction during World War II, Japan was forced to rebuild its stock and had the opportunity to incorporate into that stock the best-practice techniques. Such massive retooling was not required of the World War II winners Australia, New Zealand, and the

United States. The youthfulness of Japan's stock can be seen even in homogeneous-shay capital.

With respect to proximity, Table 4.3 compares the marginal product of average capital M_m to the real rate of interest r over the years for which information on the real rate is fairly prevalent across countries. Relying on the usual optimality criterion, where the marginal product equals the real rate, Table 4.3 shows that Korea and the United States have optimal stocks. Korea aside, the remaining maturing countries have deficient capital on balance; that is, $M_m > r$, thereby expressing in yet another way their labor intensive nature of production. By contrast, the mature economies, apart from the United States, have excessive capital on balance. For them $M_m < r$.

4.3 PROFILES BY COUNTRY GROUPS

When grouped in the manner described by Table 4.1, the data give rise to the numbers shown in Table 4.4. Since the OECD Elephants include the United States, their enormous size comes as no surprise. Judged by their real GDP of 338.6 billion dollars, they outweigh the second-place Latin Rim Bulls by more than a factor of 1.5 and exceed the Sub-Saharan Hippos by more than a multiple of 60. Similarly, the Elephants have the highest level of educational attainment across country groups, and they have the greatest stock of capital however measured. They also lead the way in labor productivity, in initial labor productivity, in the capital-output ratio, and in the saving rate. Yet in their growth rates, the Elephants are more moderate. For instance, their productivity growth rate of 2.65 percent ranks fifth, and their capital deepening rates of 3.87 percent and 6.80 percent rank fifth as well. Given their abundance of machinery, the Elephants trail the pack in their marginal products of efficient capital.

Naturally, the defining characteristic of the East Asian Tigers is their growth rates. Although diminutive with a real GDP of 54.3 billion dollars, those countries lead all metaphorical creatures in labor productivity growth, that annual rate being 5.88 percent. They likewise lead in capital deepening with annual rates of 9.14 percent for

Table 4.4 Economic Statistics by Country Group

Country Group	Y billion dollars	L million workers	E years	J_i billion dollars	J_m billion dollars	y dollars per worker	k_i decimal	k_m decimal	M_i decimal	M_m decimal	y_o dollars per worker
East Asian Tigers	54.3	5.7	5.41	154.0	3,322.2	10,249	2.61	46.52	0.120	0.056	3,475
Southeast Asian Lions	93.3	25.8	3.66	216.6	1,648.0	4,739	2.17	21.08	0.088	0.044	2,216
South Asian Gaurs	87.7	38.2	2.76	237.9	804.2	3,617	2.40	7.59	0.068	0.042	2,317
Latin Rim Bulls	214.0	18.1	4.19	701.0	6,204.9	14,079	3.28	25.26	0.101	0.050	7,910
Latin American Tapirs	15.1	1.9	4.07	55.9	422.7	7,428	3.55	25.30	0.108	0.055	4,560
Caribbean Iguanas	7.9	1.0	4.16	27.5	219.1	11,522	3.18	23.07	0.165	0.080	5,090
Middle Eastern Camels	50.4	5.1	3.80	152.5	1,515.1	12,107	3.19	26.81	0.140	0.062	4,905
Perimeter African Rhinos	36.7	5.1	3.39	102.7	919.7	7,612	2.65	21.54	0.173	0.082	3,998
Sub-Saharan Hippos	5.6	3.2	1.74	13.5	42.8	2,451	2.59	7.37	0.094	0.059	1,709
OECD Elephants	338.6	14.5	7.50	1,874.1	24,473.6	21,757	5.71	67.71	0.052	0.033	10,134
All Groups	92.8	9.1	3.80	443.4	5,391.5	8,896	3.38	26.25	0.097	0.054	4,499

Country Group	$100\,\dot{Y}$ percent	$100\,\dot{L}$ percent	$100\,\dot{E}$ percent	$100\,\dot{J}_i$ percent	$100\,\dot{J}_m$ percent	$100\,\dot{y}$ percent	$100\,\dot{k}_i$ percent	$100\,\dot{k}_m$ percent	$100\,U$ percent	$100\,X$ percent	$100\,s$ percent
East Asian Tigers	8.75	2.87	2.49	12.01	15.54	5.88	9.14	12.67	157.23	77.76	24.89
Southeast Asian Lions	6.87	2.71	3.38	11.17	13.61	4.16	8.45	10.90	59.73	31.02	23.23
South Asian Gaurs	4.30	2.18	3.78	5.70	7.47	2.11	3.52	5.29	43.60	20.54	10.94
Latin Rim Bulls	3.87	2.75	1.98	5.47	7.67	1.12	2.72	4.92	25.52	15.44	22.98
Latin American Tapirs	3.61	2.46	1.96	4.92	7.30	1.15	2.46	4.84	56.84	26.58	13.33
Caribbean Iguanas	3.57	1.84	1.98	5.63	7.96	1.73	3.79	6.12	83.17	40.93	14.84
Middle Eastern Camels	5.60	2.62	4.83	8.06	10.55	2.98	5.45	7.93	61.25	29.96	19.93
Perimeter African Rhinos	5.21	2.24	2.84	6.91	9.56	2.97	4.67	7.32	69.57	33.75	15.07
Sub-Saharan Hippos	3.85	2.43	4.07	5.71	7.38	1.42	3.28	4.95	65.96	30.57	7.12
OECD Elephants	3.73	1.08	1.21	4.95	7.89	2.65	3.87	6.80	61.64	30.03	27.36
All Groups	4.23	2.16	2.97	6.00	8.24	2.07	3.84	6.08	64.61	30.94	15.18

Notes. Group memberships appear in Table 4.1. Other details appear in the notes to Table 4.2.

homogeneous shays and 12.67 percent for mean-grade equipment. A similar picture is presented by the Southeast Asian Lions. But with a real GDP of 93.3 billion dollars, they are a bit larger than the Tigers, and with productivity growth and capital-deepening rates of 4.16 percent, 8.45 percent, and 10.90 percent sequentially, they are a bit slower. Still, the Lions grow faster than the Elephants. The same can be said of the Middle Eastern Camels, whose productivity growth rate equals 2.98 percent and whose deepening rates equal 5.45 and 7.93 percent.

Perimeter African Rhinos remain a step behind the Camels in growth and, perhaps curiously, look much like the Elephants in that way. Their labor productivity expands at an annual rate of 2.97 percent, and their capital deepens at rates of 4.67 percent and 7.32 percent annually. The Caribbean Iguanas and the South Asian Gaurs place a notch or two below the Rhinos in that context.

The disappointing performance of the Latin Rim Bulls is manifest in Table 4.4. Their closeness to the United States both geographically and economically held an early promise of high growth. Nonetheless, that promise faded into a nonmiraculous 1.12 percent annual expansion of labor productivity coupled with annual deepening rates of 2.72 and 4.92 percent. Those rates are as unflattering as those for the Latin American Tapirs or the Sub-Saharan Hippos. Seen in terms of growth rates, the Bulls look much more like Tapirs or Hippos than Tigers. All three lie at the bottom of the growth chart.

A pronounced pattern deducible from the rates of productivity growth and capital deepening reported in Table 4.4 reveals that growth is importantly driven by deepening. The two variables follow a very similar sequence across country groups. Similar too are the rankings for productivity growth and openness. For example, on both scales the Tigers, having the trade leaders Hong Kong and Singapore in their midst, stand at the top; the Elephants place fifth; the Bulls, last. By contrast, the fit between productivity growth and education growth is much less definitive. Figure 4.4 illustrates those comparisons. The positive relationship between labor productivity growth and capital deepening is obvious. Evident too is the positive match between productivity growth and openness. Lacking clarity, however, is the tie between growth and human capital. Perhaps the most noticeable aspect of that pattern is the *negative* correlation between the two series in the right half of the display. Figure 4.4, then, easily supports equation (3.26) in its call for positive relationships between labor productivity growth on the one hand and capital deepening and international trade on the other. It is decidedly less supportive of the call for a positive connection between productivity growth and human capital growth.

4.4 CONVERGENCE AND DIVERGENCE

The differential growth rates for labor productivity reported in Table 4.2 for the Asia Pacific countries imply that through time some countries move toward others in productivity while some countries move away. That is, some converge; others diverge.

As regards convergence a natural question is, How long? How long does it take for the convergence process to become complete? One answer can be obtained from equation (3.47), which posits the time t_ε needed for a country to move to *100 ε* percent of its own steady-state path. Admittedly, t_ε does not directly gauge the time required for one country to converge to another; nevertheless, its magnitudes might be thought of as a first approximation for the country-to-country case.

In activating equation (3.47) for any nation, it is imagined that the entries for $\hat{L}$ and $\hat{E}$ in Table 4.2 represent the sustained values η and ξ respectively and that the U entry is an appropriate number for computing τ. Estimates for the parameters α and θ are those associated with median capital J_5 and with the μ and δ values embedded in J_5. Details of the estimation work can be left for later, and other details concerning the t_ε evaluation can be left aside.

Table 4.5 gives the results for three different convergence standards; namely, *100 ε* magnitudes of 5 percent, 10 percent, and 20 percent. A higher ε means an eased standard—in effect, a shorter distance to travel for declared convergence—and therefore shorter convergence time. For the 5 percent criterion, time t_ε proves to be 16.3 years for Singapore and 17.6 years for its sister city-state Hong

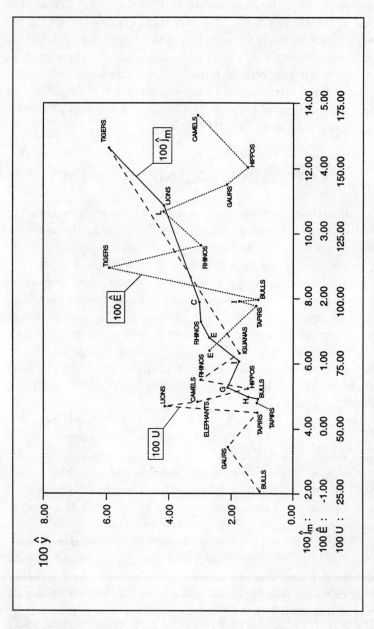

Figure 4.4 Labor Productivity Growth and Its Determinants by Country Group

Kong. Taiwan and Korea, the two other Tigers, post 21.8 years and 23.5 years respectively. These times resemble that for Japan, which registers 23.2 years. With respect to convergence, anyway, the Tigers behave like Japan. The Lions of Thailand and Indonesia display slower convergence, their times being 32.4 years and 40.3 years repectively. Similarly, the Gaur of the Philippines has an horizon of 34.0 years. Relaxing the ε grip to 10 percent and then to 20 percent lowers the Philippine estimate progressively to 26.1 years and 18.2 years.

Estimates of this sort are sensitive to the underlying conditions. Nevertheless, they suggest inter alia that convergence is a protracted process. By many measures 40 years is a long while. So may be 18 years or even 16 years. Besides, it must be remembered that such time frames presume a total absence of shocks once the convergence process has begun. Shocks may cause delay, and consequently actual movements of a country to its own steady-state path may extend beyond the theoretical milestones. The same situation may hold for country-to-country convergence.

A closer look at that issue can be obtained from a yearly mapping of the convergence index

$$CI_t = 100\left(1 - y_t^d / y_t^{US}\right) \tag{4.1}$$

Symbol CI_t denotes the convergence index at time t, y_t^d represents the labor productivity of designated country d at t, and y_t^{US} signifies the labor productivity of the United States at t. The United States serves as numéraire since, by Table 4.2, it has the highest productivity level of all countries under review. If labor productivity in the designated country equals zero, then $CI_t = 100$. However, if it equals the U.S. level, then $CI_t = 0$. Thus, a country markedly inferior to the United States in labor productivity has a high index value; the more similar the productivity, the lower the index. Furthermore, a declining index conveys convergence whereas a rise connotes divergence.

By Figure 4.5 the Tigers exhibit the lively convergence tendencies intimated by the economic profiles in Table 4.2. Hong Kong and Singapore slash their index levels in half from 82.2 and 77.6 in

Table 4.5 Convergence Time by Country

Country	Convergence Standard 100 ε		
	5 Percent	10 Percent	20 Percent
Hong Kong	17.6	13.6	9.5
Korea	23.5	18.1	12.6
Singapore	16.3	12.6	8.8
Taiwan	21.8	16.8	11.7
Indonesia	40.3	30.9	21.6
Malaysia	21.0	16.2	11.3
Thailand	32.4	24.9	17.4
Papua New Guinea	31.7	24.3	17.0
Philippines	34.0	26.1	18.2
Australia	31.3	24.1	16.8
Japan	23.2	17.8	12.5
New Zealand	31.6	24.3	17.0
United States	39.6	30.4	21.3

Notes. Calculations proceed by equation (3.47), and results are expressed in years.

1961 to 40.9 and 39.1 respectively in 1990. Korea cuts it from 88.7 to 59.9, and Taiwan slices it from 84.2 to 48.2. The annual rates of decline implicit in those patterns are noted on the display. For Hong Kong the index falls at an annual rate of 2.50 percent over the 30 years. For Singapore the rate is 2.44 percent, while for Taiwan and Korea it is 1.91 percent and 1.36 percent respectively.[4] Those rates, especially the ones for Hong Kong and Singapore, are not unlike the 2.47 percent posted by Japan, whose convergence configuration locates next to those for the Tigers. Obviously, the Tigers strongly resemble Japan in terms of convergence, and just as obviously this finding repeats the lesson learned from t_ε.

Indonesia and Malaysia, as deduced from Table 4.2, show convergence although not as sharply as do the Tigers. Their descent rates equal 0.34 percent and 0.80 percent serially. Thailand too evidences convergence, its rate of 0.36 percent matching those of the other two Lions. And true to prior reasoning, the two

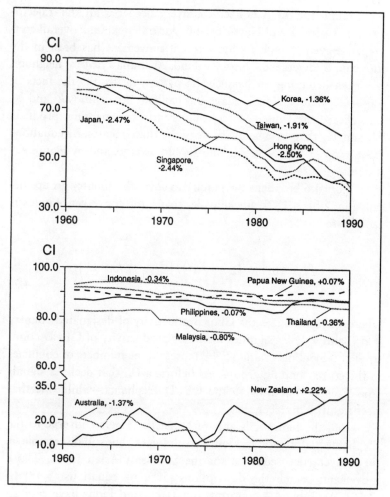

Figure 4.5 Convergence and Divergence Patterns by Country

Gaurs are essentially lifeless in convergence: their convergence lines are basically flat. That for the Philippines declines very slightly at 0.07 percent, whereas that for Papua New Guinea rises very slightly at 0.07 percent. If Papua New Guinea does anything, it diverges.

Completing the Asia Pacific convergence story are the trajectories for Australia and New Zealand. Australia exhibits overall convergence even though its most recent movement has been in the direction of divergence. New Zealand, Australia's mature neighbor, has been diverging on balance. Its pattern neatly fits the facts in Table 4.2; that is, New Zealand has capital-output ratios k_1 and k_m that exceed the United States counterparts and marginal products M_1 and M_m that drop below those of the United States. By equations (3.48) and (3.49), New Zealand should diverge, and by Figure 4.5 it does.

Figure 4.6 broadens the inquiry to cover the country groups detailed in Table 4.1. To fit the wider scope, the convergence index is reexpressed as

$$CI_t = 100\left[1 - \left(\Sigma_g y_{gt}^d / n^d\right) / \left(\Sigma_h y_{ht}^{OECD} / n^{OECD}\right)\right],$$
(4.2)

where y_{gt}^d symbolizes the labor productivity of designated country g at t, and y_{ht}^{OECD} signifies the labor productivity of OECD country h at t. Symbols n^d and n^{OECD} represent the numbers of countries in the corresponding groups. As before, a CI_t that declines signals convergence—but now to the OECD Elephants—while one that rises signifies divergence.

From the figure it is apparent that the Tigers converge to the Elephants in dramatic fashion. Less dramatic, but still discernible, is the convergence sequence for the Southeast Asian Lions. Those movements match the descriptions given by equations (3.48) to (3.50). As Table 4.4 confirms, the Tigers and Lions have capital-output ratios that fall below the Elephant benchmark, they have marginal products of efficient capital that exceed the benchmark, and they have initial labor productivity levels that fall below the benchmark. Their saving coefficients resemble the Elephants', and hence it might be maintained that the three country groups have the same steady state but that the Tigers and Lions are still en route to a steady state. Going the other way, the Latin Rim Bulls exhibit pronounced divergence. From their capital-output ratios, marginal

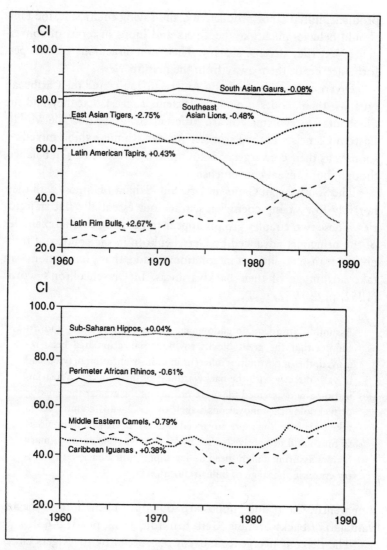

Figure 4.6 Convergence and Divergence Patterns by Country Group

products, initial labor productivity, and saving coefficient, the Bulls should behave much like the Tigers and Lions in terms of convergence. Yet they diverge sharply. Their nonmiraculous growth performance heads them away from the mature West.

Diverging too are the Latin American Tapirs and the Caribbean Iguanas; their modest saving coefficients suggest that they and the Elephants are evolving toward different steady states. The Middle Eastern Camels and the Perimeter African Rhinos exhibit mixed responses as their convergence is followed by divergence. On balance, though, both reveal convergence.

The South Asian Gaurs and the Sub-Saharan Hippos, with their horribly low saving coefficients, trace out essentially flat trajectories. These two country groups appear to be living counterexamples of the principle, advanced by Gerschenkron in the context of technology transfers through international trade, that poor nations can take advantage of their backwardness. In Gerschenkron's words (1952, p. 6; 1962, p. 8),

> Assuming an adequate endowment of usable resources, and assuming that the great blocks to industrialization had been removed, the opportunities inherent in industrialization may be said to vary directly with the backwardness of the country. Industrialization always seemed the more promising the greater the backlog of technological innovations which the backward country could take over from the more advanced country. Borrowed technology, so much and so rightly stressed by Veblen, was one of the primary factors assuring a high speed of development in a backward country entering the stage of industrialization.

Apparently, Gaurs and Hippos are too poor to benefit from the advantages of backwardness (Gerschenkron, 1962, pp. 362–63).

The fierce convergence movements shown by the Tigers either individually within the Asia Pacific region or collectively within a global setting contrast with the slow convergence runs of the Lions individually and collectively. The Lions' runs, in turn, contrast with the listless drifts of the Gaurs. Such differences highlight differences in the underlying growth rates and in the growth determinants. Those determinants are the focus of the next chapter.

CHAPTER 5

CONTRIBUTIONS
TO GROWTH

*By Heaven, Watson, I believe that I've got it! . . . Yes, it must
be so.*

Sherlock Holmes
—A. Conan Doyle, *The Adventure of the Priory School*

ECONOMIC GROWTH INVOLVES THEORETICAL PRECEPTS and empirical
evidence. Precepts constituted the subject of Chapter 3 while evidence occupied Chapter 4. The present discussion brings together
both elements to establish the contributions to growth from capital
quantity and quality, labor quantity and quality, and international
trade. At the center of that blend of theory and practice rests labor
productivity equation (3.26). Cast in general terms, however, it must
be reduced to specifics if the growth contributions are to be quantified. More plainly, values must be assigned to the coefficients. Such
a task calls for estimation work, which is treated in Section 5.1.
Next, Section 5.2 takes the coefficients estimated for labor productivity and combines them with share equations (3.27) and (3.29) to
measure the contributions. That section first looks at the individual
countries of the Asia Pacific Region and then widens the perspective
to cover the country groups. Section 5.3 repeats the exercise under

the supposition, common in the literature, that international trade need not be broken out as an explicit determinant of growth. Afterward, Section 5.4 draws upon the findings from the individual countries and the metaphorical groups to examine the contribution of total factor productivity to growth. In the process it reviews precedents surrounding that growth agent and perhaps reconciles results. Finally, Section 5.5 steps back from the numbers to reflect on the research at a distance.

5.1 ESTIMATION

Labor productivity growth depends positively upon physical capital growth, human capital growth, and international trade. That message was unmistakable from equation (3.26). Mapping those relationships for the 13 Asia Pacific nations in Figure 4.3 supported their positive correlations, but that support was sketched with a shaky hand as the configurations had saw-toothed edges and lacked stability. Broadening the scope to encompass the 120 countries produced, at least by the average magnitudes, the smoother patterns displayed in Figure 4.4. Therefore, in an effort to obtain reliable values for the labor productivity coefficients, estimation of equation (3.26) is set out to include all 120 nations.

Countries, of course, differ in a variety of ways, and so it may be prudent to expand specification (3.26) to allow for "structural" variables. One addition is initial labor productivity y_o pulled from PWT. In the spirit of convergence, its coefficient should be negative: countries having lower initial productivity should experience faster productivity growth ceteris paribus. Two other additions are the mortality rate m and a civil liberty index c, which assumes unity for the highest level of liberty and seven for the lowest. The coefficient of m should be negative as diminished health care undermines work effort. Likewise, if liberty rather than authoritarianism fosters growth, then the coefficient of c should be negative as well.[1] Both variables m and c take their data from Barro and Wolf (1989), and they, along with y_o, can be envisioned as elaborating the structural growth term ζ in equation (3.25).

Besides recommending additional structural terms, prudence encourages enhancing schedule (3.26) to recognize possible inter-country differences in growth parameters. That extension can be made by dummy variables keyed to the stage of development as reflected in income (real GDP) per capita. Dummy D_1 equals unity if a nation belongs to country group Partition 1. It assumes zero otherwise. By the same token, dummy D_2 refers to a country in Partition 2, whereas dummy D_3 pertains to a country in Partition 3.[2]

So modified, equation (3.26) becomes

$$
\begin{aligned}
\hat{y} = a + a_y y_0 + a_m m + a_c c \\
+ a_E \hat{E} + a_{E2}\left(D_2\hat{E}\right) + a_{E3}\left(D_3\hat{E}\right) \\
+ a_j \hat{j} + a_{j2}\left(D_2\hat{j}\right) + a_{j3}\left(D_3\hat{j}\right) \\
+ a_U U + a_{U2}\left(D_2 U\right) + a_{U3}\left(D_3 U\right),
\end{aligned}
\tag{5.1}
$$

U being chosen to quantify the trade variable because of its inclusive nature. Coefficient estimation takes place by least squares. However, since the sample pools countries, it has a cross-section dimension where, if Tables 4.2 and 4.4 provide any guide, size differs greatly across economies. To protect estimator precision in this circumstance, the regression data are weighted by the square root of the ratio of labor to J_1 capital. In the end, those data, extracted from the aforementioned sources, embrace a total of 120 countries annually over the 41-year period 1950–90 and, after accounting for missing information, yield a sample whose number of observations NOB equals 4,240.

Regression (5.1) is tested separately on each of the nine capital types using alternative sets of parameter restrictions. A flavor of those tests is provided by Table 5.1, which refers to homogeneous-shay capital J_1 and to median capital J_5. For either capital model, Experiment 1 fits equation (5.1) without restriction. Experiment 2 deletes the trade interactors $(a_{U2} = a_{U3} = 0)$ whereas Experiment 3 discards the knowledge interactors $(a_{E2} = a_{E3} = 0)$. Experiment 4 jettisons both sets of interactors. Capital deepening is maintained across experiments without interactor deletion because of the acceptable performance by the deepening trio in preliminary work.

Table 5.1 Regressions for Labor Productivity Growth

Coefficient or Statistic	Homogeneous-Shay Capital Experiment				Median Capital Experiment			
	1	2	3	4	1	2	3	4
a	0.0420	0.0446	0.0420	0.0447	0.0361	0.0385	0.0361	0.0387
	[4.690]	[5.071]	[4.697]	[5.089]	[4.036]	[4.380]	[4.047]	[4.409]
a_y	$-2.1 \cdot 10^{-6}$	$-3.2 \cdot 10^{-6}$	$-2.1 \cdot 10^{-6}$	$-3.2 \cdot 10^{-6}$	$-2.2 \cdot 10^{-6}$	$-3.2 \cdot 10^{-6}$	$-2.2 \cdot 10^{-6}$	$-3.2 \cdot 10^{-6}$
	[-1.885]	[-2.905]	[-1.890]	[-2.975]	[-1.972]	[-2.899]	[-1.974]	[-2.962]
a_m	-0.1695	-0.1623	-0.1692	-0.1619	-0.1575	-0.1489	-0.1568	-0.1482
	[-4.279]	[-4.134]	[-4.285]	[-4.133]	[-4.006]	[-3.816]	[-3.998]	[-3.806]
a_c	-0.0049	-0.0050	-0.0049	-0.0050	-0.0045	-0.0047	-0.0045	-0.0047
	[-4.770]	[-4.936]	[-4.780]	[-4.962]	[-4.414]	[-4.603]	[-4.445]	[-4.654]
a_j	0.4389	0.2898	0.4353	0.2777	0.3667	0.2593	0.3531	0.2407
	[3.610]	[2.853]	[3.873]	[3.173]	[4.196]	[3.554]	[4.458]	[3.908]
a_{j2}	-0.0277	0.0347	-0.0222	0.0340	-0.0374	-0.0010	-0.0240	0.0063
	[-0.183]	[0.281]	[-0.161]	[0.350]	[-0.353]	[-0.001]	[-0.251]	[0.096]
a_{j3}	-0.3202	-0.1725	-0.3166	-0.1604	-0.2486	-0.1418	-0.2351	-0.1232
	[-2.639]	[-1.697]	[-2.824]	[-1.831]	[-2.848]	[-1.939]	[-2.972]	[-1.995]
a_E	0.0618	0.0163	0.0830	0.0835	-0.0173	-0.0508	0.0830	0.0837
	[0.229]	[0.061]	[5.362]	[5.395]	[-0.063]	[-0.185]	[5.390]	[5.431]
a_{E2}	0.0267	0.0361			0.0995	0.0928		
	[0.090]	[0.122]			[0.331]	[0.310]		
a_{E3}	0.0212	0.0678			0.1006	0.1354		
	[0.079]	[0.252]			[0.367]	[0.494]		
a_U	-0.0030	0.0235	-0.0031	0.0235	-0.0044	0.0225	-0.0047	0.0225
	[-0.280]	[6.166]	[-0.288]	[6.169]	[-0.406]	[5.946]	[-0.424]	[5.945]
a_{U2}	0.0088		0.0089		0.0064		0.0065	
	[0.584]		[0.603]		[0.415]		[0.429]	
a_{U3}	0.0308		0.0309		0.0315		0.0317	
	[2.698]		[2.712]		[2.772]		[2.792]	
Addendum								
R^2	0.077	0.074	0.077	0.074	0.084	0.082	0.084	0.082
F	29.19	33.96	35.04	42.45	32.44	37.72	38.93	47.12
DW	1.93	1.92	1.93	1.92	1.93	1.92	1.93	1.93
NOB	4,240	4,240	4,240	4,240	4,240	4,240	4,240	4,240

Notes. The dependent variable is $\hat{y}$. Brackets indicate Student-t values.

Since the regression results are about the same for both capital types, the discussion concentrates on the drills for homogeneous shays. There the R^2 values are about what might be anticipated for a regression defined in terms of growth rates since growth rates are often subject to considerable variability. For instance, a series posited in levels may evolve as 100.0, 104.0, and 106.1 over three years, thus exhibiting annual changes of 4.0 and 2.1 respectively and annual growth rates of 4.0 percent and 2.0 percent respectively. Although the series itself moves smoothly by varying at or below 4 percent annually, the growth rates do not move smoothly: they vary about 50 percent year over year. It follows that an R^2 based on rates (or changes) is likely to be much lower than one based on levels.[3] Nonetheless, the F-statistic for the regression assumes gratifyingly strong numbers. Moreover, as suspected from the growth-rate character of equation (5.1), the Durbin-Watson statistic DW indicates the absence of serial correlation from the time-series dimension of the sample.

In regard to the coefficients a_y, a_m, and a_c, they all exhibit negative signs regardless of experimental format. Convergence—at least in the conditional sense of allowing for other circumstances—characterizes macro dynamics; worsening health conditions impair growth; and increased liberty, rather than strengthened authoritarianism, promotes growth. Coefficient a_j estimates the capital output-elasticity for Partition 1 nations such as Japan while a_j combined with an interactor estimates the elasticity for one of the other country sets. Thus $a_j + a_{j3}$ estimates the capital elasticity for a Partition 3 society such as the Philippines. These coefficients substantiate the hypothesis in equation (3.26) and the inference from Figures 4.3 and 4.4 that capital deepening exerts a positive effect on productivity growth.

Knowledge coefficients a_E, a_{E2}, and a_{E3} are insignificant without exception when the three are taken together. One explanation for their weak showing is statistical: ill-conditioning in the presence of interaction dummies, a worry studied by Green and Doll (1974, p. 61). Another explanation is economic. Contrary to the belief of Romer (1990, pp. S95-S96) and others in the human capital camp, labor quality may have little bearing on the *discrepancies* in productivity growth across countries. However, according to the decidedly significant a_E coefficients in Experiments 3 and 4, labor quality does exert a positive effect on growth *overall* just as equation (3.26) insists and just as Figure 4.3 sketches with hesitancy.

Trade coefficients a_U, a_{U2}, and a_{U3} behave much like the knowledge coefficients, implying that trade pertains more to overall growth than to discrepant growth. Again, in keeping with equation (3.26) and with Figure 4.3, its effect is positive.

From such reasoning Experiment 4 gives the preferred form for equation (5.1). Its selection, which is reinforced by the regression F values, yields estimates for the knowledge elasticity θ that equal 0.1156 for Partition 1 countries and 0.1213 and 0.0946 respectively for Partition 2 and Partition 3 countries under homogeneous-shay capital. For median capital the counterparts are 0.1102, 0.1112, and 0.0948. Both sequences confirm the θ hypothesis underlying production functions (3.16) and (3.19).

Other elasticities deducible from Experiment 4 are informative as well. The growth elasticity with respect to deepening measures the percent change in the rate of labor productivity growth due to a given percent change in the rate of capital deepening. Represented by σ_j, it can be calculated as a_j [mean $(\hat{j})$/mean $(\hat{y})$] for a Partition 1 country and as $(a_j + a_{j2})$ [mean $(\hat{j})$/mean$(\hat{y})$] or as $(a_j + a_{j3})$ [mean $(\hat{j})$/mean $(\hat{y})$] respectively for a Partition 2 or Partition 3 nation. In those expressions the mean operator calls for the mean of the indicated variable. Likewise, the growth elasticity with respect to labor quality, notated σ_E, becomes a_E [mean $(\hat{E})$/mean $(\hat{y})$] whereas the elasticity with respect to international trade, σ_U, follows as a_U [mean (U)/mean $(\hat{y})$]. Combining the median-capital coefficients from Experiment 4 with the means of the requisite variables for the three decades from 1961 to 1990 yields for Hong Kong $\sigma_j = 0.3692$, $\sigma_E = 0.0219$, and $\sigma_U = 0.7029$. In words, a 10 percent increase in the rate of capital deepening increases the rate of labor productivity growth by 3.7 percent. A 10 percent gain in the rate of labor quality improvement raises the productivity growth rate by 0.2 percent, but a 10 percent boost in trade openness bolsters the rate by 7.0 percent. For Indonesia the elasticity sequence reads 0.3920, 0.0992, and 0.2116. Philippines has 0.4102, 0.0997, and 0.5743; Japan posts 0.5394, 0.0140, and 0.0936.

In general, the three elasticities show labor quality to be the least powerful determinant of labor productivity growth. All 13 nations in the Asia Pacific Region place σ_E last. By contrast, seven nations rank σ_j first, and six put σ_U first. Essentially, capital deepening and international trade are tied as the leading causes of growth, and labor quality trails as an "also ran." An identical conclusion emerges from the average elasticities calculated across the 13 nations. Those averages are 0.6281 for deepening, 0.0629 for labor quality, and 0.6190 for trade. Again, deepening and trade are tied at the top, and labor quality is a distant last. This ordering of determinants is studied further in the next section, which deals with growth shares.

5.2 GROWTH SHARES

With the parameter estimates in hand from Experiment 4, it is possible to establish for the Asia Pacific nations the contribution to growth made by each of the determinants. The exact method for the purpose combines those estimates with the data behind the economic statistics presented in Table 4.2 after netting out from output growth the control set $a + a_y y_o + a_m m + a_c c$ used in the regression work. Equations (3.27) and (3.29) then generate the growth shares by type of capital using the corresponding set of coefficient values. Averaging across the nine types yields the numbers reported in Table 5.2. Several features stand out in bold relief.

As regards output growth, Table 5.2 indicates that efficient capital, foreign trade, and total labor all matter importantly. Their strengths, however, vary greatly across countries. Efficient capital ranges from highs of 68.2 percent and 54.2 percent for Japan and Korea to lows of 22.4 percent and 15.6 percent for the Philippines and Papua New Guinea. Trade ranks highest in Singapore, where it explains 49.5 percent of output growth, and lowest in the United States, where it describes 10.4 percent. Similarly, labor takes top honors in the Philippines with 55.0 percent before bottoming out in Singapore at 19.1 percent. These intercountry differences in the strength of determinants mirror the intercountry differences in the intensity of output growth shown in Table 4.2.

For the Tigers, foreign trade or efficient capital is the principal cause of growth. In particular, Hong Kong and Singapore are led by

Table 5.2 Growth Shares by Country

Country	Output Growth Share due to							Labor Productivity Growth Share due to				
	Total	Labor Quantity	Labor Quality	Capital Efficient	Capital Quantity	Capital Quality	Foreign Trade	Labor Quality	Capital Efficient	Capital Quantity	Capital Quality	Foreign Trade
Hong Kong	24.3	22.8	1.4	30.3	21.5	8.7	45.5	1.8	39.2	27.9	11.3	58.9
Korea	30.0	26.2	3.8	54.2	42.6	11.6	15.8	5.2	73.4	57.6	15.7	21.4
Singapore	19.1	17.9	1.2	31.4	25.5	5.9	49.5	1.5	38.2	31.0	7.2	60.3
Taiwan	29.9	26.8	3.2	47.7	36.9	10.7	22.4	4.3	65.1	50.4	14.7	30.6
Indonesia	47.0	39.1	7.9	36.1	31.4	4.7	16.9	13.0	59.2	51.5	7.7	27.8
Malaysia	32.9	29.5	3.4	41.1	31.1	10.0	26.0	4.8	58.3	44.1	14.1	36.9
Thailand	51.9	48.4	3.5	26.9	22.2	4.7	21.1	6.9	52.1	43.2	9.0	41.0
Papua New Guinea	43.1	39.1	4.0	15.6	10.4	5.2	41.3	6.6	25.5	17.1	8.4	68.0
Philippines	55.0	51.1	3.9	22.4	17.4	5.0	22.6	8.0	45.7	35.8	10.0	46.3
Australia	41.6	40.6	1.0	41.5	23.8	17.7	16.9	1.7	69.6	40.6	29.0	28.7
Japan	20.8	19.1	1.6	68.2	51.4	16.9	11.0	2.0	84.3	63.6	20.8	13.6
New Zealand	35.4	33.3	2.2	35.5	17.7	17.8	29.0	3.2	53.0	26.8	26.1	43.8
United States	43.1	40.5	2.6	46.6	23.9	22.7	10.4	4.4	77.8	41.2	36.6	17.8

Notes. All entries, written as percentages, are averages calculated across the nine capital types and over the 30-year period 1961–90. Foreign trade is measured by the openness variable U.

trade while Korea and Taiwan are led by capital. For the Lions the leader is typically labor, and for the two Gaurs it is always labor. For the mature Elephants the major cause is almost always efficient capital. The pattern, therefore, appears to be that the growth experiences of the rich, mature Elephants are governed mainly by capital; those of the rapidly moving Tigers, by capital or trade; and those of the poor, maturing Lions and Gaurs, by labor.

Narrowing the focus within the output growth determinants to the distinction between quantity and quality reveals that quantity dominates quality by a wide margin regardless of whether capital or labor is the input.[4] To illustrate, Hong Kong has a labor quantity share of 22.8 percent compared with a labor quality share of only 1.4 percent. Moreover, its corresponding capital split is 21.5 percent against 8.7 percent. Even where the quality share attains its maximum, it is still dominated by quantity. For labor that quality maximum happens in the Indonesia case, but the 7.9 percent share is nonetheless outstripped by the quantity share of 39.1 percent. Capital quality reaches its maximum of 22.7 percent in the United States case only to give the edge to a quantity share of 23.9 percent. Comparing the two quantity variables shows that labor quantity outweighs capital quantity in 8 of the 13 tries. But comparing the two quality measures reveals that labor quality loses to capital quality in every instance save the Indonesia episode. Apart from that lone exception, labor quality is the weakest of the growth determinants.

This same property holds for productivity growth accounting: Labor quality is dominated by capital quality in virtually every instance, and it is almost always the weakest determinant. Widening the perspective finds that foreign trade ranks first in four cases while efficient capital is first in nine. This disparity between foreign trade and efficient capital on the one hand and labor quality on the other resembles the finding derived from the growth elasticities in the previous section.

Averaging the growth shares within country groups corroborates the findings from the individual Asia Pacific nations and offers further insights into the contributions to growth. Table 5.3 has that information.

Table 5.3 Growth Shares by Country Group

Country Group	Total	Output Growth Share due to — Labor Quantity	Labor Quality	Capital Efficient	Capital Quantity	Capital Quality	Foreign Trade	Labor Productivity Growth — Labor Quality	Capital Efficient	Capital Quantity	Capital Quality	Foreign Trade
East Asian Tigers	25.8	23.4	2.4	40.9	31.6	9.3	33.3	3.2	54.0	41.7	12.3	42.8
Southeast Asian Lions	43.9	39.0	4.9	34.7	28.2	6.5	21.4	8.2	56.5	46.3	10.3	35.2
South Asian Gaurs	55.9	47.7	8.2	21.7	16.1	5.6	22.4	15.5	42.2	31.4	10.9	42.2
Latin Rim Bulls	45.7	42.2	3.5	41.7	28.0	13.8	12.6	6.2	71.7	48.3	23.3	22.2
Latin American Tapirs	39.3	35.8	3.4	35.2	22.2	13.0	25.5	5.4	55.4	35.4	20.1	39.1
Caribbean Iguanas	28.4	25.2	3.3	37.0	25.2	11.8	34.5	4.3	49.3	33.4	15.8	46.4
Middle Eastern Camels	36.4	30.3	6.0	41.5	30.9	10.6	22.2	8.8	60.1	44.8	15.2	31.1
Perimeter African Rhinos	33.0	29.2	3.9	40.5	29.1	11.4	26.5	5.6	58.1	41.7	16.4	36.3
Sub-Saharan Hippos	52.6	45.3	7.4	17.1	12.3	4.8	30.3	13.8	30.6	21.7	8.9	55.7
OECD Elephants	21.9	19.4	2.5	45.8	27.6	18.1	32.3	3.1	57.2	34.6	22.6	39.7
All Groups	40.8	35.6	5.2	30.8	20.9	9.9	28.3	8.9	46.5	31.7	14.8	44.6

Notes. Expressed as percentages, all entries are averages calculated across the nine capital types and over the 30-year period 1961–90 within each country group, whose membership is listed in Table 4.1. As before, foreign trade is gauged by the openness variable U.

Confirming an initial conclusion from the previous display, Table 5.3 shows that efficient capital, foreign trade, and total labor matter for output growth. In addition, it confirms that the magnitudes involved exhibit considerable variation across groups. For instance, efficient capital has a 45.8 percent share for the OECD Elephants but a 17.1 percent figure for the Sub-Saharan Hippos. Similarly, trade accounts for 34.5 percent of output growth in the islands of the Iguanas but 12.6 percent in the land of the Bulls. And labor's responsibility ranges from 55.9 percent for the Gaurs to 21.9 percent for the Elephants.

Another look at Table 5.3 reveals important similarities in the ranking of the five determinants of output growth. With the lone exception of the Bulls, all country groups rank international trade, capital quantity, and labor quantity as the top three determinants, and they classify capital quality and labor quality as the bottom two forces. Moreover, labor quality is ranked last in eight of the ten instances. Thus trade and quantities count most for output growth whereas qualities, especially labor quality, count least.

But deeper insight can be gained from Table 5.3. By the accounts presented in Chapters 1 and 4, it is fair to say that the East Asian Tigers have enjoyed a successful growth history. The Elephants too have seen growth success. According to Table 5.3, both successes can be linked to the same rule of order for the growth determinants: trade is first; capital quantity, a close second; labor quantity, a more distant third; capital quality, fourth; and labor quality, a negligible fifth. Hence trade and capital quantity might be thought of as the two main drivers of a successful growth program. At the opposite end of the success spectrum rest the Gaurs and Hippos. Their low growth rates and lifeless convergence drifts documented in Chapter 4 describe unsuccessful growth histories. From Table 5.3 such lack of achievement can be related to a rule of order common to the two groups. Labor quantity is a decided first that accounts for almost half of output growth. Trade is a distant second; capital quantity, third; labor quality, fourth; and capital quality, fifth.

On closer inspection, then, labor quantity appears to be a weak foundation on which to build strong growth. That thought is clearly reinforced by the lackluster growth performance and resolute divergence trajectories of the Bulls and Tapirs, which likewise have labor quantity as the leading growth agent. The thought is also reinforced by Gerschenkron's principle because labor quantity provides little opportunity for a developing country to take advantage of its backwardness. Borrowing technology, a critical proviso behind Gerschenkron's reasoning, is much less likely to be geared to labor quantity than to the "big two": foreign trade and capital quantity.

Attention turned to labor productivity growth for the country groups repeats the lessons learned from Table 5.2 for the individual Asia Pacific nations. Trade and efficient capital are the two top determinants, and labor quality is last.

5.3 GROWTH SHARES WITHOUT TRADE

In both its theoretical and empirical forms, the inquiry has postulated international trade as an explicit determinant of economic growth. Trade entered the production structure through its effect on allocative efficiency, and justification for such treatment came from Dornbusch (1993, pp. 87–88) and Western (1996b, p. 6). Further justification could be inferred from the strength of trade in the growth accountancy. Nonetheless, an alternative approach popular in the literature makes no explicit allowance for trade. That alternative is followed, for example, by Kim and Lau (1994, pp. 240–41), who shape their study of East Asian growth around a meta-production function involving capital and labor inputs without reference to trade factors. Likewise, Krugman (1994) and Young (1995, pp. 646–48) do not break out trade in studying the East Asian growth experience, and Gapinski (1997d, pp. 148–50) too bypasses direct consideration of that agent in the Asia Pacific context and beyond. Consistency with those precedents encourages a reworking of the present growth accountancy in a way that makes no specific allowance for trade. Curiosity and completeness dictate that it be done. In addition, such an endeavor could provide useful information for the discussion of total factor productivity in the next section.

Recalculation entails two steps. Step 1 is the reestimation of equation (5.1) with the trade variables removed. The sample remains at 4,240 observations as before, and as before the equation is tested separately on each of the nine capital types. Again, the results are similar across types, and hence the rendering for median capital J_5 can be thought of as representative. In Experiment 4 format it becomes

$$\hat{y} = 0.0577 - 2.8 \times 10^{-6} y_o - 0.1587m - 0.0062c$$
$$\begin{bmatrix} 7.026 \end{bmatrix} \begin{bmatrix} -2.599 \end{bmatrix} \qquad \begin{bmatrix} -4.062 \end{bmatrix} \begin{bmatrix} -6.330 \end{bmatrix}$$

$$+ 0.0810\hat{E} + 0.2373\hat{j} - 0.0046(D_2\hat{j}) - 0.1195(D_3\hat{j}).$$
$$\begin{bmatrix} 5.238 \end{bmatrix} \begin{bmatrix} 3.837 \end{bmatrix} \begin{bmatrix} -0.070 \end{bmatrix} \qquad \begin{bmatrix} -1.929 \end{bmatrix} \qquad (5.2)$$

Student-t statistics appear in brackets below the coefficients. Moreover, $R^2 = 0.074$, $F = 48.41$, and $DW = 1.91$. Plainly, the properties delineated in Table 5.1 for the original equation in Experiment 4 carry over to the abridgment. Of particular consequence is the similarity of the corresponding coefficients. For example, the capital coefficient a_j changes from 0.2407 to 0.2373, the Partition 3 interaction coefficient goes from −0.1232 to −0.1195, and the labor quality coefficient switches from 0.0837 to 0.0810. Thus, although the median regression without trade differs from its counterpart with trade, it does not differ by much.

Step 2 in revising the accountancy calls for recalculation of the growth shares. Intuition suggests that the share previously attributed to trade becomes projected into the remaining shares, thereby increasing them proportionally. In this case, anyway, mathematics confirms intuition. Eliminating the trade share $\zeta_F F/\hat{Y}$ from the share equation (3.27) proceeds by moving it to the left-hand side and then dividing out $1 - \zeta_F F/\hat{Y}$. What results is

$$1 = \Phi\left[(1-\alpha)\hat{L} / \hat{Y}\right] + \Phi\left[(1-\alpha)\theta\hat{E} / \hat{Y}\right] + \Phi\left[\alpha\hat{j}_K / \hat{Y}\right] + \Phi\left[\alpha\hat{j}_\mu / \hat{Y}\right], \qquad (5.3)$$

where the proportional adjustment multiple Φ equals $(1 - \zeta_F F/\hat{Y})^{-1}$. Since the coefficients do not change much between the trade and no-trade drills, the transformations embedded in equation (5.3) should be order preserving on balance. That is, the rules of order established for output growth from equation (3.27) and spelled out in Tables 5.2 and 5.3 should remain largely intact except for the obvious removal of the trade component. Similar logic applies to the rules for labor productivity growth.

Table 5.4 presents the revised growth shares for the Asia Pacific countries while its twin, Table 5.5, gives the new numbers for the country groups. Arithmetically, there are no surprises. The previous trade shares become absorbed by the remaining terms. To illustrate, Hong Kong's trade contribution to output growth, which equals 45.5 percent in Table 5.2, splits into a 19.5 percentage point increase in labor quantity from 22.8 percent to 42.3 percent, a 1.1 point increase in labor quality, an 18.1 point increase in capital quantity, and a 6.9 point increase in capital quality. Similarly, its trade contribution of 58.9 percent to labor productivity growth translates into a 2.6 point gain for labor quality from 1.8 percent to 4.4 percent and into 41.0 point and 15.4 point increments in capital quantity and quality respectively.

Perhaps the most impressive feature in the new numbers is the strength of capital quantity. As regards the individual Asia Pacific nations, capital quantity leads the way for output growth in five instances. For productivity growth it leads in all 13 situations. In the country-group setting, capital quantity leads the successful programs of output growth for the Tigers and Elephants, and it leads labor productivity growth for all ten metaphorical creatures. With trade removed from consideration, the "big two" forces reduce to the "big one": capital quantity. This conclusion echoes the sentiment expressed by Krugman (1994, p. 70) when he asserted in connection with Singapore's miraculous growth that

> ... the miracle turns out to have been based on perspiration rather than inspiration: Singapore grew through a mobilization of resources that would have done Stalin proud. ... *Above all,* the country had made an awesome investment in physical capital ... (emphasis added).

Table 5.4 Growth Shares by Country Without Allowance for Trade

Country	Output Growth Share due to							Labor Productivity Growth Share due to				
	Total	Labor		Efficient	Capital		Foreign Trade	Labor Quality	Efficient	Capital		Foreign Trade
		Quantity	Quality		Quantity	Quality				Quantity	Quality	
Hong Kong	44.8	42.3	2.5	55.2	39.6	15.6	0.0	4.4	95.6	68.9	26.7	0.0
Korea	35.9	31.5	4.4	64.1	50.5	13.6	0.0	6.5	93.5	73.6	20.0	0.0
Singapore	38.1	35.7	2.3	61.9	50.4	11.6	0.0	3.6	96.4	78.2	18.1	0.0
Taiwan	38.8	34.8	4.0	61.2	47.5	13.7	0.0	6.1	93.9	72.9	21.0	0.0
Indonesia	56.4	47.1	9.3	43.6	37.9	5.7	0.0	17.5	82.5	71.9	10.6	0.0
Malaysia	44.7	40.3	4.5	55.3	42.1	13.2	0.0	7.5	92.5	70.4	22.1	0.0
Thailand	65.8	61.4	4.4	34.2	28.3	6.0	0.0	11.4	88.6	73.7	14.9	0.0
Papua New Guinea	73.5	66.9	6.6	26.5	17.8	8.7	0.0	20.3	79.7	55.0	24.7	0.0
Philippines	71.0	66.1	4.9	29.0	22.6	6.4	0.0	14.6	85.4	67.4	18.0	0.0
Australia	50.5	49.3	1.2	49.5	28.7	20.8	0.0	2.4	97.6	58.4	39.2	0.0
Japan	23.5	21.7	1.8	76.5	57.7	18.8	0.0	2.3	97.7	73.7	24.0	0.0
New Zealand	50.5	47.6	3.0	49.5	25.3	24.2	0.0	5.9	94.1	50.6	43.6	0.0
United States	48.4	45.6	2.8	51.6	26.7	24.8	0.0	5.4	94.6	51.4	43.2	0.0

Notes. Entries represent averages computed across the nine capital types and over the 30-year period 1961–90. All are percentages.

Table 5.5 Growth Shares by Country Group Without Allowance for Trade

Country Group		Output Growth Share due to						Labor Productivity Growth Share due to				
		Labor		Capital			Foreign	Labor	Capital			Foreign
	Total	Quantity	Quality	Efficient	Quantity	Quality	Trade	Quality	Efficient	Quantity	Quality	Trade
East Asian Tigers	39.4	36.1	3.3	60.6	47.0	13.6	0.0	5.2	94.8	73.4	21.5	0.0
Southeast Asian Lions	55.6	49.6	6.0	44.4	36.1	8.3	0.0	12.1	87.9	72.0	15.9	0.0
South Asian Gaurs	72.1	62.5	9.6	27.9	20.7	7.2	0.0	24.2	75.8	56.5	19.3	0.0
Latin Rim Bulls	54.2	50.2	3.9	45.8	30.7	15.2	0.0	8.5	91.5	61.8	29.8	0.0
Latin American Tapirs	54.7	50.1	4.6	45.3	28.4	16.8	0.0	9.3	90.7	58.2	32.5	0.0
Caribbean Iguanas	45.9	41.1	4.9	54.1	36.6	17.4	0.0	8.5	91.5	61.6	29.9	0.0
Middle Eastern Camels	48.0	40.5	7.5	52.0	38.5	13.5	0.0	12.6	87.4	64.9	22.6	0.0
Perimeter African Rhinos	45.6	40.5	5.1	54.4	39.2	15.3	0.0	8.6	91.4	65.8	25.7	0.0
Sub-Saharan Hippos	75.8	65.4	10.4	24.2	17.4	6.9	0.0	35.0	65.0	42.8	22.2	0.0
OECD Elephants	32.5	28.8	3.7	67.5	40.9	26.6	0.0	5.2	94.8	57.8	36.9	0.0
All Groups	57.5	50.5	7.1	42.5	28.7	13.8	0.0	18.9	81.1	54.4	26.7	0.0

Notes. All entries reflect averages computed across the nine capital types and the 30-year period 1961–90 within each country group. They are given in percentages. Group memberships appear in Table 4.1.

The conclusion about the strength of capital quantity also supports the front part of the adage offered by the popular press to summarize Krugman's thesis; namely, that "if you invest in more sausage machines . . . , of course you will make more sausages" (*Economist*, 1995, p. 33).

Machines are one component of the sausage story. Total factor productivity TFP is another, and to it the discussion now turns.

5.4 TOTAL FACTOR PRODUCTIVITY

About 40 years ago Solow (1957) sought to split the growth in labor productivity into the contribution from capital deepening and the contribution from technical change. Technical change was defined as any kind of shift in the production function, and hence the endeavor could be seen as an effort to separate movements along a production function from shifts in the function. Anchoring Solow's inquiry was an aggregate production function posited in his notation as

$$Q = A(t)f(K,L),\qquad(5.4)$$

where Q denoted the quantity of output, K and L signified the physical quantities of capital and labor respectively, f represented a functional relationship, and $A(t)$ designated an index of technology at time t. From this arrangement he obtained, with w_k referring to capital's income share and with hats here marking growth rates,

$$\hat{Q} - \hat{L} = \hat{A} + w_k\left(\hat{K} - \hat{L}\right)\qquad(5.5)$$

For the rate of technical change, this expression implied that

$$\hat{A} = \left(\hat{Q} - \hat{L}\right) - w_k\left(\hat{K} - \hat{L}\right),\qquad(5.6)$$

$$\hat{A} = \hat{Q} - w_k\hat{K} - \left(1 - w_k\right)\hat{L}.\qquad(5.7)$$

Working through the logic and combining it with an economic profile of the United States for the years from 1909 to 1949, Solow concluded that technical change was by far the greater determinant of labor productivity growth. In particular, 87.5 percent of that growth was attributable to technical change and only 12.5 percent came from capital deepening (Solow, 1957, p. 320). The shift in the production function overwhelmed movements along the surface.

Although Solow's compelling study may be the most celebrated piece on the subject, it surely was not the first. Solow (1957, p. 317) himself cites an earlier undertaking by Fabricant, who also concluded that technical progress accounted for most of productivity growth—about 90 percent. Griliches (1996) offers a fuller review of the precursors to Solow. Besides Fabricant, they include Tinbergen, Stigler, Schmookler, Kendrick, and Abramovitz, and they all held that technical change was responsible for more than 85 percent of labor productivity growth (Griliches, 1996, p. 1327). Terminology was a bit slippery, however. Some referred to technical change as efficiency the way Tinbergen did (Griliches, 1996, p. 1326), and some called it a measure of ignorance as Abramovitz (1956, p. 11) did. But regardless of the label used, the concept $\hat{A}$ in equation (5.7) was the amount of output growth unexplained by the quantities of inputs. It was the amount left over; it was the residual.

Explaining the unexplained became the object of much research following Solow's seminal piece. For instance, Griliches (1967, pp. 308–17), examining U.S. manufacturing over the period 1947–60, starts with the conventional definition of the residual in equation (5.7) and finds that the residual accounted for 61 percent of output growth. Adjusting the calculations to allow for input quality, economies of scale, and the like brings the residual contribution down to 18 percent. The unexplained was now largely explained. In Griliches's (1967, p. 316) own words, " . . . by a more careful accounting we have been able to eliminate a substantial part of the unknown, assigning the bulk of it to improvements in the quality of labor and capital." Ignorance dropped from 61 percent to 18 percent in no small way by recognizing labor quality and capital quality. In related pursuits Jorgenson and Griliches (1967, pp. 271–72) cut ignorance to 2.8 percent while Griliches (1963, pp. 344–46) drove it to zero or below zero. The unexplained was either completely explained or more than completely explained.

Comparing equation (5.7) for the residual with formula (3.30) for total factor productivity growth $T\hat{F}P$ indicates why the history of the residual suits a discussion of total factor productivity: the residual *is* TFP growth as Dowling and Summers (1997, pp. 3–4) along with Dornbusch et al. (1998, p. 46) note. And given that equivalence, the attempts to explain the residual and to reduce to zero the unexplained portion of economic growth can be seen as efforts to discover and measure all of the components of TFP growth. Among those discoveries, according to Griliches (1967, p. 316), are labor quality and capital quality, two of the three elements of $T\hat{F}P$ shown in equation (3.31). Consequently, that representation meshes nicely with the precedents.

Besides agreeing with the precedents, equation (3.31) can assist in breathing numerical life into the growth contributions of TFP. To derive the contribution to output growth for the Asia Pacific nations, it suggests adding together the entries in columns 3, 6, and 7 of Table 5.2. Thus, in the case of Hong Kong, TFP explains 55.6 percent of output growth. As regards productivity growth, the equation says to add columns 8, 11, and 12 yielding a Hong Kong figure of 72 percent. Complete results for the Asia Pacific countries appear in Table 5.6.

Perhaps the most prominent aspect of Table 5.6 is the size of the numbers. For output growth the TFP share never falls below 29.0 percent, and it dominates the quantities share in three cases: Hong Kong, Singapore, and Papua New Guinea, where it necessarily passes the 50.0 percent mark. For labor productivity growth the TFP share has an even more impressive record as it surpasses 50.0 percent in all but four cases: Korea, Taiwan, Indonesia, and Japan. TFP matters appreciably. Much of its strength originates in trade as the last column of the table indicates. According to those entries, calculated by dividing the share of output growth from trade (column 7 in Table 5.2) by the share for TFP growth (columns 3, 6, and 7),[5] Hong Kong has 81.8 percent of its TFP growth rooted in trade, and Singapore along with Papua New Guinea have 87.4 percent and 81.9 percent. Even the trade-reluctant United States owes about 30

Table 5.6 Total Factor Productivity Accounting by Country

Country	Output Growth Share due to		Labor Productivity Growth Share due to		Share of TFP Growth due to	
	Quantities	TFP	Quantities	TFP	Qualities	Trade
Hong Kong	44.4	55.6	27.9	72.1	18.2	81.8
Korea	68.8	31.2	57.6	42.4	49.4	50.6
Singapore	43.3	56.7	31.0	69.0	12.6	87.4
Taiwan	63.7	36.3	50.4	49.6	38.3	61.7
Indonesia	70.4	29.6	51.5	48.5	42.7	57.3
Malaysia	60.6	39.4	44.1	55.9	33.9	66.1
Thailand	70.6	29.4	43.2	56.8	28.1	71.9
Papua New Guinea	49.5	50.5	17.1	82.9	18.1	81.9
Philippines	68.6	31.4	35.8	64.2	28.2	71.8
Australia	64.4	35.6	40.6	59.4	52.5	47.5
Japan	70.5	29.5	63.6	36.4	62.7	37.3
New Zealand	51.0	49.0	26.8	73.2	40.7	59.3
United States	64.3	35.7	41.2	58.8	70.9	29.1

Source. Table 5.2.

percent of its TFP growth to trade. TFP is important for output growth and for productivity growth, and trade is important for TFP.

 Roughly the same conclusions apply to the larger community looked at by Table 5.7, which is derived from Table 5.3 by the aforementioned procedure. Again, for output growth the TFP role never drops below 29.0 percent, and the successful programs of the Tigers and Elephants have TFP roles of approximately 50 percent. As before, labor productivity reveals even greater dependency on TFP, those figures exceeding the 50 percent mark in all ten circumstances. And once more, trade is typically the dominant driver of TFP growth.

 The importance of TFP in the processes of output growth and labor productivity growth for the East Asian Tigers specifically and

Table 5.7 Total Factor Productivity Accounting by Country Group

Country Group	Output Growth Share due to		Labor Productivity Growth Share due to		Share of TFP Growth due to	
	Quantities	TFP	Quantities	TFP	Qualities	Trade
East Asian Tigers	55.0	45.0	41.7	58.3	25.9	74.1
Southeast Asian Lions	67.2	32.8	46.3	53.7	34.8	65.2
South Asian Gaurs	63.8	36.2	31.4	68.6	37.9	62.1
Latin Rim Bulls	70.2	29.8	48.3	51.7	57.8	44.2
Latin American Tapirs	58.0	42.0	35.4	64.6	39.1	60.9
Caribbean Iguanas	50.4	49.6	33.4	66.6	30.4	69.6
Middle Eastern Camels	61.2	38.8	44.8	55.2	42.8	57.2
Perimeter African Rhinos	58.2	41.8	41.7	58.3	36.6	63.4
Sub-Saharan Hippos	57.6	42.4	21.7	78.3	28.6	71.4
OECD Elephants	47.1	52.9	34.6	65.4	38.9	61.1
All Groups	56.6	43.4	31.7	68.3	34.8	65.2

Source. Table 5.3.

for the whole collection of metaphorical creatures generally seems to run counter to the popular pronouncements of Krugman (1994, pp. 68–70). Opening his discussion of the Asian miracle by reflecting on the economic history of the Soviet Union Bear, Krugman alludes to the 1957 finding by Solow and then volunteers the following observation:

> Just as capitalist growth had been based on growth in both inputs and efficiency, with efficiency the main source of rising per capita income, [economists] expected to find that rapid Soviet growth reflected both rapid input growth and rapid growth in efficiency.
>
> But what they actually found was that Soviet growth was based on rapid growth in inputs—end of story. The rate of efficiency growth was not only unspectacular, it was well below the rates achieved in Western economies. Indeed, by some estimates, it was virtually nonexistent.

Perceiving common ground between the Bear and the Tigers, he goes on to assert that

> Asian growth, like that of the Soviet Union in its high-growth era, seems to be driven by extraordinary growth in inputs like labor and capital rather than by gains in efficiency.

Efficiency, alias technical change or total factor productivity, does not matter for East Asian growth, and such reasoning leads to the remarks about perspiration and physical capital cited in Section 5.3.

Albeit pitched at a nontechnical level for a wide audience, the argument advanced by Krugman is tied to the rigorous work of Kim and Lau (1994, pp. 240–41, 264), whose translog meta-production function indicates that "technical progress (or increase in efficiency) has played an insignificant role in the postwar aggregate economic growth of the East Asian [Tigers]." It is also founded on the sophisticated effort of Young (1995, pp. 646–48, 671), whose translog production function suggests that the premise of extraordinarily high productivity growth in the Tigers "is largely incorrect."[6]

Reconciling the strong TFP results in Tables 5.6 and 5.7 with the unenthusiastic TFP showing in the expositions by Krugman and company revolves around international trade, because while trade enters the present setting as a separate growth agent that proves to have considerable power, it does not enter as a separate element in those other formulations.

Tables 5.4 and 5.5 provide the basis for "tradeless" TFP calculations since they contain the growth shares established under the proviso that trade is not an explicit cause of growth. As already discussed, that proviso means that the previous trade share becomes assimilated by the remaining growth determinants. It also means by equation (3.31) that TFP growth now depends only upon capital and labor qualities. Since those elements have been the weakest ones considered, it is natural to imagine the TFP growth contribution to plummet in the tradeless framework. It does. Tables 5.8 and 5.9 help to make the point.

An explicit accounting of international trade in Table 5.6 found that Hong Kong had TFP contribute 55.6 percent to output growth whereas capital and labor quantities contributed the smaller portion 44.4 percent. Moreover, Singapore led the TFP contributions with 56.7 percent, and no Asia Pacific country saw a TFP figure below 29.0 percent. But when the allowance for trade is suspended to produce Table 5.8, Hong Kong observes the TFP involvement in output growth decline from 55.6 percent to 18.1 percent and the quantities involvement rise from 44.4 percent to 81.9 percent. Singapore's TFP figure of 56.7 percent shrinks to 13.9 percent, moving that Tiger from the top spot in the TFP ledger to eleventh. Furthermore, no Asia Pacific country manages to place the TFP share *above* 29.0 percent. Similar swings are evident for labor productivity growth.

The country groups repeat the story. Comparing Tables 5.7 and 5.9 discloses for the Tigers that the TFP share of output growth decreases from 45.0 percent to 16.9 percent while for the Lions it reduces from 32.8 percent to 14.3 percent. And whereas the TFP contribution to output growth never falls below 29.0 percent in the trade case, it almost never rises *above* 29.0 percent in the tradeless case.

Table 5.8 Total Factor Productivity Accounting by Country Without Allowance for Trade

Country	Output Growth Share due to		Labor Productivity Growth Share due to		Share of TFP Growth due to	
	Quantities	TFP	Quantities	TFP	Qualities	Trade
Hong Kong	81.9	18.1	68.9	31.1	100.0	0.0
Korea	81.9	18.1	73.6	26.4	100.0	0.0
Singapore	86.1	13.9	78.2	21.8	100.0	0.0
Taiwan	82.4	17.6	72.9	27.1	100.0	0.0
Indonesia	85.1	14.9	71.9	28.1	100.0	0.0
Malaysia	82.3	17.7	70.4	29.6	100.0	0.0
Thailand	89.7	10.3	73.7	26.3	100.0	0.0
Papua New Guinea	84.7	15.3	55.0	45.0	100.0	0.0
Philippines	88.7	11.3	67.4	32.7	100.0	0.0
Australia	78.0	22.0	58.4	41.6	100.0	0.0
Japan	79.4	20.6	73.7	26.3	100.0	0.0
New Zealand	72.9	27.1	50.6	49.4	100.0	0.0
United States	72.4	27.7	51.4	48.6	100.0	0.0

Source. Table 5.4.

Making no allowance for trade in the growth analysis takes the steam out of total factor productivity. It also helps to reconcile the results across studies. For instance, Kim and Lau (1994, pp. 246, 249, 251) dismiss on strict statistical grounds the hypothesis of technical progress in the four Tigers. Nonetheless, in computing growth shares they run through a relaxed sequence that includes progress effects, and in that connection they find the contribution of technical progress to output growth to average 21.8 percent across the four nations (Kim and Lau, 1994, pp. 258–59). Likewise, Young (1995, pp. 657, 658, 660, 661) estimates the TFP share for each Tiger, those estimates averaging 19.5 percent. Plainly, such numbers, corroborated by Dowling and Summers (1997, p. 18), lie within hailing distance of the 16.9 percent value posted in Table 5.9. Thus,

Table 5.9 Total Factor Productivity Accounting by Country Group Without Allowance for Trade

Country Group	Output Growth Share due to		Labor Productivity Growth Share due to		Share of TFP Growth due to	
	Quantities	TFP	Quantities	TFP	Qualities	Trade
East Asian Tigers	83.1	16.9	73.4	26.6	100.0	0.0
Southeast Asian Lions	85.7	14.3	72.0	28.0	100.0	0.0
South Asian Gaurs	83.2	16.8	56.5	43.5	100.0	0.0
Latin Rim Bulls	80.9	19.1	61.8	38.2	100.0	0.0
Latin American Tapirs	78.6	21.4	58.2	41.8	100.0	0.0
Caribbean Iguanas	77.7	22.3	61.6	38.4	100.0	0.0
Middle Eastern Camels	79.0	21.0	64.9	35.1	100.0	0.0
Perimeter African Rhinos	79.6	20.4	65.8	34.2	100.0	0.0
Sub-Saharan Hippos	82.7	17.3	42.8	57.2	100.0	0.0
OECD Elephants	69.7	30.3	57.8	42.2	100.0	0.0
All Groups	79.1	20.9	54.4	45.6	100.0	0.0

Source. Table 5.5.

incorporating international trade into the growth analysis on the basis of allocative efficiency puts a powerful force into TFP and produces a high percentage contribution to growth. By contrast, ignoring trade as an explicit growth agent leaves TFP to be governed by quality factors alone and relegates its growth contribution to a much lower percentage.[7]

5.5 REFLECTIONS

Economic growth theory has evolved through many twists and turns. An early formulation by Harrod and, by extension, Domar imagined steady equilibrium growth as a knife edge that an economy might attain only by accident. The neoclassical response to that precarious balance envisioned steady growth as a center of gravity to which a nation would naturally tend. "Old" models of endogenous progress brought richness and realism to the discussion, and their "new" counterparts added depth. From homogeneous shays to putty and clay, from production functions to technical progress functions, and from distinctions between workers and capitalists to fascination about the representative agent, theory twisted and turned to explain economic growth. It sought the causes. Empirical inquiry, built on theory, aided the search to a point at which scores of causes were tested and millions of regressions were run. Levine and Renelt (1992, pp. 942, 960–61) and Sala-i-Martin (1997, p. 180) easily vouch for the enthusiasm of the empirical undertakings.

In a sense, the study at hand is less ambitious. It does not sift through dozens of causes, nor does it fill archives with estimated equations. Instead, it tailors theory to fit the facts of growth. Then it focuses on a small set of causes and uses a small set of empirical renderings to help establish the importance of those determinants for individual countries in the Asia Pacific Region and for country groups from Asia eastward to Europe and Africa. In this sense of mission, the study may not be unambitious.

Included among the determinants are three control variables that serve to capture structural differences across countries. One of those controls is the initial level of labor productivity, whose presence in the regression work can be explained by the convergence property implied by theory. Conditional convergence is affirmed across the pool of countries under review. Moreover, graphical sketches substantiate the convergence tendencies of Asia Pacific nations such as Hong Kong, Singapore, and Japan and likewise verify those leanings for the Tigers and Lions taken collectively. At the same time, however, the divergence depictions for Papua New Guinea and the Sub-Saharan Hippos constitute a reminder that the notion of country-to-country convergence can be at odds with the idea of steady state convergence. The country-to-country circumstance presumes ceteris paribus conditions that may not hold in practice, the equality of saving coefficients across nations being only one such requisite.

Another control variable is the mortality rate. On testing, it indicates that improved health improves economic growth. While this result can be interpreted as merely confirming common sense, it nonetheless goes further to give quantitative content to the relationship.

The clarity of common sense surrounding health does not carry over to the third control variable: civil liberty. Talk about Soviet economic supremacy over the West and the image of Nikita Khrushchev pounding a shoe on the podium at the United Nations and saying "We will bury you" fostered a belief that authoritarianism promotes growth (Krugman, 1994, pp. 64–65). The success of Yugoslavia under Tito fortified that belief. Surely, Yugoslavia's miraculous productivity growth rate, which exceeded 5.0 percent annually during the 1960s and 1970s (Gapinski, 1993a, pp. 7–10), left little doubt about the merits of strong control. In the end, however, liberty won out as the regressions here find that strengthening liberty enhances growth. The collapse of the Soviet and Yugoslav systems dramatically underscores that statistical result.

Although the control variables are more than incidental to the inquiry, they are not the determinants of primary concern. The primary determinants are international trade, capital quantity, capital quality, labor quantity, and labor quality. International trade proves to be a powerful force in the growth process just as Clark and Kim (1995b, pp. 3–10, 19–21) and Western (1996a, pp. 3–7, 74–85,

100–01) argue. Entering the production structure through its effect on allocative efficiency, trade works its way into the arithmetic of steady growth and convergence. Put simply, more trade means faster long-run growth and bolder convergence movements, and the empirical measures along with the observed convergence configurations support those theoretical propositions. Trade matters. Accordingly, strategies intended to improve growth prospects might be designed to recognize a nation's involvement in the international community. In that setting the promotion of trade openness in general and exports in particular and the stabilization of exchange rates may not be inappropriate themes for guiding policy.

Capital quantity, like trade, proves to be a major factor in economic growth. This finding reaffirms the assertions by De Long and Summers (1991, pp. 445–47, 479, 484–86; 1992, pp. 157–59, 194), Wolff (1991, pp. 565–67, 577–78), and Dollar and Wolff (1994, pp. 197–99, 214, 216–17), who likewise stress the role of capital in growth. Acquisitions, by definition, enhance capital quantity. But, because of embodiment, they simultaneously enhance capital quality, and hence they must be understood as accessing two sources of growth. Acquisitions matter—for two reasons. Moreover, the empirical evidence implies that the maturing countries in the Asia Pacific Region tend to be deficient in capital, as the marginal product of efficient capital exceeds the real rate of interest. For those nations acquisitions are needed on optimization grounds. And to the extent that acquisitions are accomplished through international trade, they represent a transfer of technology enabling the maturing states, consonant with Gerschenkron's principle, to take advantage of their backwardness. Acquisitions therefore matter in four respects: capital quantity, capital quality, stock deficiency, and technology transfers. Given the multiple dimensions of acquisitions, domestic strategies geared to raise thrift or to lower capital costs should not be treated lightly. Nor should they be perceived as being unrelated to international strategies.

Capital acquisitions allow the Asia Pacific nations to stretch scarce labor as they strive to restore international competitiveness. Another way to stretch scarce labor is through education to compensate through quality what might be lacking in quantity. Certainly, opportunities to increase the educational level of a population should be pursued, and numerous reasons can be advanced to justify such action. Still, the analysis here suggests that education may not provide a fast track for economic growth. In point of fact, labor quality consistently tests as the weakest of the primary determinants. By inference, the growth benefits of education may be low, and they may fall below the requisite costs. In their comment on Denison's notion of the advance of knowledge, Jorgenson and Griliches (1967, p. 274) remark:

> Our conclusion is not that advances in knowledge are negligible, but that the accumulation of knowledge is governed by the same economic laws as any other process of capital accumulation. Costs must be incurred if benefits are to be achieved.

Barro (1992, pp. 204–05; 1994, p. 11) voices the same opinion in saying

> The conclusions about imbalances between human and physical capital are reinforced if the accumulation of human capital involves adjustment costs that are much higher than those applicable to physical capital. (Machines and buildings can be assembled quickly, but people cannot be educated rapidly without encountering a sharp drop-off in the rate of return to investment.)

Optimality criteria may be much less kind to human capital than to physical capital in the context of economic growth.

Theory and the empirical analysis built on it identify the causes of economic growth and show them to have different strengths that themselves differ across individual countries and across country groups. Necessarily, then, the policy implications from that mix of theory and evidence carry weight that differs from country to country and from metaphorical creature to metaphorical creature. Nonetheless, applied resolutely, the policy recommendations may hold bright promise, as the poet Cecil Francis Alexander might say, for all creatures great and small.

PART III

SPECIAL STUDIES

CHAPTER 6

A TIGERS' TALE OF TWO CITIES

I will look into this matter. . . . On the face of it, it would appear to be a case of a very exceptional nature.

Sherlock Holmes
—A. Conan Doyle, *The Adventure of the Devil's Foot*

HONG KONG AND SINGAPORE, two of the East Asian Tigers, have enjoyed ferocious economic growth that has been called miraculous. As Table 4.2 confirms, for the period 1961–90 Hong Kong saw real output grow at an annual rate of 8.85 percent and real labor productivity grow at a yearly rate of 6.03 percent. Similarly, Singapore saw rates of 8.62 percent and 5.32 percent respectively. Such achievements, while impressive by themselves, become even more impressive when they are put alongside the corresponding rates for the United States, 3.28 percent and 1.54 percent. In terms of economic growth, the two Tigers have easily bested America.

But there is more to the miracle. The stunning growth successes of Hong Kong and Singapore have been accompanied by remarkable declines in the unemployment rate and, perhaps more remarkably, by *leftward* shifts in the Phillips curve. Figure 6.1 illustrates for recent years through 1995 using measures that are denominated as

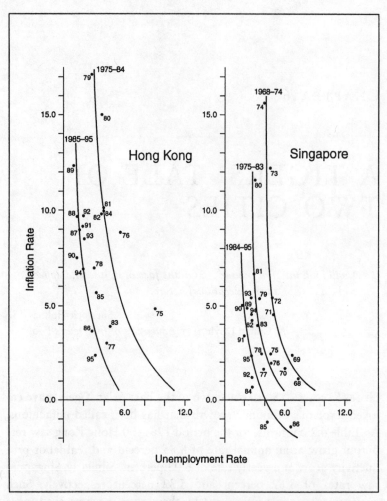

Figure 6.1 Phillips Curves for Hong Kong and Singapore

percentages. The shifts are quite evident. Meanwhile, as those patterns developed, real wages in both countries increased. For Hong Kong the real wage, indexed at unity for 1985, equaled 0.574 in 1974, whereas in 1995 it equaled 1.332. Singapore had comparable values of 0.520 and 1.623.[1]

High output growth, rapid labor productivity growth, declining unemployment rates, leftward Phillips shifts, and rising real wages can be explained by the acquisition of physical capital. More machinery bolsters output through the production function. It quickens output growth and labor productivity growth, it boosts the marginal product of labor, and it propels the labor demand curve rightward thereby driving unemployment down and the real wage up. That same sequence also can be explained by technical progress. To add clarity to the concept, technical progress can be defined as the amount of output growth *not* accounted for by the growth in input quantities. In that residual sense of Solow (1957, pp. 312–13), it is synonymous with the growth of TFP, total factor productivity. Seemingly, then, TFP growth matters in the chain of economic events.

Nevertheless, scholarly opinion on the contribution of TFP, at least in the growth context, is mixed. Krugman (1994, pp. 66–67, 69–72), for instance, dismisses TFP as a causal determinant in East Asian growth and instead contends, in the language of the popular press (*Economist,* 1995, p. 33), that the production of more sausages involves little more than the mobilization of more sausage machines and more sausage makers. Chen (1977, pp. 125–26) and Western (1996b, pp. 1, 6–7), by contrast, insist that TFP has been an important force behind the miracle. Young (1992, pp. 16, 34–37; 1995, pp. 656–59, 671–73), in studying Hong Kong and Singapore, concludes that TFP matters for the former but not for the latter. Meanwhile, Kim and Lau (1994, pp. 248–51, 257–60) believe that TFP matters for neither Tiger.[2]

The present chapter extends the precedents by examining further the contribution of TFP to growth. However, its scope is broader than TFP alone, as it covers the contributions to growth due to capital quantity, capital quality, labor quantity, labor quality, and international trade. In that broad context TFP becomes a determinant because it derives from the quality variables and from trade. Hong Kong and Singapore provide the setting. Their contemporary histories are presented in Section 6.1 to orient the inquiry. With history in hand, Section 6.2 explores economic features of the Tigers including their convergence tendencies. Section 6.3 describes a growth accounting that quantifies the growth shares from the various determinants treated separately and from the portmanteau determinant, TFP. Section 6.4 offers thoughts on policy.

6.1 HISTORICAL TALES

Hong Kong has a fascinating history. The contemporary passages of its tale revolve around opium, an indulgence that profiteering British traders endeavored to impose on the unwilling Chinese. In due course tension mounted between Britain and China leading to hostilities known as the Opium War. The Crown won handily. To the victor go the spoils, and by the Treaty of Nanking, signed in 1842, the island of Hong Kong was ceded to Britain. Fourteen years later a small craft named the *Arrow,* traversing the seas under the protection of the Union Jack, was boarded by Chinese authorities at Canton. The incident sparked the Second Opium War, and again the British were victorious. By the resulting Convention of Peking of 1860, Britain took possession of the tip of Kowloon Peninsula, thereby giving it a secure land mass to the immediate north of the Fragrant Harbour. But the Colony of Hong Kong was to grow yet again. Concerned about the escapades of France and Russia in the Far East, Britain sought to further insulate Hong Kong, and to that end it leased the New Territories from China. The lease ran for 99 years starting from July 1, 1898.

At the time of the first war, Lord Palmerston, the British foreign secretary, characterized Hong Kong as a "barren island with hardly a house upon it."[3] It would not remain barren. Rather, it would become an economic jewel in the Royal Crown. That jewel, however, had a return date, and as the years advanced, Britain and China began deliberations on reversion. Round upon round of negotiations ensued that culminated in the Joint Declaration of 1984. By that accord, which was forged around the concept of "one country, two systems" envisioned by Deng Xiaoping, China's paramount leader, Britain agreed to hand over the entire colony. For its part, China agreed to a 50-year period wherein Hong Kong would have a high degree of autonomy and would maintain its capitalist orientation. In 1990 China pounded out the Basic Law, which defined the legal and constitutional framework for the new Hong Kong, formally a special administrative region (SAR). By its language, the Basic Law laid down specifics consonant with the spirit of the Joint Declaration and, in a way, set into stone the principle of one country, two systems.[4]

Sentiment about the impending changeover was mixed.[5] Hope and exuberance mingled with worry and fear. Then, amid the mixed emotions, came July 1, 1997. The stroke of midnight ushering in that Tuesday also ushered in the Chinese and escorted out the British. Revelry erupted and remained intense despite driving rain. Then came the morning after. Cooler heads prevailed and wondered about the prospects. Some continue to wonder.[6]

Singapore, like Hong Kong, has an engaging tale to tell. The contemporary chapters, like those for Hong Kong, begin in the early 1800s because it was then that history encountered Sir Thomas Stamford Raffles. In 1805 the young Raffles was sent from London to fill a government post in Penang, an island located at the northern entrance to the Straits of Malacca along the western shore of the Malay Peninsula. By 1818 Raffles had become Lieutenant Governor of Bencoolen, a station situated on the western side of Sumatra and therefore rather removed from the major trade routes through the Straits. Feeling the need for Britain to control a port at the southern gateway to the Straits, Raffles took it upon himself to act, and on January 28, 1819, he navigated up at least what is now called the Singapore River and landed on the northern bank. With that landing Singapore came into being.

Events moved quickly on the tiger-inhabited island. In February of 1819 a deal was struck enabling the British to build a factory and granting the Crown jurisdiction inland within a range of a cannon shot. Subsequent jurisdictional disputes with the Dutch were resolved in March of 1824 by the Treaty of London. More important, perhaps, was the treaty that followed only a few months later. By that compact, signed in August of 1824, the sultan of Johor ceded to Britain the entire island of Singapore and everything in the surrounding seas within ten miles of its coast. Two years later, in 1826,

Singapore joined Penang and Malacca, a Malay port city positioned midway along the north-south run through the Straits, as the Straits Settlements. In 1867 the settlements became a Crown colony. Prior to that occurrence, however, Singapore served as a base for Britain in its fight with China over opium.

The dawn of the new century proved to be rather uneventful for the City of the Lion, a translation of the eleventh-century name *Singapura* that probably involved mistaking a tiger for a lion. Singapore was largely unaffected by World War I although it did suffer under the Depression. Suffering took a sharp turn during World War II. Having no military defenses along its northern exposure to the Malay Peninsula, Singapore was overrun by the Japanese across that line and surrendered in February of 1942. The island city remained under Japanese occupation until September 1945, when the British military took control and set the stage for restoration of civilian governance on April 1, 1946. Promptly the Straits Settlements was dissolved, and Singapore was proclaimed a Crown colony—again. Notably and prophetically, Britain maintained that its action regarding Singapore would not prevent the island from merging with other states at some future date if such a union might prove to be beneficial.

Thomas Stamford Raffles is undeniably one of the founding fathers of Singapore. Another father, this one providing much more recent parentage, is Lee Kuan Yew. Sensing a political void that demanded filling, Lee Kuan Yew and several others established the People's Action Party (PAP), which held its initial meeting in Singapore during November of 1954. On June 5, 1959, PAP assumed political authority over the new State of Singapore while Lee held the reins as prime minister and head of government. Since PAP had championed the idea of merger with Malaya as an immediate cure for economic ills, its ascent pushed that idea closer to reality. A precipitous shove came quite innocuously at a banquet hosted by Singapore in May of 1961. At that gathering the prime minister of the Federation of Malaya suggested that Singapore, Malaya, and other territories might unite as Malaysia. This surprise comment delighted PAP, which seized it as a formal invitation. On September 1, 1962, a Singapore referendum approved the merger, which took effect on

September 16, 1963. On that day Malaysia was created, and Singapore was part of the new creation.

Marriages sometimes are not meant to last; Singapore's would last only 23 months. Grumbles over political philosophy, operational style, and economic issues escalated into irreconcilable differences. On August 7, 1965, a separation agreement was reached, and on August 9, 1965, the divorce became final. At that blink in history, Singapore became a fully independent sovereign state.

Soon after the Singapore independence, the British military hauled anchor and sailed into the sunrise, taking with it a considerable number of civilian jobs. Political issues evolved, and for the election of September 1988, debate focused on the notion of an elected president. PAP won that contest, and Lee continued as prime minister until November of 1990, when Goh Chok Tong accepted the post. The first popular election of a president took place in August of 1993. Those ballots brought Ong Teng Cheong into office, which he held as Hong Kong reverted to China.[7]

History, then, finds numerous similarities between the two Tigers. Both Hong Kong and Singapore came to prominence during the early part of the nineteenth century through maneuverings of the British. Both islands were strategic centers militarily and economically. Both became Crown colonies, and both ceased being Crown colonies. Therein, however, lies a difference. Hong Kong, on gaining independence from Britain, returned to China. For Hong Kong, independence from Britain did not mean independence. For Singapore it did. As of August 9, 1965, Singapore found itself independent, alone, and adrift on the economic sea.

Having had the responsibility for the country's economic survival thrust upon it, the Singapore government under Lee thrust itself into business affairs ranging from international trade to industry targeting to labor conduct. In fact, the visible hand of the government went beyond the immediate circle of business and touched the citizens of Singapore in their social and personal lives. Littering, toilet habits, hair styles, family size, and even family quality became areas of government concern and policy. In part, government intervention was dictated by the circumstance. Nonetheless, it stands in marked contrast to the laissez faire that Raffles had in mind when he first set foot on Singapore soil and that Hong Kong had practiced as positive noninterventionism at least until reversion.[8] Indeed, it may be argued, as Krause (1988, pp. S60-S64) does, that this contrast is one of the main differences between the two Tigers. By the same token, it may be argued, as the introductory remarks imply, that one of the main similarities between the two is their fierce economic growth. To that growth and to its causes the discussion now turns.

6.2 ECONOMIC RECORDS

The growth paradigm presented in Section 3.4 identifies variables that explain the ferocious performance of the two Tigers. Tables 6.1 and 6.2 here present the economic records for those variables and for several related measures. As before, the underlying data come from the Penn World Table Mark 5.5 (PWT) compiled by Summers and Heston (1993), and from Barro and Lee (1993). All currency magnitudes are denominated in billions of 1985 international dollars, and consequently they are comparable between countries. Output Y is gauged by gross domestic product; labor quantity L, by millions of workers; and labor quality E, by average years of schooling. Efficient capital J is constructed according to equation (3.21). Capital type J_1 sets to zero the rate of embodied technical progress and the rate of physical deterioration. Involving no embodiment and no daily decay, it is homogeneous-shay capital. Measure J_m represents the mean of the nine capital types. Circumflexes—or hats—indicate growth rates in proportionate terms. Multiplication by 100 converts the rates into percentages.

Tables 6.1 and 6.2 are instructive. They indicate Hong Kong to be the larger economy having a greater abundance of resources, human and mechanistic. For example, over the 30-year period from 1961–90, Hong Kong generated output Y on the order of 35.5 billion dollars annually compared against 13.5 billion for Singapore. For the recent half decade 1986–90, the Hong Kong dominance continued, its 76.2 billion dollars outdistancing the Singapore 27.7

Table 6.1 Economic Record of Hong Kong

Period	Y billion dollars	L million workers	E years	J_l billion dollars	J_m billion dollars	y dollars per worker	100 s percent	M_l decimal	M_m decimal	r decimal
1961-90	35.5	2.7	6.16	98.3	1,824.3	11,896	24.79	0.099	0.052	
1961-65	9.7	1.8	5.02	29.3	209.5	5,318	24.92	0.092	0.051	
1966-70	15.1	2.0	5.06	43.3	386.0	7,441	24.27	0.097	0.053	
1971-75	22.5	2.3	5.44	62.2	703.7	9,562	24.74	0.101	0.054	
1976-80	35.8	2.9	6.29	94.7	1,447.7	12,489	26.05	0.105	0.053	-0.047
1981-85	53.4	3.4	7.20	148.5	2,986.6	15,884	23.59	0.100	0.048	0.015
1986-90	76.2	3.7	7.98	211.8	5,212.1	20,680	25.15	0.100	0.050	-0.031

	100 $\hat{Y}$ percent	100 $\hat{L}$ percent	100 $\hat{E}$ percent	100 $\hat{J}_l$ percent	100 $\hat{J}_m$ percent	100 $\hat{y}$ percent	100 $\hat{j}_l$ percent	100 $\hat{j}_m$ percent	100 U percent	100 X percent
1961-90	8.85	2.82	1.58	8.22	11.81	6.03	5.40	8.99	188.39	95.49
1961-65	13.00	3.21	-1.14	9.16	13.97	9.79	5.95	10.76	168.37	83.48
1966-70	7.28	1.88	1.08	6.93	8.80	5.40	5.05	6.92	175.30	90.01
1971-75	6.79	3.63	1.68	7.91	11.83	3.17	4.28	8.21	169.36	86.46
1976-80	12.82	4.46	3.67	9.67	15.15	8.36	5.21	10.69	173.91	87.85
1981-85	5.60	2.34	2.22	8.41	11.21	3.26	6.06	8.87	194.17	97.77
1986-90	7.62	1.42	2.00	7.24	9.88	6.20	5.81	8.46	249.20	127.36

Note. Each entry is an annual average over the corresponding period.

Table 6.2 Economic Record of Singapore

Period	Y billion dollars	L million workers	E years	J_l billion dollars	J_m billion dollars	y dollars per worker	100 s percent	M_l decimal	M_m decimal	r decimal
1961-90	13.5	1.0	3.96	49.6	1,141.0	12,422	25.98	0.120	0.050	
1961-65	3.4	0.6	3.15	4.1	39.8	5,600	4.44	0.244	0.103	
1966-70	5.2	0.7	3.57	9.5	119.8	7,424	17.63	0.154	0.063	
1971-75	9.4	0.8	3.95	24.3	398.9	11,073	24.18	0.109	0.042	
1976-80	14.3	1.0	3.84	46.8	888.0	13,708	32.29	0.085	0.035	0.014
1981-85	20.8	1.2	4.21	83.7	1,946.4	16,867	38.94	0.070	0.030	0.046
1986-90	27.7	1.4	5.07	129.0	3,453.0	19,859	38.39	0.059	0.028	0.007

Period	100 $\hat{Y}$ percent	100 $\hat{L}$ percent	100 $\hat{E}$ percent	100 $\hat{J}_l$ percent	100 $\hat{J}_m$ percent	100 $\hat{y}$ percent	100 $\hat{j}_l$ percent	100 $\hat{j}_m$ percent	100 U percent	100 X percent
1961-90	8.62	3.30	2.02	15.13	18.15	5.32	11.83	14.84	307.41	149.78
1961-65	5.37	3.34	1.68	20.02	25.00	2.02	16.68	21.66	274.66	129.75
1966-70	12.44	2.48	3.07	19.48	24.15	9.96	17.00	21.67	237.07	112.46
1971-75	11.67	4.83	1.44	19.06	22.33	6.84	14.23	17.50	260.92	122.23
1976-80	8.20	3.96	-1.89	12.48	14.05	4.24	8.52	10.09	359.24	177.62
1981-85	5.88	3.22	4.28	11.83	14.38	2.66	8.61	11.16	357.16	177.00
1986-90	8.19	1.98	3.52	7.92	8.97	6.21	5.94	6.99	355.37	179.65

Note. See Table 6.1.

billion. Hong Kong had more labor quantity L, 2.7 million workers on balance as opposed to 1.0 million, and it had higher labor quality E, 6.16 years rather than 3.96 years. Furthermore, its stock of homogeneous-shay capital J_1, registering 98.3 billion dollars, doubled the Singapore level, and its average stock of efficient capital J_m, equaling 1,824.3 billion, stood 60 percent higher than Singapore's counterpart.

In short, Hong Kong enjoyed greater levels. By contrast, Singapore tended to experience greater rates. Over the 30 years labor quantity in the City of the Lion expanded at 3.30 percent per year while the Fragrant Harbour showed 2.82 percent. Labor quality advanced at 2.02 percent in Singapore and 1.58 percent in Hong Kong, and homogeneous shays exploded at 15.13 percent instead of 8.22 percent. For mean efficient capital the growth spread was 18.15 percent versus 11.81 percent. Along the same line, Singapore's rate of capital deepening, $100 \; \hat{j}_1$ for homogeneous shays or $100 \; \hat{j}_m$ for mean capital, handily beat Hong Kong's. So did its trade volume as measured by openness U, which combines exports and imports and expresses the combination as a fraction of output. Its percent variant $100 \; U$ appears alongside the export component $100 \; X$, which reports exports as a percent of output. On that score too, Singapore proved to be much stronger.

Having seen more favorable growth determinants over the 30-year period, Singapore—by equations (3.24) through (3.26)—should have experienced faster growth of output and labor productivity than did Hong Kong. Yet it did not. Singapore grew more slowly. Its output growth was 8.62 percent whereas Hong Kong's was 8.85 percent, and its productivity growth was 5.32 percent while Hong Kong's was 6.03 percent. Explaining this paradox requires looking at government intervention in everyday life.

By the history recounted in the previous section, Singapore found itself abruptly independent, and economic survival prompted the government under Lee Kuan Yew to engineer activity. As Table 6.2 discloses, that orchestration quickly increased the saving rate $100 \; s$ from a meager 4.44 percent just before independence to 17.63 percent immediately afterward and then to a high of 38.94 percent in the early 1980s. Such colossal thriftiness helped to finance the fantastic rates of capital expansion and must be regarded as a positive consequence of intervention. At the same time, however, heavy social engineering meant the curtailment of civil liberties noted earlier. Ascribing some precision to the forfeiture, Barro and Wolf (1989) show for Singapore a civil liberty rating c of 5.0 on a scale that uses 1.0 to signify greatest liberty and 7.0 to mark least liberty. Likewise Gwartney and Lawson (1997, pp. 249–50), appealing to a reverse-order system whose index f ranges from 0.0 to 10.0 for least and greatest civil liberty respectively, assign Singapore an f value of 0.0. Tellingly, Hong Kong, with its positive noninterventionist brand of laissez faire, at least before reversion, boasts a c rating of 2.0 and an f index of 7.5. Liberty, then, was much less prevalent in Singapore than in Hong Kong. This situation, combined with the empirical finding by Gapinski (1996, pp. 573–75) that reduced liberty undermines economic growth, readily explains the paradox.

Other aspects of the economic records deserve review. Labor productivity y rides an upward trend for both countries but plays leapfrog in the process. Productivity begins in the early half decade 1961–65 with Singapore in front 5,600 dollars to 5,318 dollars. Hong Kong leaps ahead in the next half decade, but Singapore leaps over Hong Kong in 1971–75. Hong Kong then waits its turn until the late 1980s, when it again leaps over Singapore. Leapfrogging can be interpreted as a "lumpy" way of keeping the labor productivity profiles similar across the two Tigers.

Hardly similar across the two are the profiles for the marginal product of efficient capital, denoted M_1 for homogeneous-shay machinery and M_m for mean equipment. Intervention by the Singapore government drove up the capital stock in a manner unimaginable in Hong Kong. Correspondingly, the marginal product of capital in Singapore fell dramatically from 0.244 during 1961–65 to 0.059 during 1986–90 for homogeneous shays and from 0.103 to 0.028 for mean capital. Such declines did not occur in Hong Kong. Declines notwithstanding, Singapore usually managed to post marginal products above the real interest rate r, thereby confirming the consonance of capital acquisitions with the customary rule of optimization. Hong Kong too acquired capital consonant with the rule.[9]

The leapfrogging behavior of the two Tigers with regard to labor productivity has implications for convergence. It may be recalled that convergence is the tendency for a country having low initial labor productivity to catch up to a country having high initial productivity. Convergence is accomplished, of course, by the laggard growing in productivity faster than the leader. Relative to the United States, Hong Kong and Singapore began as true laggards. According to Table 4.2 their initial labor productivity levels were 4,105 dollars and 5,171 dollars respectively while that for the United States was 20,152. Therefore, in the tradition of neoclassical growth theory, a tradition which Section 3.5 shows as carrying over to the present vintage-capital theory, the two Tigers should record productivity growth rates higher than the U.S. rate. By the numbers quoted in the introduction, they do. They converge toward the United States. Relative to each other, however, the two Tigers are rather alike in initial labor productivity. Appropriately, they are rather alike also in overall productivity growth, and leapfrogging over the half decades implies that Hong Kong and Singapore should show alternating periods of convergence and divergence. They do.

Figure 4.5, which tracks the convergence index CI posited in equation (4.1) with the United States as numéraire, illustrates that the convergence run of Hong Kong and Singapore toward the United States has been fierce indeed. Over the 30 years from 1961 to 1990, the two Tigers have been able to cut their indices in half from about 80.0 to around 40.0. Moreover, the runs have been roughly parallel apart from the crossovers associated with frog leaps. At those leap points, though, the trajectories weave around each other creating alternating phases of convergence and divergence between the Tigers.

6.3 GROWTH SHARES

Data of the sort presented in the economic records join with the paradigm to produce growth shares. However, as equations (3.27) and (3.29) indicate, the shares call for parameter estimation, which proceeds in the manner described by Section 5.1. For Hong Kong and

Singapore, that estimation on homogeneous-shay capital leads to
the expression

$$\hat{y} = 0.0447 - 3.2 \times 10^{-6}y_o - 0.1619m - 0.0050c$$
$$\quad [5.089] \quad [-2.975] \quad\quad [-4.133] \quad [-4.962]$$
$$+ 0.0835\hat{E} + 0.2777\hat{j}_1 + 0.0235U,$$
$$\quad [5.395] \quad [3.173] \quad [6.169]$$

$$(6.1)$$

whose $R^2 = 0.074$, $F = 42.45$, and $DW = 1.92$. Student-t values appear in brackets. Plainly, all coefficients carry the anticipated signs.
For instance, the negative coefficient for initial labor productivity
reflects, in the fashion of Barro (1991, pp. 409, 437; 1992, pp.
202–03), productivity convergence conditional upon ceteris
paribus. That the coefficient is taken to be identical for Hong Kong
and Singapore manifests the lesson that the two island states are
much alike in their convergence tendencies. The negative sign for
mortality rate m says that worsened health conditions compromise
growth. The negative for civil liberty index c gives numerical content to the paradox explanation; namely, moving from the ample
liberty of Hong Kong, where $c = 2.0$, to the constrained liberty of
Singapore, where $c = 5.0$, reduces annual labor productivity growth
by 1.5 percentage points ceteris paribus. The coefficient for capital
deepening $\hat{j}_1$ is α, the output elasticity of efficient capital. Its value
of 0.2777 falls naturally within the tradition of the Cobb-Douglas.
Together with the coefficient for labor growth $\hat{E}$, it puts the estimate of the knowledge elasticity θ at 0.1157, again confirming anticipations. Easily confirming the trade hypothesis that $\zeta_F > 0$ is the
coefficient of openness U.

With the parameter estimates in hand, share equations (3.27)
and (3.29) become operative and produce Tables 6.3 and 6.4. Those
displays report the shares for output growth and for labor productivity growth net of the control factors. Furthermore, they provide
that information for homogeneous-shay capital and for mean capital, the latter numbers actually being the mean shares calculated
across all nine capital types using all nine sets of parameter values.

Table 6.3 Growth Shares for Hong Kong

Period	Total	Output Growth Share due to Labor Quantity	Labor Quality	Capital Efficient	Capital Quantity	Capital Quality	Foreign Trade	Labor Productivity Growth Share due to Labor Quality	Capital Efficient	Capital Quantity	Capital Quality	Foreign Trade
				Homogeneous-Shay Capital, J_l								
1961-90	24.5	23.0	1.5	25.7	25.7	0.0	49.8	1.9	33.4	33.4	0.0	64.7
1961-65	25.5	26.6	-1.1	29.2	29.2	0.0	45.3	-1.5	39.8	39.8	0.0	61.7
1966-70	19.3	18.1	1.2	25.7	25.7	0.0	55.0	1.5	31.4	31.4	0.0	67.1
1971-75	30.9	29.3	1.6	24.6	24.6	0.0	44.5	2.2	34.8	34.8	0.0	63.0
1976-80	34.3	31.3	3.0	26.1	26.1	0.0	39.7	4.3	38.0	38.0	0.0	57.7
1981-85	21.4	19.3	2.1	26.6	26.6	0.0	52.0	2.6	33.0	33.0	0.0	64.4
1986-90	13.2	11.3	1.8	22.2	22.2	0.0	64.6	2.1	25.0	25.0	0.0	72.9
				Mean Capital, J_m								
1961-90	24.3	22.8	1.4	30.3	21.5	8.7	45.5	1.8	39.2	27.9	11.3	58.9
1961-65	24.6	25.6	-1.0	35.4	25.8	9.6	40.1	-1.4	47.5	34.7	12.8	53.8
1966-70	20.0	18.8	1.2	27.6	18.6	9.1	52.3	1.5	34.0	22.9	11.2	64.5
1971-75	30.2	28.8	1.5	29.7	20.9	8.8	40.1	2.1	41.7	29.3	12.4	56.2
1976-80	32.7	30.0	2.7	32.4	23.9	8.5	34.9	3.9	46.2	34.1	12.1	49.9
1981-85	21.7	19.7	2.1	29.7	21.4	8.3	48.5	2.6	37.0	26.7	10.4	60.4
1986-90	13.5	11.7	1.8	25.6	17.4	8.2	61.0	2.1	28.9	19.7	9.3	69.0

Note. Expressed as a percentage, each number represents an annual average over the appropriate period.

Table 6.4 Growth Shares for Singapore

Period		Output Growth Share due to						Labor Productivity Growth Share due to				
		Labor		Capital			Foreign	Labor	Capital			Foreign
	Total	Quantity	Quality	Efficient	Quantity	Quality	Trade	Quality	Efficient	Quantity	Quality	Trade
					Homogeneous-Shay Capital, J_l							
1961-90	18.3	17.1	1.2	30.1	30.1	0.0	51.6	1.5	36.3	36.3	0.0	62.3
1961-65	17.5	16.6	1.0	38.2	38.2	0.0	44.3	1.2	45.8	45.8	0.0	53.1
1966-70	15.7	13.8	2.0	41.5	41.5	0.0	42.7	2.3	48.2	48.2	0.0	50.0
1971-75	24.0	23.2	0.8	35.2	35.2	0.0	40.8	1.0	45.9	45.9	0.0	53.1
1976-80	18.5	19.6	-1.1	23.7	23.7	0.0	57.8	-1.3	29.5	29.5	0.0	71.8
1981-85	18.7	16.2	2.5	22.9	22.9	0.0	58.4	3.0	27.3	27.3	0.0	69.7
1986-90	14.1	11.7	2.4	17.9	17.9	0.0	68.0	2.7	20.3	20.3	0.0	77.0
					Mean Capital, J_m							
1961-90	19.1	17.9	1.2	31.4	25.5	5.9	49.5	1.5	38.2	31.0	7.2	60.3
1961-65	17.9	16.9	0.9	40.6	34.0	6.6	41.5	1.1	49.9	40.9	8.0	49.9
1966-70	16.0	14.1	1.9	43.9	36.7	7.3	40.1	2.2	51.1	42.6	8.5	46.6
1971-75	25.0	24.2	0.8	35.9	30.3	5.7	39.0	1.1	47.4	39.9	7.5	51.5
1976-80	19.8	20.9	-1.1	23.6	18.6	5.0	56.5	-1.4	29.9	23.5	6.4	71.5
1981-85	19.5	17.0	2.5	24.2	18.7	5.5	56.3	3.0	29.2	22.6	6.6	67.8
1986-90	15.0	12.6	2.5	17.9	12.3	5.6	67.1	2.8	20.4	14.1	6.4	76.7

Note. See Table 6.3.

According to the tables, foreign trade proves to be the leading cause of growth. Over the 30-year period 1961–90, homogeneous-shay capital sees trade explain 49.8 percent of output growth for Hong Kong and 51.6 percent for Singapore. In either case roughly half of output growth stems from foreign trade. Second in line is capital quantity explaining 25.7 percent of output growth in Hong Kong and 30.1 percent in Singapore. Third comes labor quantity at 23.0 percent for Hong Kong and 17.1 percent for Singapore; fourth comes labor quality at 1.5 percent and 1.2 percent respectively; and last, by definition, comes capital quality at zero. With the embodiment rate restricted to zero under homogeneous-shay capital, capital quality is eliminated as a growth determinant.

This causal ordering applicable to the 30-year period under homogeneous shays applies in general terms to the half decades. Additionally, it often holds for the case of mean capital with the obvious exception that capital quality, which no longer is eliminated on definitional grounds, assumes the fourth spot ahead of labor quality. Still, a uniform causal ordering can be detected across capital types, across periods, and across the two nations. That is, international trade ranks first; quantities—either capital or labor—rank second; and qualities—either capital or labor—rank last. When capital quality is permitted, it finishes ahead of labor quality. The same sequence holds for labor productivity growth, which, of course, abstracts from labor quantity growth as a determinant. Foreign trade places first followed serially by capital quantity, capital quality (when posited), and labor quality. Manifestly, labor quality never gives a strong showing; its improvement through education has a consistently weak effect on growth.

The likeness of the shares for Hong Kong and Singapore is apparent in Tables 6.3 and 6.4. It can be verified statistically. For instance, the output growth shares might be interpreted as frequencies from a probability distribution, and they may be compared for Hong Kong and Singapore by a goodness-of-fit test. For the 30 years 1961–90 under homogeneous shays, the appropriate χ^2 statistic equals 2.817 against the critical value of 5.991, thereby accepting the null hypothesis that the two distributions—the share patterns—are the same. Mean capital for that period has a χ^2 of

3.654 against the critical mark of 7.815. Again, the patterns of output shares are statistically identical across the two countries. The same conclusion holds for the labor productivity shares over the 30-year history. Hong Kong and Singapore are similar in their growth shares.

They also are similar in TFP. Equation (3.31) of the model notes that TFP growth originates in qualities and trade, and equations (3.33) and (3.34) observe that the individual shares can be arranged into components for quantities and TFP. Tables 6.5 and 6.6 present those results. Three features stand out. The first pertains to the sheer size of the TFP contribution: It is enormous for either output growth or labor productivity growth, for any period, for either type of capital, and for either country. Roughly half or much more than half of growth derives from TFP. The second feature to emerge from the tables concerns the sources of TFP growth. Dividing the combined output growth share due to qualities by the output share due to TFP growth generates the share of TFP growth due to qualities. In an analogous manner dividing the output growth share from trade by the share from TFP growth yields the share of TFP growth from trade. As the tables show, trade is decisive; it never accounts for less than 75 percent of TFP growth. The third feature of Tables 6.5 and 6.6 is implicit in the first two: Hong Kong and Singapore are TFP twins. For both countries TFP growth contributes roughly the same to output growth, it contributes roughly the same to labor productivity growth, and it originates from trade in roughly the same proportion. In the Fragrant Harbour and the City of the Lion, TFP matters for growth, and trade matters for TFP.

6.4 TRADE, TURBULENCE, AND POLICY

International trade is the main cause of growth in Hong Kong and Singapore. It also is the main determinant of TFP growth and the dominant component of the residual. That finding adds support to the thought by Dornbusch (1993, p. 87) that trade may offer a satisfactory explanation for the residual, and it may transform into a flat rejection the lingering skepticism of Lovell and Tang (1997, p.

Table 6.5 Total Factor Productivity Accounting for Hong Kong

Period	Output Growth Share due to		Labor Productivity Growth Share due to		Share of TFP Growth due to	
	Quantities	TFP	Quantities	TFP	Qualities	Trade
			Homogeneous-Shay Capital, J_1			
1961-90	48.7	51.3	33.4	66.6	2.9	97.1
1961-65	55.8	44.2	39.8	60.2	-2.5	102.5
1966-70	43.8	56.2	31.4	68.6	2.1	97.9
1971-75	53.9	46.1	34.8	65.2	3.4	96.6
1976-80	57.4	42.6	38.0	62.0	7.0	93.0
1981-85	45.9	54.1	33.0	67.0	3.9	96.1
1986-90	33.5	66.5	25.0	75.0	2.8	97.2
			Mean Capital, J_m			
1961-90	44.4	55.6	27.9	72.1	18.2	81.8
1961-65	51.4	48.6	34.7	65.3	17.6	82.4
1966-70	37.4	62.6	22.9	77.1	16.4	83.6
1971-75	49.6	50.4	29.3	70.7	20.5	79.5
1976-80	53.9	46.1	34.1	65.9	24.3	75.7
1981-85	41.1	58.9	26.7	73.3	17.6	82.4
1986-90	29.1	70.9	19.7	80.3	14.1	85.9

Note. All magnitudes are percentages. Each indicates an annual average over the designated period.

22) about the claim by Krugman and associates that TFP growth is inconsequential in the East Asian context. Moreover, trade fits the facts of the Phillips curve, as the Phillips shifts illustrated in Figure 6.1 roughly correspond to jumps in the openness and export measures reported in Tables 6.1 and 6.2. Allocative efficiency from international trade counts. That notion is hardly new. What may be new is the extent to which it counts.

Of course, the importance of trade in Hong Kong and Singapore means that their growth is vulnerable to unfavorable world happenings, and the recent currency crisis that swept across Asia serves as only one, albeit a dramatic, example of such happenings. Global turbulence, then, cautions against treating the other growth determinants lightly.

As regards physical capital, acquisitions might be encouraged through tax concessions or other initiatives. State-of-the-science acquisitions would expand capital quantity, but they also would

Table 6.6 Total Factor Productivity Accounting for Singapore

Period	Output Growth Share due to		Labor Productivity Growth Share due to		Share of TFP Growth due to	
	Quantities	TFP	Quantities	TFP	Qualities	Trade
	Homogeneous-Shay Capital, J_1					
1961-90	47.1	52.9	36.3	63.7	2.3	97.7
1961-65	54.8	45.2	45.8	54.2	2.1	97.9
1966-70	55.3	44.7	48.2	51.8	4.4	95.6
1971-75	58.4	41.6	45.9	54.1	1.9	98.1
1976-80	43.3	56.7	29.5	70.5	-1.9	101.9
1981-85	39.1	60.9	27.3	72.7	4.1	95.9
1986-90	29.6	70.4	20.3	79.7	3.4	96.6
	Mean Capital, J_m					
1961-90	43.3	56.7	31.0	69.0	12.6	87.4
1961-65	51.0	49.0	40.9	59.1	15.4	84.6
1966-70	50.7	49.3	42.6	57.4	18.6	81.4
1971-75	54.5	45.5	39.9	60.1	14.2	85.8
1976-80	39.5	60.5	23.5	76.5	6.5	93.5
1981-85	35.7	64.3	22.6	77.4	12.5	87.5
1986-90	24.8	75.2	14.1	86.0	10.7	89.3

Note. See Table 6.5.

improve capital quality, thereby giving a double boost to growth. Here the two Tigers might part company as Singapore, with its history of aggressive intervention and industry targeting, may be better prepared to implement capital incentives than might Hong Kong, whose laissez faire of the old colonial days may not provide much guidance for the new special administrative region. In contrast to physical capital, human capital—that is, education—holds little promise for growth policy. It proves to be nothing more than a uniformly weak determinant of growth, and given the amount of resources that it can absorb (Barro, 1992, pp. 204–05), policy might generate a greater bang per Hong Kong or Singapore dollar by pursuing other opportunities. Evidently, the arithmetic elegance of formulations by new growth theorists such as Romer (1990, S78-S93) does not survive the test of policy relevance. In criticizing new growth, anyway, Krugman (1992) may be right.

The two Tigers have enjoyed the best of times while avoiding the worst of times as they leapfrogged along their convergence paths from the economic hinterland to the economic foreground. They have both succeeded by making astute choices within markedly different philosophies of growth management. However, their continued success at a time when the global community draws closer together, when shocks quickly spread through the network of nations, and when business grapples with the business of restructuring (Clark and Kim, 1995b, pp. 5–9) may require even more astute choices. Failure to make them might leave the Tigers leapfrogging, in the words of the original *Tale of Two Cities* by Charles Dickens, not direct to Heaven but rather direct the other way.

CHAPTER 7

HONG KONG GROWTH UNDER REVERSION

> *"We are coming now rather into the region of guess work,"* said Dr. Mortimer.
> *"Say, rather, into the region where we balance probabilities and choose the most likely. It is the scientific use of the imagination, but we have always some material basis on which to start our speculations."*
>
> Sherlock Holmes
> —A. Conan Doyle, *The Hound of the Baskervilles*

IN THE MONTHS, WEEKS, AND DAYS preceding the reversion of Hong Kong from British colonial rule to Chinese sovereignty, emotions about the event were mixed. Hope and exuberance mingled with worry and fear. Deng Xiaoping's advocacy of the principle "one country, two systems" struck a hopeful chord that Hong Kong would remain economically healthy under Beijing rule. Logic reinforced hope. China needed Hong Kong to stay healthy. The Tiger served as the entry point to China, as a magnet for business ventures from the four corners of the globe, and as a center for finance and trade. Surely China had much to lose if Hong Kong's fortunes faded. Exuberance wrapped in patriotism believed that the Motherland would stick to her end of the bargain, that property rights would be honored, and that unification would build strength. As the slogan went, "What is good for Hong Kong is good for China, and what is good for China is very good for Hong Kong."

Yet worry could be sensed in the wind. Business, already facing serious problems of restructuring, now would have to contend with a new political order that took a dim view of the personal freedoms that are basic to the enterprise system. And despite the aphorism of Deng, the memory of the Tiananmen Square Massacre in 1989 stirred a lingering fear that words written down by a totalitarian government may be nothing more than ink on paper. Deng's death only added to the chill.[1]

Then came July 1, 1997. The Prince of Wales made a solemn speech in the pouring rain, the Union Jack was struck, and the British departed, leaving the Chinese in charge. Jubilantly Victoria Harbour exploded in fireworks that celebrated a changing of the guard fit for the history books. Lan Kwai Fong partied, D'Aguilar Street pulsated, and Nathan Road sold souvenirs as dragons danced. But then the merriment subsided, and sober minds asked, What now? Would the Tiger continue its phenomenal run and keep step with the other three members of the Tiger family: Korea, Singapore, and Taiwan? Would its already miraculous pace quicken? Or would the Tiger stumble and tumble?

Conjecture was easy to find. It still is. This chapter attempts to place formal bounds on conjecture by using theory and empirical evidence to study the effects of reversion on the growth prospects for Hong Kong. It begins with a sensitivity analysis and in Section 7.1 identifies the baseline conditions; namely, the conditions that conceivably would have applied had reversion not occurred. Section 7.2 looks at the worst case and best case scenarios. Recognizing that extremes are unlikely to occur in practice, Section 7.3 studies more moderate sequences. Section 7.4 then moves away from the sensitivity analysis to present viewpoints from other research. Section 7.5 closes the discussion by underscoring the importance of separating out complicating occurrences before reaching conclusions about the effects of reversion.

7.1 THE BASELINE

Many things matter for economic growth. However, by the causal ordering established for Hong Kong in Chapter 6, the determinants are not equally important, and hence an event that affects international trade probably would be more significant than would be a similarly powered happening that influences education. Some events are sweeping in the sense that they encompass multiple determinants simultaneously; by their nature they have the potential to alter growth greatly. By its nature reversion falls into that category. Reversion may affect many factors, unfavorably or favorably, moderately or substantially. Or—perhaps—it may affect them not at all. Literally, the possible outcomes of reversion are countless. Nonetheless, some are much more likely than others, and the growth inquiry of the previous chapter can help to reduce the possibilities to manageable proportions.

Equation (6.1) of that inquiry focused on six factors: initial labor productivity y_o, civil liberty c, health care represented by the mortality rate m, labor quality growth $\hat{E}$, capital deepening $\hat{\jmath}_1$, and trade tracked by openness U. The first three elements y_o, c, and m were givens behind the intercountry growth experiences, and hence they were appropriately netted out before calculating the growth shares for Hong Kong alone. Reversion, though, may alter even the givens, bringing to five the number of factors that require attention: c, m, $\hat{E}$, $\hat{\jmath}_1$, and U. Still, five factors are hardly as formidable as "many." Initial labor productivity can be ignored because it is a bygone.

To deal with the magnitude of the reversion effects on the five determinants and thereby provide a numerical reference for the notions of moderate and substantial changes, calibrations begin with the status quo, which defines the baseline situation. Through the years Hong Kong enjoyed considerable civil liberty reflected in a c value of 2.0. A value of 1.0 corresponds to free societies such as the

United States, Japan, and Australia whereas a 7.0 represents the greatest infringement on rights. By that scale Hong Kong has been the freest of the four Tigers. Taiwan's index has been 4.9 compared to 5.0 for Korea and Singapore. As regards health care, Hong Kong historically posted a mortality rate m of 0.0185, somewhat worse than the Taiwan and Singapore records of 0.0155 and 0.0175 respectively but noticeably better than the Korea position of 0.0450. Thus baseline assignments for the growth givens are $c = 2.0$ and $m = 0.0185$.

Baseline assignments for the primary determinants $\hat{E}$, $\hat{\jmath}_1$, and U come from the 30-year period 1961–90 in Table 6.1. Specifically, baseline $\hat{E}$ equals 0.0158. That rate is the lowest among the Tigers, the highest in the family being 0.0347 for Korea. Still, it is more enthusiastic than the anemic 0.0051 evidenced by Australia. The baseline rate for the deepening of homogeneous shays $\hat{\jmath}_1$ equals 0.0540. That figure also happens to be the lowest among the Tigers, while Korea's rate of 0.1030 places near the top. Nonetheless, the Hong Kong magnitude towers over the New Zealand mark of 0.0114. Rounding out the list is openness U, whose baseline rendering is 1.8839, in the Tiger community second only to the Singapore entry of 3.0741 and well above the Korea and Taiwan figures of 0.5322 and 0.7645 respectively.

7.2 EXTREME CASES

The baseline marks serve as a center around which magnitudes representing the deterioration or improvement of conditions due to reversion can be established. Those bracketing values are chosen not from hypothetical musings but rather from actual accounts in the Asia Pacific Region. The logic behind such a strategy is that actuals found elsewhere in the area are likely to provide more realistic bounds for the new Hong Kong than would numbers created in a vacuum by some abstract criterion. Thus the worst case scenario for Hong Kong involves settings that rank among the least favorable conditions observed in the Region. That is, c assumes the 5.0 value of Korea, m takes 0.0450 also from Korea, $\hat{E}$ uses 0.0050 as a stylized version of the Australia statistic, $\hat{j}_1$ presumes 0.0115 from New Zealand, and U takes 0.7500 from Taiwan. By contrast, the best case scenario draws from the most favorable circumstances in the area. More precisely, c repeats the baseline 2.0, m becomes the Taiwan 0.0155, $\hat{E}$ adopts the Korea 0.0350, $\hat{j}_1$ assumes the Korea 0.1050, and U equals 2.500 in tempered reflection of the Singapore extreme.

Averaging in stylized fashion the worst case setting against the baseline assignments produces a more modest vision of a deteriorated economic climate. Similarly, averaging the best case against the baseline yields a more guarded sense of improvement. Variations on those four themes then depict other possible environments for the new Hong Kong. The reversion matrix in Table 7.1 presents 31 possibilities including the baseline to allow for perpetuation of the status quo.

Growth implications of the different environments are calibrated by two yardsticks, D and Q_h. Measure D is the difference in growth rates:

$$D = 100\left(\hat{y}_R - \hat{y}_B\right), \tag{7.1}$$

where $\hat{y}_R$ denotes the growth rate of labor productivity under reversion and where $\hat{y}_B$ signifies the baseline rate, which naturally presumes the absence of reversion. Both $\hat{y}_R$ and $\hat{y}_B$ derive from regression (6.1) by imposing the underlying conditions identified in the matrix. Measure Q_h is the ratio of productivity levels in the two situations h years after reversion:

$$Q_h = 100\left(y_R^h / y_B^h\right), \tag{7.2}$$

with y_R^h and y_B^h signifying respectively labor productivity levels under reversion and along baseline h years out. But because the productivities are identical at the moment of the event, it follows that smooth growth at the rates $\hat{y}_R$ and $\hat{y}_B$ leaves

$$Q_h = 100\left[\left(1 + \hat{y}_R\right) / \left(1 + \hat{y}_B\right)\right]^h. \tag{7.3}$$

Table 7.1 Reversion Matrix for Hong Kong

Row	c	100 m	100 $\hat{E}$	100 $\hat{j}_1$	100 U	D	Q at 5 years	10 years	20 years
					Baseline				
1	2.0	1.85	1.58	5.40	188.39	0	100.00	100.00	100.00
					Moderate Deterioration				
2	2.0	1.85	1.00	3.25	125.00	-2.14	90.49	81.89	67.05
3	3.5	1.85	1.00	3.25	125.00	-2.89	87.33	76.26	58.16
4	5.0	1.85	1.00	3.25	125.00	-3.64	84.25	70.99	50.39
5	2.0	3.15	1.00	3.25	125.00	-2.35	89.59	80.27	64.44
6	3.5	3.15	1.00	3.25	125.00	-3.10	86.46	74.75	55.87
7	5.0	3.15	1.00	3.25	125.00	-3.85	83.41	69.57	48.40
					Substantial Deterioration				
8	2.0	1.85	0.50	1.15	75.00	-3.94	83.05	68.97	47.57
9	3.5	1.85	0.50	1.15	75.00	-4.69	80.10	64.16	41.16
10	5.0	1.85	0.50	1.15	75.00	-5.44	77.23	59.64	35.57
11	2.0	3.15	0.50	1.15	75.00	-4.15	82.21	67.59	45.68
12	3.5	3.15	0.50	1.15	75.00	-4.90	79.28	62.86	39.51
13	5.0	3.15	0.50	1.15	75.00	-5.65	76.44	58.43	34.14
14	2.0	4.50	0.50	1.15	75.00	-4.36	81.35	66.18	43.80
15	3.5	4.50	0.50	1.15	75.00	-5.11	78.45	61.54	37.87
16	5.0	4.50	0.50	1.15	75.00	-5.86	75.63	57.19	32.71
					Moderate Improvement				
17	2.0	1.85	2.50	8.00	220.00	1.54	107.35	115.24	132.80
18	3.5	1.85	2.50	8.00	220.00	0.79	103.72	107.58	115.74
19	5.0	1.85	2.50	8.00	220.00	0.04	100.19	100.39	100.78
20	2.0	1.70	2.50	8.00	220.00	1.57	107.47	115.50	133.39
21	3.5	1.70	2.50	8.00	220.00	0.82	103.84	107.82	116.26
22	5.0	1.70	2.50	8.00	220.00	0.07	100.31	100.61	101.23
					Substantial Improvement				
23	2.0	1.85	3.50	10.50	250.00	3.02	114.82	131.84	173.81
24	3.5	1.85	3.50	10.50	250.00	2.27	110.99	123.19	151.76
25	5.0	1.85	3.50	10.50	250.00	1.52	107.27	115.06	132.39
26	2.0	1.70	3.50	10.50	250.00	3.05	114.95	132.13	174.57
27	3.5	1.70	3.50	10.50	250.00	2.30	111.11	123.46	152.43
28	5.0	1.70	3.50	10.50	250.00	1.55	107.38	115.31	132.97
29	2.0	1.55	3.50	10.50	250.00	3.07	115.07	132.42	175.34
30	3.5	1.55	3.50	10.50	250.00	2.32	111.24	123.74	153.10
31	5.0	1.55	3.50	10.50	250.00	1.57	107.50	115.57	133.57

Notes. Apart from *c*, which is an index that ranges between 1.0 and 7.0, and *D*, which expresses growth rate differences by percentage points, the variables are denominated as percentages. Descriptions such as moderate deterioration and substantial improvement refer to the extent of change in the underlying conditions and not necessarily to the size of the resulting productivity effects. Capital is homogeneous shay in character.

Worsened conditions mean a D that is negative and a Q_h that lies below 100. Improvement means the exact opposite. Of course, the status quo baseline has $D = 0$ and, for any h value, $Q_h = 100$.

The reversion matrix, although founded on homogeneous-shay capital, changes little by changing the capital type to median machines, and hence it has general applicability. Within that general framework, it shows that the worst case, Row 16, is really bad. Although the rate of productivity growth $\hat{y}_R$ remains positive, it falls 5.86 percentage points below the baseline rate. Accordingly, the productivity level drops to 75.63 percent of the baseline standard 5 years after reversion and continues declining to 57.19 percent and to 32.71 percent at the 10-year and 20-year anniversaries. Two decades after reversion, labor productivity is about a third of what it would have been had Hong Kong stayed British. By the same token, the best case, Row 29, is truly stellar. Now the growth rate exceeds baseline by 3.07 points, and at the twentieth-anniversary celebration, the productivity level is 175.34 percent of what British governance would have provided.

7.3 MODERATION

Life is neither black nor white. Economic life under reversion probably is neither as negative nor as positive as the worst and best cases imagine. Moderation in impact seems to be more likely. Some suppression of civil liberty is almost certain, but sacrifice of health care is rather remote. Consequently, a sensible estimate for c is 3.5 or 5.0; for m it is 0.0185. As regards the primary determinants, some retrenchment might be expected. The government's philosophy of positive nonintervention that helped to make the Tiger what it had become has given way to tighter controls that may be perceived to threaten property rights. Moreover, administrative efficiencies gained from decades of learning by doing have been jeopardized by arrivals who have a different attitude toward the art and science of business. In effect, the learning-by-doing process has begun anew, thereby subjecting Hong Kong to the inefficiencies inherent in any maiden voyage. In the wake of the changed sovereignty, the primary elements may suffer across the board. Labor quality growth $\hat{E}$ may fall from 0.0158 to 0.0100, capital deepening $\hat{j}_1$ may slow from 0.0540 to 0.0325, and openness U may close from 1.8839 to 1.2500. Under these circumstances, depicted by Rows 3 and 4 of Table 7.1, growth loses between 2.89 and 3.64 percentage points against the status quo. Furthermore, labor productivity in five years declines to 87.33 percent or 84.25 percent of its British norm. In 20 years it erodes to 58.16 percent or 50.39 percent of British norm. Though higher than its value at the time when Hong Kong changed hands, labor productivity amounts to roughly half of the level that would have prevailed had Britain stayed in charge.

Yet it is also credible to argue that reversion can have favorable effects on Hong Kong. Surely the Panda recognizes the economic significance of the Tiger and feels a need to nurture and promote its success. Encouraging news that China has the astuteness necessary to nurture and promote comes from its own economic indicators, which according to Y. Wu (1997, pp. 11–13) show annual growth rates for real GDP and real physical capital of 10.3 percent and 21.5 percent respectively. Indeed the indicators reported in Table 1.2 confirm the encouraging news by disclosing annual rates of output growth and labor productivity growth respectively amounting to 12.0 percent and 10.1 percent in real terms over the first half of the 1990s. Such stunning achievements cannot be lightly dismissed. In addition, by wresting control from Britain, China relegated the handover to the past and drove the hesitancy surrounding that event into the past as well. At the same time, it replaced hesitancy with a reaffirmed promise that the principle of one country, two systems would preserve the basics for enabling private enterprise to flourish well into the future. In the fresh, less uncertain climate thus created, Hong Kong may see education strengthened, investment quickened, technical progress stimulated, and trade intensified.

Other points bolster the argument for a positive outlook. For instance, the United States has a huge economic interest in Hong Kong and would not take kindly to the prospect of having that interest compromised. The Most Favored Nation status of China is only one lever of influence that America has at its disposal. But

China's management of Hong Kong should have ramifications even closer to home; that is, on the island where the Taiwan Question remains unsettled. A favorable precedent in Hong Kong might facilitate a resolution across the Taiwan Strait (Hsiung, 1998, pp. 240–42). And it must not be forgotten that economic unification between mainland China and Hong Kong had been under way for years and had reached a stage at which the lowering and raising of flags at the midnight hour may have been much more symbolic than substantive. In a sense true reversion occurred long ago, and had economic disaster been an integral part of the process, it already would have manifested itself. It did not, of course.

Optimistic thoughts such as these suggest that the primary growth determinants, if they change at all, would rise rather than fall: $\hat{E}$ from 0.0158 to 0.0250, $\hat{\jmath}_1$ from 0.0540 to 0.0800, and U from 1.8839 to 2.2200. With c taken as either 3.5 or 5.0 and with m holding at 0.0185, Rows 18 and 19 of the matrix become operative. According to Row 18 the rate of productivity growth rises by 0.79 percentage point, prompting a productivity level that runs 15.74 percent higher in 20 years. Row 19, by contrast, shows almost no increase in either the productivity rate or level. Manifestly, the setback in liberty almost completely wipes out the gains from the improved performance of the primaries.[2]

At this point it may be prudent to note that the reversion matrix implicitly supposes that the effects of reclaimed sovereignty take hold instantly and completely. Such an assumption obviously oversimplifies practice, in which delays steer events. Interviews with merchants in Hong Kong just prior to reunification suggest little noticeable change over the first few years.[3] In that case the h clock behind the Q ratio must be adjusted suitably although the general conclusions remain largely intact. Further, the matrix quantifies alternatives that have not been discussed. Those options have merit nonetheless because they help to define reasonable bounds for the consequences of reversion and because they may enable researchers to add a numerical dimension to their own interpretations of reversion. Some of those other interpretations are presented next.

7.4 INTERPRETATIONS FROM OTHER SOURCES

Ever since the inking of the Joint Declaration, and possibly even before that landmark occasion, Hong Kong experienced an appreciable decline in its manufacturing sector. Sung and Wong (1998, p. 30), for instance, indicate that manufacturing accounted for 22.4 percent of Hong Kong GDP in 1980. By 1990, however, that figure had shrunk to 16.9 percent, and in 1996 it stood at only 6.7 percent. Correspondingly, manufacturing employed 46.6 percent of the labor force in 1980 but 28.9 percent and 12.7 percent in 1990 and 1996 respectively. Yet despite its loss of manufacturing clout, the nation continued to prosper. In that regard, Hong Kong has been compared to Manhattan in New York City.[4] Such a comparison is useful for the discussion at hand because it helps to gauge the difficulty inherent in assessing reversion outcomes. Evaluating the effects on Hong Kong of reversion to China can be construed as roughly equivalent to judging the effects on Manhattan of secession from New York State. Although the directions of movement in those exercises are exactly opposite, the questions being asked are equally comprehensive. Much is involved. And since much is involved, a single perspective, even one that allows for numerous variations on the theme, may miss much. Thus it seems fitting to present other interpretations.

Looking into the next millennium, Lin and Chou (1996, pp. 2, 4–5) forecast the Hong Kong economy to grow "at much more moderate rates in the future as compared with the historical experiences." More specifically, from their 1996 vantage point, they predict real GDP to grow at 4.3 percent in 1997 and 1998 and then at about 4.0 percent through 2004. Importantly, though, the scholars do not envision a precipitous drop in growth occurring at or after reversion. Rather, the retrenchment that they project is hardly inconsistent with the growth pattern that might be anticipated in conjunction with productivity convergence. Lin and Chou prepared their numbers as input for Project LINK, a global forecasting endeavor that brings together econometric models of some 80 nations to endogenize trade flows and to quantify economic interdependencies across countries. For its part, Project LINK (1996, p. 60) agrees with Lin and Chou: It sees a gradual decline in real GDP growth for Hong Kong but no sudden break happening at or after reversion.

In analyzing the handover the OECD (1996, pp. 125–28) maintains that the short-term consequences for Hong Kong are likely to be minor inasmuch as a considerable amount of the requisite adjustments had been taking place well in advance of the formal ceremony. Actually, in 1996 the OECD forecasts real GDP growth in Hong Kong to *increase* in 1997 and again in 1998, the exact sequence being 4.5 percent for 1996, 4.7 percent for 1997, and 5.0 percent for 1998. To the OECD, Hong Kong does not miss a beat under reversion; instead, it may beat slightly faster. Concurring with that appraisal is Tang (1995, pp. 120–25), who aims research at potential GDP. Extending a study conducted by Hang Seng Bank, Tang decomposes potential GDP growth into its contributions from the labor force, factor productivity, capital stock, technical progress, and industrial restructuring. Quantifying those contributions for the reversion half decade 1996–2000 puts the average annual growth rate for potential GDP between 5.1 percent and 6.1 percent and roughly duplicates the spread between 4.7 percent and 5.7 percent applicable to the preceding half decade 1991–95.

The inquiry leading to the reversion matrix in Table 7.1 begins with an equation, expression (6.1), that for Hong Kong links labor productivity growth to its determinants and then adjusts those determinants to allow for reversion. Sung and Wong (1998, pp. 7, 18–26, 37) follow a similar approach. For them, though, the determinants of concern are Hong Kong's foreign direct investment (FDI) in mainland China, entrepôt activity, and Chinese immigration. The FDI matters for Hong Kong because it encourages domestic investment, and while FDI may prompt business to relocate plants to the mainland in pursuit of lower labor costs, it nonetheless remains a positive force behind Hong Kong growth. By contrast, entrepôt services have little bearing on growth. As for immigration from the mainland, it affects labor productivity growth negatively, although the magnitude of that impact depends upon the skill levels of the immigrants.

Against this backdrop Sung and Wong take up the reversion question. In their judgment reversion has weak influence on FDI, and its connection with entrepôt operations can be summarily dismissed. Still, it may stimulate immigration from China by virtue of a provision contained in the Basic Law. Therefore reversion, working through the three growth determinants taken together, may compromise Hong Kong growth. But Sung and Wong go on to add that reversion may have other consequences, which might bolster growth. For instance, the government of the special administrative region is more interventionist than was its British predecessor, and as a result it may lean toward a more active technology policy. Likewise, immigration from China may drift toward higher skill levels. Either of those happenings would be welcome developments. To Sung and Wong, then, reversion means pluses and minuses for Hong Kong growth.

Studies accentuating the positive include one by Ho and another by Hsiung. In the former, L.-S. Ho (1998, pp. 228–29) observes that Hong Kong experienced a loss of attractiveness to business during the middle 1990s. More precisely, it lost ground concerning entrepreneurial perceptions of features such as labor cost, infrastructure, financial facilities, availability of technical skills, government policy, and geographic location. Reversion, however, is helping to reverse the trend. Ho (1998, pp. 233–34) ends by voicing optimism: "The reversion of Hong Kong to Chinese sovereignty will benefit both Hong Kong and China economically. Hong Kong benefits because reunification with China greatly enhances Hong Kong's locational advantage." Similarly sanguine is Hsiung (1998, pp. 241–43), who notes that reversion brings together Hong Kong and mainland China to form an economic powerhouse with foreign exchange reserves totaling a colossal 220 billion U.S. dollars. In addition, the miraculous economic success of the Fragrant Harbour stems from objective factors unassailable by reversion—factors that include strategic location, extensive transportation and communication networks, solid infrastructure, strong entrepreneurship, and renowned competitiveness. Driving home the point, Hsiung (1998, p. 238) insists that "the international prominence of Hong Kong has only increased after its 1 July 1997 reversion to China."

Yet another ray of sunshine emanates from the offering by C. Wu (1997, pp. 130–32). In Wu's opinion the mainland and Hong

Kong have vested interests in preserving the status quo. Moreover, reversion "should not produce significant effects on trade. The factors that drove the economic growth of Hong Kong . . . will remain largely intact." Wu concludes by emphasizing that changed sovereignty presents the Fragrant Harbour with new opportunities to strengthen itself as a premier business center in the China area.

Disagreeing with these jubilant sentiments is Kiyoshi (1998, pp. 39–42), who feels that mainland China and Hong Kong are headed for collapse. According to that writer, China embraced the market economy in a way that permits slipshod management practices to flourish alongside bribery and corruption. Given that environment, one only can be pessimistic about economic prospects. However, much of Kiyoshi's reasoning about collapse centers on a belief that the Chinese yuan is vulnerable to devaluation, and therefore his argument relates less to reversion proper and more to the Asian currency crisis. With respect to that crisis, which the next chapter treats at length, it is possible to infer from the information provided by Kiyoshi (1998, pp. 38–39) and from the estimate of foreign exchange reserves supplied by Hsiung (1998, p. 241) that reversion may have given the Hong Kong dollar some immunity by fostering a sense that the special administrative region had ready access to mainland reserves. From that standpoint reversion might be viewed as being beneficial to Hong Kong.

7.5 REVERSION ALONE

The allusion by Kiyoshi (1998, p. 42) to the currency crisis indicates the importance of disentangling confounding influences in arriving at conclusions about reversion effects. Sung and Wong (1998, p. 23) themselves are clear on this score. Although they project that Hong Kong FDI will stagnate or decline, they attribute the setback to the currency crisis and appropriately exclude its negative implication from their assessment of reversion. In point of fact, the actual economic experience of Hong Kong necessarily reflects joint consequences from multiple causes. Financial shocks, productivity convergence, and bird flus are only some of those confounding events. Yet on the condition that complications are held in abeyance, the views from elsewhere seem to suggest that while reversion may have negative or positive effects, the magnitudes will not be dramatic. Expressed in terms of the reversion matrix in Table 7.1, those interpretations collectively suggest a reversion result somewhere between the pessimism of a Row 3 sort and the optimism of a Row 18 kind. Tellingly, that range contains the likes of Row 1, the baseline.

How the Hong Kong Tiger truly fares in the land of the China Panda is a complex matter that admits alternative outcomes. Nevertheless, in the parlance of Sherlock Holmes, the scientific use of imagination through growth theory combined with a material basis from empirical evidence lead to a balance of probabilities that narrow the outcomes to the more likely. Those prospects include potential losses and potential gains. They also include perpetuation of the status quo.

CHAPTER 8

THE ASIAN CURRENCY CRISIS

It is a formidable difficulty, and I fear that you ask too much when you expect me to solve it. The past and the present are within the field of inquiry, but what a man may do in the future is a hard question to answer.

Sherlock Holmes
—A. Conan Doyle, *The Hound of the Baskervilles*

HONG KONG REVERTED TO CHINA on July 1, 1997, amid an explosion of fireworks across Victoria Harbour. The very next day, another explosion of fireworks of a different sort occurred across the South China Sea. On that day the Thailand baht began a colossal depreciation and in the process ignited the Asian currency crisis. Soon headlines spread the news that the Asian Tiger was one sick puppy, that the Tigers were adrift, that the economic miracle was headed for the deep freeze, and that a cloud hung over Indonesia as the rupiah plunged. Jakarta burned from the torches of rioters, and Suharto, seemingly president for life, resigned. The Asian sky was falling. The only question that remained unanswered was, Where will it fall next? George Soros was to blame for the chaos, at least according to Malaysian prime minister Mahathir Mohamad, who called the American financier a moron. Responding in kind, Soros replied that Mahathir was a menace to his own country.[1] Sparks flew, fortunes faded, and personalities clashed.

Asia's currency crisis is a fascinating story. It also is a complicated one having many dimensions. The particular dimension that bears on the present volume concerns its impact on economic growth: the growth consequences. However, since joining a story somewhere other than at the beginning may be misinformative, Section 8.1 opens the discussion with a review of happenings. Section 8.2 follows with an examination of causes. Section 8.3 then turns to the growth effects. Anchoring that exposition is a crisis matrix based on equation (5.1) and patterned after the reversion matrix in Table 7.1. Because economic growth contributes to the international competitiveness of a country, consequences of the crisis for that aspect of growth are studied in Section 8.4. Prospects for future growth in the Asia Pacific Region help to occupy Section 8.5, which goes on to close the analysis with reflections on policy conduct, external heterodoxy, and opportunities for further research.[2]

8.1 HAPPENINGS

After years of maintaining a "25" peg to the U.S. dollar (USD), the Thailand baht, under pressure from intense selling by foreigners, began a ruinous free-fall and triggered the Asian currency crisis.[3] The day was Wednesday, July 2, 1997, and by the close of business the baht had lost more than 15 percent of its value. The fall continued with only brief breaks, and by the close of the year, the once-constant 25 baht stood at 46—46.0 baht per USD. The loss of value had become acute, but more bad news was yet to come. As the new year dawned, the plunge persisted, and on Monday, January 12, the baht registered 55.8, less than half its value of the previous summer. Fortunes then reversed. The baht strengthened, notwithstanding some setbacks, and on Tuesday, June 30, 1998, it stood at 42.2. Still, the 12 months had not been good to the baht. Panel A of Figure 8.1 shows just how bad they had been.[4]

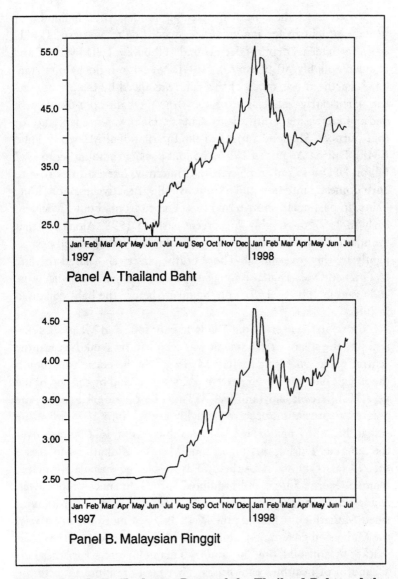

Figure 8.1 Daily Exchange Rates of the Thailand Baht and the Malaysian Ringgit Against the United States Dollar. Source: Antweiler, © 1998. Used by permission.

When the baht started its precipitous descent, Thailand was heavily in debt to foreign creditors. According to Western (1998b, p. 4), its external debt totaled around 100 billion USD by 1997 and equaled roughly 50 percent of its GDP, a large ratio by any standard. Furthermore, much of this debt was owed by the private sector, particularly financial institutions. As the baht nose-dived, debt became increasingly difficult to manage. Help was needed, and for that purpose Thailand turned to the International Monetary Fund (IMF). During August of 1997 a bailout package amounting to 17.2 billion USD was put in place. Concomitantly, interest rates rose to curb domestic inflation and to improve the attractiveness of holding bahts. In particular, short-term rates climbed from about 12 percent early in 1997 to roughly 25 percent early in 1998. Alongside that event, scores of the country's finance companies were closed permanently by the government. Those outfits effectively shared the fate of Finance One, Thailand's biggest finance company. Finance One collapsed in June of 1997 only moments before the baht collapsed in July.

Close on the heels of the Thailand baht followed Malaysia's currency as the steadfast 2.5 ringgit was set adrift by Bank Negara, the central bank, on Monday, July 14, 1997. By the end of the month the ringgit had forfeited 5 percent of its worth, and by the end of the year 35.5 percent had vanished. As Panel B of Figure 8.1 shows, the greatest depreciation occurred roughly a week into 1998 when the ringgit hit 4.657 against the USD, a value loss of 46.2 percent over the 2.5 rate. During this time Prime Minister Mahathir Mohamad offered less than calming rhetoric as he blasted speculative greed, blamed George Soros, and prompted Soros's "menace" reply. Even Madeleine Albright, the tolerant U.S. Secretary of State, admonished Mahathir for faulting the West. Perhaps more constructively, the Malaysian government announced plans to restructure the credit market by consolidating the country's many finance companies into a handful of healthier enterprises. That plan drew praise from the IMF. And despite the shock waves of both the financial and rhetorical sort that swept over Malaysia, the government kept the rise in short-term interest rates within a narrow band from about 7 percent at the start of 1997 to around 12 percent one year later.

Although the Thailand episode triggered the Asian crisis and the Malaysia incident provoked public name-calling, the Indonesia experience involved arguably the most spectacular currency decline and the most violent public reaction.

Year 1997 opened quietly enough for the rupiah as the currency held fast at a rate of about 2,400 rupiahs per USD. It continued to maintain value even when the baht teetered on July 2 and when the ringgit tottered on July 14. But on August 14, exactly one month after the Malaysia shock, Indonesia scrapped its program of a managed exchange rate, and the rupiah stumbled. In the following days it suffered a cumulative tumble but nonetheless stayed below the 4,000 threshold through November and into the first week of December. At that point, though, it took a meteoric plunge into oblivion. On Thursday, January 8, 1998, the rupiah traded against the USD at a rate of 10,676.8. Two weeks later, on Friday, January 23, the rate registered 14,555.0 as the rupiah's value fell to only 18.2 percent of its worth during the previous August: More than 80 percent of its value had disappeared. Some improvement came through April, but the forfeiture resumed in May. On Wednesday, June 17, the rate stood at 16,097.4. While the rupiah still had value, it was a shadow of its former self. Panel A of Figure 8.2 sketches the profile.

Fallout from the rupiah's implosion was extensive. In October 1997 the IMF announced a rescue package totaling 40 billion USD. Moreover, financially weak banks were closed, interest rates rose from just under 15 percent early in 1997 to 35 percent one year later, and prices rocketed. Soaring prices, in turn, helped to fuel social unrest over the government's handling of the crisis. Months of almost daily student protests led to days of riots that left 500 people dead and thousands of buildings destroyed. The people of Indonesia had turned against President Suharto. Similarly, Parliament and even his own party turned against him. With such writing clearly on the wall, Suharto on May 21, 1998, smiled, shook hands, and relinquished his office to Vice President B. J. Habibie. The falling rupiah took the long-standing president with it.

All three Southeast Asian Lions sustained sizable currency hits in 1997 and 1998. Yet the Asian sky was not falling everywhere, as the Tigers of Hong Kong, Singapore, and Taiwan demonstrated.

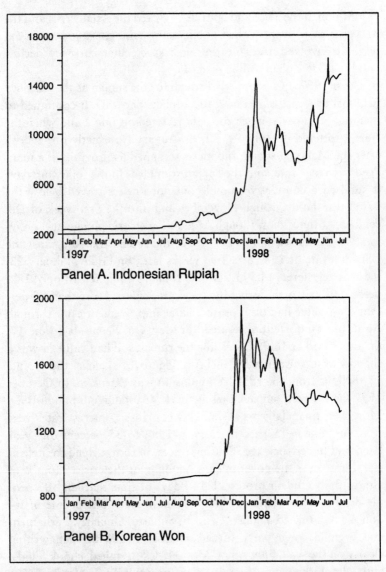

Figure 8.2 Daily Exchange Rates of the Indonesian Rupiah and the Korean Won Against the United States Dollar. Source: Antweiler, © 1998. Used by permission.

The Hong Kong dollar never veered from its 7.7 peg to the USD.[5] And while the Singapore dollar and the Taiwan dollar did depreciate, their declines were modest. Perhaps mirroring their higher states of development indicated in Tables 4.1 and 4.2, those three Tigers managed to escape the brunt of the crisis. The China Panda, too, escaped as the yuan continued to trade against the USD at about the same rate that it had ever since its devaluation in 1994. Indeed, the 8.3 yuan proved to be a fixture of 1997 and 1998.

At first blush there were sound reasons to believe that Korea would behave much like Hong Kong, Singapore, and Taiwan as the crisis unfolded. After all, it formed part of the Tiger family, its rate of productivity growth *exceeded* the rates posted by the other family members as Table 4.2 manifests, and its convergence to the United States was energetic as Figure 4.5 illustrates. Yet in the crisis situation, Korea performed more like Thailand and Indonesia than like the island trio. It behaved like a weak Lion rather than a fierce Tiger.

Shakiness already could be seen in January 1997 when Hanbo Steel, a chaebol, or business conglomerate, went bankrupt under pressure from debts amounting to six billion USD. Shortly thereafter Sammi Steel, another chaebol, failed. Nonetheless, the won, which traded against the USD at a rate of 893.7 at the beginning of April, withstood the initial shocks to the baht, ringgit, and rupiah by registering 885.7, 889.2, and 893.1 respectively on July 2, July 14, and August 14. In other words, even when the rupiah declined, the won maintained the value that it enjoyed before any currency fell. Panel B of Figure 8.2 illustrates that steadiness. But then Monday, November 17, arrived. On that day Korea abandoned the defense of its currency, and immediately the won rose past the thousand mark. On Thursday, December 11, it hit a record 1,713.1, which represented only 57.3 percent of the value seen just before Black Monday. A new record came two days before Christmas when the won roared to 1,952.7, half its former worth. On the cheerier side, 1998 began with the won improving, albeit in an unsteady fashion, and by July 2, the anniversary of the crisis, it had strengthened to 1,367.0.

As the won started to vaporize in November, Korea, whose foreign debt approximated 120 billion USD, turned to the IMF for relief. On December 3, 1997, it entered into a bailout agreement equaling 57 billion USD. That figure easily surpassed the 17.2 billion USD Thailand package and the 40 billion USD Indonesia accord. It even topped the 50 billion USD rescue effort that the IMF arranged for Mexico during 1995. In fact, the Korea bailout was a record. Punctuating developments, merchant banks folded, and Korea First Bank along with Seoul Bank, major commercial institutions, showed cracks in their cornerstones. Moreover, chaebol after chaebol ran into financial difficulty. Clark and Kim (1995a, pp. 271–72) note that chaebols often encompassed inefficient and globally uncompetitive firms thereby compromising the performance of the collective unit. The won plunge seems to have underscored that weakness.

Rounding out the won story were two other events. The first concerned Korean interest rates, which doubled by the end of 1997. The second also drew attention to year's end. It was the presidential election, which took place on December 18 and concluded with Kim Dae Joong replacing Kim Young Sam as the country's leader. Unhappy about economic conditions, the citizenry affected political change as it did in Indonesia. Again, Korea resembled a weak Lion.

The Philippine Gaur suffered through its own share of turbulence. During the first half of 1997, the peso adhered to a 26.3 rate against the USD. Then on Friday, July 11, the central bank declared that the peso would be allowed to move more widely against the USD, and more widely it did move. On Tuesday, January 6, it traded at 45.2, its poorest showing through the anniversary of the Asian turmoil. The Philippine situation prompted IMF intervention on July 14, the day of the ringgit shock, but the package of 1.1 billion USD would pale against the programs engineered for Thailand, Indonesia, and Korea. Almost as a matter of routine, interest rates rose as the peso incident evolved.

In one sense the erosion of the Philippine peso constituted the median experience of the nine currency cases. The value of a currency on January 2, 1997, may be measured in relation to the value on the date of greatest departure from the "initial" reading. By that exercise the China yuan registers 100.3 percent while the Hong Kong dollar posts 99.8 percent: Neither currency changes value against the USD apart from noise. The Taiwan dollar shows 78.8 percent as it depreciates at most to 78.8 percent of its initial level. Singapore has 78.1 percent, and the Philippines, 58.0 percent. The four worst performers are Malaysia, Thailand, Korea, and Indonesia with respective percentages of 54.2, 46.1, 43.1, and 14.7. These grave situations warranted the pictorial representations in Figures 8.1 and 8.2. The bottom three nations—Thailand, Korea, and Indonesia—appear together repeatedly in what follows.

8.2 CAUSES

Causes of the Asian currency crisis have formed an urgent subject for discussion in both the popular press and the professional literature. Scholars have responded amply, thereby generating a rather lengthy list of possibilities. Some of the possibilities possess strong intuitive appeal while others seem to be more tenuous. Nevertheless, a few taken together have something to say. And although their statement may not fit all facts in all cases, it can provide a point of focus.

The synthesis view begins by looking back at a change in world order. The thawing of the Cold War, the transition of command economies to markets, the implementation of the North American Free Trade Agreement, and other developments altered the attitudes and preferences of the West and posed a threat to Asian exports, a key driver of economic success according to the growth shares in Tables 5.2, 5.3, and 5.6. Expressed a bit differently, critical events occurring in the West and beyond started rotating the political economy of world trade against the maturing Asian nations. Clark and Kim (1995b, p. 20) are emphatic on this point:

> Whereas the growth and development of Asian NIEs (Newly Industrializing Economies) with respect to the markets of the Western economic world was guaranteed for decades by the cold war and the pivotal place of the NIEs and Japan in Asia, the collapse

of the U.S.S.R. and eastern Europe has made the Asian NIEs less significant to the West. Indeed, as the Cold War is replaced by trade wars, the Asian NIEs are peculiarly exposed to the competition for markets between the large trading blocs.

Similarly, Western (1998b, p. 9), writing about the effect of shifting alliances in connection with Thailand, remarks that

> blue collar workers in the West have often borne the brunt of a more open world economy and so more Asian exports to developed nations have aroused worker anxiety about wages and job security. Protectionist sentiment is ever present in the West.

The Centre for Economic Policy Research (CEPR) concurs with the caution about protectionism (CEPR, 1998, p. 1).

Another threat to the exports of maturing Asian nations arose much closer to home. From 1991 through 1993 China steered the yuan around a 5.5 rate against the U.S. dollar. Then in 1994 it devalued the currency to 8.6, a drop of 33.1 percent from the 1993 level. That move, which took place in conjunction with economic reform that unified the Panda's dual-track exchange rate system, followed the inking of a sizable negative trade balance in 1993 and turned the balance from red to black. Along the same line, Japan, under pressure from its own sluggish economic condition, let the yen depreciate from 84.4 per USD in the second quarter of 1995 to 121.2 in the first quarter of 1997, a value loss of 30.3 percent. Both exchange rate maneuvers weakened the export position of the maturing nations. In the case of Thailand, for example, Western (1998b, p. 5) observes that the yuan action hurt because Thailand and China compete in labor-intensive products whereas the yen gambit hurt because Thailand and Japan compete in items at the higher end of the product ladder. Presumably the same situation applied to other members of the Asian community.

According to CEPR (1998, p. 2) export retrenchment is a critical factor behind a currency crisis. In its judgment another major element provoking a crisis is overvaluation of the real exchange rate.

The real exchange rate x_r can be expressed in standard fashion as

$$x_r = x_n\left(p_d / p_f\right). \tag{8.1}$$

Symbol x_n denotes the nominal exchange rate, which gives the foreign currency price of a unit of domestic currency. In the case of Thailand, for example, x_n refers to the number of U.S. dollars needed to buy one baht. The p_d signifies domestic price—to continue the example—in bahts per unit of product, and p_f designates foreign price in dollars per unit. From expression (8.1) the percent change in the real exchange rate can be written as

$$100\hat{x}_r = 100\hat{x}_n + 100\hat{p}_d - 100\hat{p}_f, \tag{8.2}$$

with circumflexes continuing to identify decimal rates of change. Work by Yoshimine (1998) suggests that equation (8.2) can be used to measure the extent of cumulative overvaluation by calculating percentages relative to a fixed moment in time. Table 8.1 takes that base to be 1985, the same year that functions as base for the PWT Mark 5.5.

Because the experiences of Thailand, Indonesia, and Korea have been particularly chaotic, attention naturally swirls around them. As regards overvaluation all three countries exhibited an increasing tendency on balance. Line 2 of Table 8.1 reveals that Korea's won was overvalued by 32.3 percent in 1992 and by 47.0 percent in 1996, the year immediately preceding the crisis. Indonesia's rupiah actually began the decade being undervalued but became slightly overvalued by 3.6 percent in 1993 before reaching 38.2 percent in 1996. Thailand's baht too became progressively overvalued from 7.8 percent in 1991 to 23.4 percent in 1996.

Moreover, all three countries witnessed reductions in export growth in 1996. Korea, for instance, saw its export growth rate plunge from 30.3 percent in 1995 to only 3.7 percent in 1996. Indonesia's rate dropped more modestly from 13.4 percent to 9.7 percent as it was protected by a 12.3 percent boost in the petroleum component of its export package. Evidently, petroleum is a great export anchor in Asia. Thailand, by contrast, saw export growth reverse direction from a decade high of 25.1 percent in 1995 to –1.3

Table 8.1 Economic Statistics on Causes of the Asian Currency Crisis

Country	1991	1992	1993	1994	1995	1996	1997
				Overvaluation			
Hong Kong	30.9	42.2	53.0	64.9	78.5	87.5	97.4
Korea	34.4	32.3	32.5	39.0	47.2	47.0	35.0
Singapore	11.0	17.4	17.0	25.2	34.5	32.8	24.0
Taiwan	37.5	48.6	40.7	42.1	42.9	37.4	28.1
Indonesia	-12.9	-7.2	3.6	14.2	23.1	38.2	41.0
Malaysia	-21.3	-12.5	-13.2	-13.7	-8.7	-8.7	-18.8
Thailand	7.8	9.7	10.5	15.0	20.4	23.4	8.5
Philippines	10.9	27.6	33.3	49.8	65.4	79.6	81.3
China	-0.6	4.6	25.0	55.0	96.4	117.4	123.3
				Export Growth			
Hong Kong	20.0	21.2	13.2	11.9	14.8	4.0	4.0
Korea	10.5	6.6	7.3	16.8	30.3	3.7	5.3
Singapore	3.5	-0.8	13.1	19.6	11.8	3.7	3.3
Taiwan	9.2	-4.0	6.3	5.4	15.8	4.5	na
Indonesia	13.5	16.6	8.4	8.8	13.4	9.7	7.3
Malaysia	13.7	4.7	13.0	22.4	16.2	2.9	9.4
Thailand	23.2	14.2	13.3	22.7	25.1	-1.3	3.2
Philippines	-3.5	-5.6	13.4	6.0	19.1	9.3	32.6
China	15.8	18.1	7.1	33.1	22.9	1.6	21.0
				Trade Balance			
Hong Kong	-1.7	-3.3	-2.5	-6.9	-10.9	-9.8	-10.9
Korea	-13.4	-6.7	-1.9	-6.6	-8.0	-15.9	-5.9
Singapore	-12.1	-13.7	-15.2	-6.2	-5.3	-5.1	-5.9
Taiwan	17.2	11.3	9.1	7.9	7.0	11.4	na
Indonesia	11.2	19.7	23.1	20.2	10.5	13.8	22.0
Malaysia	-6.7	2.1	3.2	-1.3	-5.1	-0.1	0.2
Thailand	-32.2	-25.3	-24.9	-20.7	-25.4	-29.8	-9.2
Philippines	-46.2	-58.5	-68.8	-70.4	-62.0	-67.5	-53.1
China	11.3	5.1	-13.3	4.4	13.2	8.1	22.2

Notes. All entries are percentages. Those for overvaluation reflect inflation rates measured by the consumer price index (CPI), those for export growth refer to real exports, and those for the trade balance use the level of exports as base. *na* means not available.

Sources. Data for overvaluation originate mainly from *Key Indicators of Developing Asian and Pacific Countries* by the Asian Development Bank. Additional information on the nominal exchange rate stems from *International Financial Statistics (IFS)* of the IMF and from the PACIFIC Exchange Rate Service (1998). Additional information on CPI inflation derives from *IFS*, the *International Financial Statistics Yearbook* of the IMF, and OECD (1998). The U.S. CPI obtains principally from United States President (1998). Sources for export growth and the trade balance are again *IFS* and *Key Indicators*. Requisite deflation involves the CPI from the aforementioned authorities.

percent in 1996. For Thailand, exports actually fell. As an obvious corollary, its trade balance in 1996 sank deeper into the red, registering –29.8 percent of the export level. Korea likewise had its trade balance worsen to –15.9 percent in 1996 from –8.0 percent the year before. Nonetheless, oil-endowed Indonesia, where petroleum accounted for about half of total exports, never faced a trade deficit in the decade.

From these statistics it is apparent that Thailand and Korea fit the pattern of crisis determinants: They had overvalued currencies, they suffered export retrenchment, and consonantly their trade balance turned even more unfavorable. But Indonesia, whose currency collapse was the most violent, did not fit the scheme as well. Its export retrenchment was rather tempered, and its trade balance remained consistently healthy.

The experience of Indonesia breaks step with Thailand and Korea and in the process reinforces the disconcerting claim by Chang and Velasco (1998b, p. 2) that "there is no unique pattern of behavior for basic macroeconomic variables in the buildup to a crisis. Sometimes the current account is in deficit, but not always." Equally disconcerting is the observation from Table 8.1 that Hong Kong and Singapore experienced currency overvaluation, export setbacks, and trade deficits, but they still managed to keep their currencies largely immune to the Asian contagion or, in the word of Krugman (1998a, p. 1), bahtulism. Thus, while export softening, trade deficits, and overvaluation may be causes of a currency crisis, they may not be the only causes. Something else might be involved. That something might be financial fragility.

The headline on the business pages said "Southeast Asian Banks Contribute to a Bust in the Economic Boom" and "Financial-Sector Weaknesses Are Roiling Currencies; Regulation Has Been Lax." The accompanying story by McDermott and Wessel (1997) went on to observe that anxiety in financial markets across Southeast Asia hinged not on trade deficits or political rhetoric but rather on weaknesses of the banking systems. High economic growth and perceptions of high rates of return attracted massive amounts of funds from the West. Zealous local financial institutions channeled the funds in many directions including real estate and stock markets. Risky ventures were pursued on a routine basis as a natural outcome of lax government supervision combined with a perceived assurance of government protection. As Western (1998b, p. 3) asserts for Thailand, "With the appearance that banks were government

backed or had strong links with the political leadership there was a
moral hazard problem whereby bank loan officers were encouraged
to take enormous lending [and] investment risks . . . a 'heads I win,
tails the taxpayer loses' mentality prevailed."[6] Debts to the West
loomed large, and loans stood a good chance of failing. Com-
pounding the situation, as Corsetti et al. (1998a, p. 9) affirm, was
the inclination for liabilities to have short-term maturity and to be
denominated in hard Western currency. All things considered, then,
banking sectors in Thailand and elsewhere in the maturing Asian
community balanced on a Harrodian knife edge of a different sort
(Solow, 1956, p. 65). Just how precarious was the balance and just
how fragile were the financial systems became evident by the degree
of liquidations alluded to in the previous section.

Fragility held the key to the Asian crisis according to Chang and
Velasco (1998a, pp. 1–2, 17–18). To them fragility means international illiquidity, a circumstance in which a financial system has potential short-term obligations in foreign currency exceeding the
amount of foreign currency that can be gathered on short notice.
Actually, by their assessment international illiquidity is a necessary
and sufficient condition for a financial crisis.[7]

Compelling evidence by Chang and Velasco (1998a, p. 57) on
the debt-reserves ratio, which divides the volume of short-term international loans by the volume of international reserves, shows that
the financial systems of several maturing Asian nations did become
progressively more illiquid as the summer of 1997 approached.
Thailand, for instance, watched its ratio more than double from
0.59 in June 1990 to 1.45 in June 1997. Similarly, Korea observed
its ratio almost double from 1.06 to 2.06 over those months. Indonesia, though, cut the ratio from 2.21 to 1.70. Still, as of June
1997 all three countries posted figures above unity, indicating to
Chang and Velasco (1998a, p. 25) financial fragility "in the sense
that international reserves would not have been sufficient to repay
the short-term debt had foreign banks decided not to roll it over."

Equally compelling evidence on fragility can be deduced from
data reported by Corsetti et al. (1998a, Table 31). Their information
pertains to foreign liabilities and foreign assets. In regard to Thailand the implied ratio of liabilities to assets registered 10.75 in 1996

and respectively 9.62 and 11.13 in the first two quarters of 1997: Just before the collapse Thailand's foreign liabilities were roughly ten times larger than its foreign assets. Korea recorded corresponding ratios of 3.63, 3.36, and 3.19 as Indonesia tallied 4.19, 4.70, and 5.53. Thus, Korea and Indonesia had foreign liabilities outweigh foreign assets by factors of about three and five respectively. That these magnitudes were huge can be inferred from the situations in Hong Kong, Singapore, and Taiwan, where the numbers averaged 1.64, 1.55, and even 0.66 sequentially. In like manner China averaged 1.26.

Taking logic a step further, Chang and Velasco (1998a, pp. 36–37) argue that the internationally illiquid financial systems were vulnerable to exogenous economic shocks. They also were vulnerable to a loss of confidence among international creditors. In other words, they were subject to panics.

Expressed in condensed form, then, the synthesis view, which should be understood as only one of many possible interpretations of causes, initially looks at the declines in export growth and the attendant worsening of the trade balances.[8] Those events put strain on currencies and raised the likelihood of depreciation. Rampant overvaluation added to the sense of urgency. Confidence in currencies eroded, and the erosion was intensified, or perhaps even sparked, by fragility of the financial systems. Foreign speculators, led by reason or driven by panic, headed for the exits to unload currencies, thereby sealing those currencies' fates: values plunged. Thailand was the first to fall. However, once it succumbed, other nations in like circumstances were almost certain to fall as well because the evaporating baht placed still more stress on *their* already beleaguered exports and trade balances. Maintaining competitive trade positions while the baht imploded became yet another point of pressure on their own currencies. In due course the rupiah dove, the won swooned, and other moneys roiled. Declining currencies, in turn, magnified the burden of the foreign-denominated debt within the financial sectors. Unable to handle the now-onerous liabilities, imperiled nations sought out the IMF, which responded with rescue packages tied to austerity measures. Concomitantly, interest rates rose to curb domestic inflation and to shore up local currency.

The higher rates of interest associated with the crisis bear on capital goods acquisitions and, by equation (5.1), affect labor productivity growth. The reaction of exports—and imports—to the changed conditions affect productivity growth as well. To those growth consequences the discussion now turns.

8.3 CONSEQUENCES FOR ECONOMIC GROWTH

Responding to the self-posed question of what is going to happen to Asia in the wake of the crisis, Krugman (1998b, p. 1) first confesses "I don't really know" but then hastens to emphasize that "*nobody* really knows." Such a response, intended for a business gathering at the Fragrant Harbour, echoes the sentiment expressed by Sherlock Holmes for a small gathering at Baker Street and underscores the difficulty of making predictions amidst calamity. Nevertheless, Krugman (1998b, pp. 5–6) ventures to suggest three possible scenarios including one that, facetiously, foresees the fall of civilization and the transformation of businessmen into boat people. Backing away from that disaster scenario, Krugman opts for a sequence that envisions two or three years of lost economic growth.

In its own vision of Asia, OECD (1998, pp. 106, 144) is more specific. To illustrate, for 1998 it has output undergoing negative growth in Korea, Indonesia, and Thailand at the respective percentage rates of –0.2, –8.5, and –1.5. At the same time, inflation intensifies, making those nations the victims of stagflation. The situation improves somewhat for 1999 as the rate of output growth turns positive for all three economies, and together with that improvement the three inflation rates moderate as well. Project LINK (1998, pp. 59–69) is more grim in its output assessment; yet it too senses improvement for 1999. Apparently, the accounts claiming the fall of civilization have been greatly exaggerated.

Another look at the growth consequences of the Asian currency crisis can be gleaned from equation (5.1), which expresses $\hat{y}$, the rate of labor productivity growth, as a general linear function of its determinants. By way of review, those determinants consist of y_o, the initial level of labor productivity; m, the mortality rate; c, the degree of civil liberty; $\hat{E}$, the growth rate of labor quality as reflected by education; $\hat{\jmath}$, the rate of capital deepening; and U, openness. Dummy variables D_2 and D_3 allow for stage of development. However, according to Table 4.1, the maturing nations of the Asia Pacific Region fit either development Stage 1—that is, Partition 1—or Stage 3, and therefore dummy D_2 becomes inoperative. Consonant with the exposition in Section 5.1, the coefficient values come from Experiment 4 in Table 5.1, and consonant with the exposition of the Hong Kong reversion matrix in Table 7.1, physical capital assumes the form of homogeneous shays although the choice of capital model involves no loss of generality. Such considerations give equation (5.1) the specific form

$$
\begin{aligned}
\hat{y} = {} & 0.0447 - 3.2 \times 10^{-6} y_0 - 0.1619m - 0.0050c + 0.0835\hat{E} + \\
& \left(0.2777 - 0.1604D_3\right)\hat{\jmath}_1 + 0.0235U.
\end{aligned}
\tag{8.3}
$$

From the happenings referred to earlier in this chapter, Hong Kong, Singapore, Taiwan, and China managed to withstand "bahtulism" reasonably well. By contrast, Korea, Indonesia, Malaysia, Thailand, and the Philippines became more seriously infected, and hence to those five nations equation (8.3) is applied.

The currency crisis can be understood to shock a country away from its baseline path, and on that interpretation the growth consequences can be quantified by comparing against the baseline the path traversed under the crisis. Baseline values for the explanatory variables come from the vital statistics in Table 1.1, from the economic statistics in Table 4.2, and from the mortality information provided by Barro and Wolf (1989). In essence, they refer to the solid growth experience enjoyed over the miraculous years from 1961 to 1990 and thus duplicate in character the baseline that focused the discussion of reversion in Chapter 7. The crisis path departs from the baseline as the growth determinants depart from the magnitudes posted during the miracle decades.

Domestic austerity introduced by directions from the IMF or by the decisions of local officials likely means a cutback of social services including health care and education. For the rates associated with m and $\hat{E}$, that cutback translates into a respective 10 percent rise and 10 percent fall from the baseline marks during 1998 and converts into 5 percent deviations from base during 1999. The subsequent return to norm follows one of three routes. Path 2000 supposes rapid bounce back wherein the determinants m and $\hat{E}$ resume their baseline values in Year 2000. Path 2002 covers a five-year horizon with the resumption of baseline settings coming in 2002. Path 2007 involves protracted adjustment that spans ten years, restoration of baseline values taking place in 2007. As regards civil liberty $c,$ efforts to curb financial excesses, to tighten economic discipline, and to bolster public confidence in the sitting government can be imagined to infringe on liberty. The sacking and later jailing of Anwar Ibrahim, Malaysia's dissident deputy prime minister, in September of 1998 (Mydans, 1998b) lends substance to the reasoning, which suggests raising c relative to base by 20 percent for 1998, by 10 percent for 1999, and by 5 percent for 2000, 2002, or 2007 depending upon the crisis path being traversed. For the years between 1999 and the terminus, c takes values by linear interpolation. At bottom, the crisis is postulated to involve a long-term reduction in liberty albeit of a small proportion.

The increased rates of interest and the overall loss of confidence surrounding the crisis take their toll on capital goods acquisitions. Investment weakens, pulling down $\hat{\jmath}_1$. How sharply $\hat{\jmath}_1$ recoils depends upon country-specific circumstances, and clues to that effect derive from OECD (1998, pp. 106, 144), Project LINK (1998, pp. 59–69), and elsewhere. Consistently, though, the heaviest blow occurs in 1998. Within that year the greatest $\hat{\jmath}_1$ setback happens for Indonesia. Fairly close behind Indonesia are Thailand and Korea sequentially. Philippines and Malaysia follow next in line but at some distance: Compared to the capital reductions for Indonesia, Thailand, and Korea, those for the Philippines and Malaysia are modest indeed. Year 1999 represents a much healthier time for capital across all five countries, and the terminal year—2000, 2002, or 2007—proves to be even healthier. Still, $\hat{\jmath}_1$ never regains its baseline vigor. For Indonesia $\hat{\jmath}_1$ recovers to a rate that is the equivalent of three percentage points below baseline. Korea restores $\hat{\jmath}_1$ to a mark two points below base, whereas Malaysia and Thailand fall one point short. The Philippines narrowly misses; it undershoots by a half point. As in the case of civil liberty, the crisis has a lasting effect on capital growth.

Rounding out the determinants of labor productivity growth is openness U. At first blush, currency devaluations of Asian dimension might be presumed to produce an export boom that bolsters openness. But while agreeing with this general proposition, McDermott and Wessell (1997) caution that "in Southeast Asia, the potential export gains are, for now, overwhelmed by the devastating effects of devaluation on fragile banks that relied heavily on overseas money." International upheaval, then, might be interpreted as reducing openness by 15 percent from baseline in 1998 and 7.5 percent in 1999. Afterward openness returns to its base value at the terminus. That sequence applies to all five maturing countries.

Creating a crisis path is one thing. Quantifying the implied growth consequences is another thing, and to that end the yardsticks used in connection with Hong Kong reversion in Chapter 7 are returned to service. D indicates the percentage-point difference between the labor productivity growth rates along the crisis path and the baseline:

$$D = 100(\hat{y}_C - \hat{y}_B), \tag{8.4}$$

with $\hat{y}_C$ and $\hat{y}_B$ denoting respectively the rates under crisis and at baseline. Similarly, Q gauges in percent the level of labor productivity under crisis relative to baseline; namely,

$$Q = 100(y_C / y_B), \tag{8.5}$$

y_C and y_B signifying the corresponding productivity levels. D and Q are computed for each year along each crisis path of each country. Table 8.2 presents the results for the middle scenario, Path 2002. The other two runs generate alternatively more favorable and less favorable conditions for the years 2000 and beyond.

Three features of Table 8.2 stand out. First, the greatest consequence for economic growth occurs in the year immediately following

Table 8.2 Crisis Matrix for Selected Maturing Countries in the Asia Pacific Region

Country	1998	1999	2000	2001	2002	2007
	Growth Rate Differences for Labor Productivity: D					
Korea	-9.9	-4.3	-3.1	-1.9	-0.7	-0.7
Indonesia	-7.4	-1.9	-1.5	-1.0	-0.5	-0.5
Malaysia	-4.4	-3.0	-2.1	-1.3	-0.4	-0.4
Thailand	-5.0	-1.7	-1.2	-0.7	-0.2	-0.2
Philippines	-2.2	-0.8	-0.6	-0.4	-0.2	-0.2
	Relative Levels for Labor Productivity: Q					
Korea	90.5	86.8	84.3	82.8	82.2	79.6
Indonesia	92.8	91.0	89.7	88.8	88.4	86.3
Malaysia	95.8	93.0	91.1	90.0	89.7	88.1
Thailand	95.1	93.6	92.5	91.9	91.7	90.7
Philippines	97.9	97.1	96.5	96.1	95.9	95.1

Notes. Entries for D are expressed as percentage points whereas those for Q are written as percentages. Both measures compare Path 2002 magnitudes against the corresponding baseline values.

the currency collapses. There—in 1998—the downward departure of the labor productivity growth rate from its baseline is largest. In the ensuing years the departure becomes progressively smaller until it stabilizes, and from that point forward, economic growth continues at a rate that lies below the reference mark by a constant amount. Pictorially, the currency crisis can be viewed as pivoting the long-run growth trajectory clockwise. This motion has implications for productivity levels, which, by the Q index in Table 8.2, continually fall away from the baseline targets.

Second, the growth consequences of the currency crisis differ substantially across countries. For 1998, Korea finds that its growth rate drops 9.9 percentage points below baseline whereas the Philippines has it fall only 2.2 points.[9] A noteworthy reason for that discrepant reaction rests with capital: Korea experiences a much larger capital shock than does the Philippines, and the $\hat{j}_1$ coefficient in equation (8.3) indicates that its productivity growth is more sensitive than the Philippines' to any given capital perturbation. Correspondingly, Korea's productivity level drops much further below the reference point than does the Philippines'. For 1998 the Korean level registers 90.5 percent of base while the Philippine level equals 97.9 percent. For 2007 the respective percentages become 79.6 and 95.1. Plainly, the rotation of growth path is far more pronounced in the case of Korea.

Feature 3 of Table 8.2 strikes a happy note: With respect to economic growth, the lasting harm of the currency crisis tends to be slight. Despite the massive depreciations of currencies, despite the colossal failures of financial institutions, despite the major losses of confidence, and despite other calamities, the maturing economies in the Asia Pacific Region tend to recover rather well. A half decade after the fact—that is, in 2002—four of the five principles have their productivity levels around or above 90 percent of baseline, and if the reversion matrix in Table 7.1 provides any guide, those results signal moderate deterioration at worst. Korea, which posts 82.2 percent in 2002, is more severely affected, of course. Nonetheless, the lesson of Feature 3 goes the other way. Rather than projecting that most maturing countries will have their economic growth seriously impaired by the crisis, it says that most will experience only slight forfeitures. That lesson reiterates the position taken by Radelet and Sachs (1997, p. 46), who maintain that "the currency upheavals probably reflect short-run financial considerations rather than a long-term crisis of regional growth." The fall of civilization is not imminent, and the Asian sky is not falling everywhere—at least not always.

8.4 CONSEQUENCES FOR INTERNATIONAL COMPETITIVENESS

Since the Asian currency crisis affects output growth and labor productivity growth, it necessarily affects international competitiveness. At one level international competitiveness is a vague idea that means different things to different people. At another level, however, it is a fairly specific construct that has intuitive appeal. Certainly, anyone acquainted with the principles of economics has a feel for the notion of competitiveness, and it may not take much to extend that notion into the international context.

In the global setting, countries may be viewed as having different degrees of competitiveness: Some may enjoy high levels of success while others may post dismal records. It therefore follows that nations might be ranked by an Index of International COMpetitiveness, nicknamed ICOM. Concentrating on the Asia Pacific Region, ICOM begins with a definition of concept. It specifies series to make the definition quantifiable and gathers data on those series. It then combines the numbers under various weight structures.

International competitiveness can be defined in numerous ways, as the contributions by Hopkins and Cabalu (1993, pp. 10–12, 27) and Manzur (1996, p. 1) illustrate. Such definitions have merit because they bring precision to the concept. For present purposes international competitiveness is defined as *the ability to provide internationally a quality product promptly at a reasonable price.* According to this proposition the concept has five dimensions: ability to provide, international scope, quality product, promptness, and reasonable price.

From the very outset ICOM was envisioned to be highly manageable, and therefore it was designed to encompass a small number of series whose data would be readily available from standard sources. On those criteria 11 series make their way into the index. *Ability to provide* is represented by (1) the rate of growth of real GDP expressed in percent. Plainly, a greater rate of production implies a greater ability to supply goods and services internationally. Also included is (2) the unemployment rate in percent, to reflect slackness in the labor market. A higher unemployment rate means that more output can be forthcoming without heating up unit cost and price. *International scope* is captured by (3) openness, calculated as exports and imports taken in combination as a percent, rather than fraction, of GDP. Greater openness signifies greater involvement in foreign trade. The other international series is (4) exchange rate volatility, defined as the ratio of the current exchange rate relative to the exchange rate in the reference year, 1989. Exchange rate volatility is bad for trade because of the uncertainty and turmoil that it causes.

Quality of product is gauged by three series. One is (5) gross fixed capital formation as a percent of GDP, the thought being that smart (new) capital creates smart (quality) products. Next comes (6) public expenditure on education as a percent of GDP: Quality labor implies quality output. Ostensibly (7) patents, taken as the number per million of population, reflect new and better products. *Promptness* strives to capture the speed with which orders are filled. To that end (8) electricity production in thousand kilowatt hours per person comes into play in the belief that electricity generation serves to indicate the speed of communication. In addition, (9) change in stocks as a percent of GDP reflects the prevalence of stocks on hand to fill orders. *Reasonable price* is manifested by (10) the CPI inflation rate as a percent and by (11) the growth rate of labor productivity in percent. Productivity growth, of course, bears on price through the standard markup rule.[10]

This ICOM list of 11 series has much in common with the catalog of international competitiveness measures developed by Bloch and Kenyon (1998). Their Measures 1 and 2 revolve around labor productivity and their later remarks stress labor productivity growth, which constitutes Series 11 of ICOM. Measure 5 of Bloch and Kenyon is the real exchange rate, and Series 4 and 10 of ICOM obviously relate to it. Moreover, their Measures 8 and 9 speak about research and development activity, an endeavor closely aligned with patents, Series 7 of ICOM. Thus, even though the reasoning of Bloch and Kenyon on the one hand and the musings behind ICOM on the other start at different points, they tend to come together, and it seems safe to say that, in a sense, ICOM puts into practice the ideas offered by Bloch and Kenyon. In the same way it seems safe to say that ICOM puts into practice ideas advanced earlier by Hopkins and Cabalu (1993, pp. 27–29).

Data sources for the ICOM 11 include "The International Economic Data Bank" from Australian National University, *International Financial Statistics* by the IMF, and *Key Indicators* by the Asian Development Bank. They also include *Main Economic Indicators* by the OECD, the Penn World Table Mark 5.5 by Summers and Heston (1993), and the *Statistical Yearbook* by the United Nations Educational, Scientific and Cultural Organization. These sources provide information on years 1975, 1985, and 1995—midpoints of the respective decades. Years 1998 and 1999 are also considered, using forecast information from OECD (1998). As already noted, that material gives forecasts for real GDP growth and the inflation rate inter alia. From those anchors predictions can be made for labor productivity growth and the unemployment rate, the latter following rough forms of either Okun's Law or the Phillips curve. Other series are presumed to move similarly or to exhibit more secular patterns.

Bringing together the data and the series to quantify ICOM consonant with the definition of international competitiveness are the weights ω_i, the i identifying the series number. In keeping with the mission of ICOM to have an international flavor, the two external variables, Series 3 and 4, receive double weight. Moreover, reflecting the consistently weak contribution that labor quality makes to economic growth, a weakness demonstrated in growth share Tables 5.2 through 5.5, the education component, Series 6, carries half weight. Each of the other eight elements takes single weight. Thus $\omega_3 = \omega_4 = 2/12.5$, $\omega_6 = 0.5/12.5$, and $\omega_i = 1/12.5$ for each remaining i.

Expressed mathematically, the Index of International Competitiveness becomes

$$ICOM_j^z = \Sigma_{i=1}^{i=11} \omega_i z_{ij}, \tag{8.6}$$

where, for some time t such as the year 1995, Z_{ij} denotes the normalized value of Series i for Country j. Being denominated in different units, the various series are first normalized to put them on equal footing. Normalization observes the usual rule: Subtract the mean and divide by the standard deviation. More precisely, $z_{ij} = (s_{ij} - \mu_i)/\sigma_i$, where s_{ij} represents the original, data-based series and where μ_i and σ_i indicate respectively the mean and standard deviation calculated over all countries. Plainly, $ICOM_j^z$ is a convex combination of its z factors, and consequently for any nation it must lie between the highest and lowest z values applicable to that nation. By implication, $ICOM_j^z$ may be negative. Hence for purposes of presentation, $ICOM_j^z$ is scaled to give the top-ranked country a score of 100 and the bottom-placed economy a score of zero. That transformation is

$$ICOM_j = \frac{100 \left[ICOM_j^z - min\left(ICOM_j^z\right)\right]}{\left[max\left(ICOM_j^z\right) - min\left(ICOM_j^z\right)\right]},$$

(8.7)

symbols *min* and *max* designating sequentially the minimum and maximum operators.[11]

ICOM results appear in Table 8.3. There Singapore is the uniform winner. It takes top honors in each of the years 1975, 1985, and 1995, and it likewise commands the top spot in the years 1998 and 1999. Hong Kong does well too as it tends to move up in competitiveness rank and score through time. Going the other way temporally is Indonesia. It begins in third place during 1975 but slips in 1985. It slips again in 1995 and then plummets to the bottom of the scale in 1998 and 1999. The turbulence surrounding Indonesia during the Asian currency crisis costs it dearly in terms of international competitiveness. Much the same can be said for Korea and Thailand, which join Indonesia at the back of the pack for 1998 and 1999. The crisis badly hurts two Lions and a Tiger.[12]

By contrast, the China Panda improves its international competitiveness after 1995 and remains tenacious during the chaos. Similarly, the Elephants of Australia, New Zealand, and the United States gain strength after 1995 despite circumstances. Nevertheless, Japan loses ground from its 1995 peak as recession woes undermine its standing.

8.5 CLOSING THOUGHTS

The currency crisis has important implications that concern international competitiveness and economic growth. For some maturing countries in the Asia Pacific Region, competitiveness suffers greatly. Similarly, growth suffers. Yet Feature 3 of Table 8.2 suggests that grave setbacks to growth need not be lasting and that nations can shed most of the ill effects as the new millennium dawns. Undoubtedly, the Tigers, the Lions, a Gaur, and the Panda have learned from

Table 8.3 International Competitiveness Rankings and Scores by ICOM for Various Years

Rank	1975	1985	1995	1998	1999
1	Singapore (100.0)	Singapore (100.0)	Singapore (100.0)	Singapore (100.0)	Singapore (100.0)
2	China (58.2)	USA (91.5)	Malaysia (93.7)	Hong Kong (99.0)	Hong Kong (91.7)
3	Indonesia (56.0)	China (91.3)	Hong Kong (86.1)	Malaysia (88.9)	Malaysia (75.4)
4	Philippines (55.5)	Indonesia (87.9)	Thailand (55.1)	China (76.5)	China (69.4)
5	Hong Kong (45.0)	Hong Kong (79.2)	Indonesia (42.4)	USA (75.4)	Taiwan (60.3)
6	Australia (34.4)	Australia (66.7)	Japan (41.0)	Taiwan (74.3)	USA (45.2)
7	Korea (33.5)	Japan (53.3)	Korea (38.6)	Australia (73.6)	Australia (44.9)
8	USA (29.9)	Korea (46.1)	Taiwan (34.5)	New Zealand (72.8)	Philippines (43.7)
9	Malaysia (14.1)	Malaysia (45.2)	Philippines (24.7)	Philippines (66.4)	New Zealand (42.7)
10	Thailand (10.1)	New Zealand (38.1)	USA (22.6)	Japan (65.6)	Japan (39.1)
11	New Zealand (9.7)	Thailand (21.1)	New Zealand	Korea (37.1)	Thailand (22.4)
12	Japan (4.4)	Taiwan (7.9)	Australia (19.9)	Thailand (29.7)	Korea (17.0)
13	Taiwan (0.0)	Philippines (0.0)	China (0.0)	Indonesia (0.0)	Indonesia (0.0)

Notes. ICOM uses double weights for the trade variables and half weight for the education measure. Parentheses indicate competitiveness score.

the episode, and they are likely to use the lessons to strengthen themselves. Asia's future is bright, maintain Radelet and Sachs (1997), and Western (1998a) sees it in much the same light. Indeed, the future may be bright. However, optimism prudently stops short of saying that the maturing metaphorical creatures will return to the heady growth days of the decades before 1990. Through the years they have been accumulating physical capital, they have been watching their marginal products of capital change, and they have been moving along their convergence paths. Naturally, then, their growth would be inclined to ease in the future. This circumstance was discussed at length in Chapter 4. It is underscored by Radelet and Sachs (1997, pp. 49–52), who offer projections of future growth reductions across the Region due to capital deepening and to demographic changes. Compared against the heyday rates for per capita output growth, the Tigers lose 3.8 percentage points into the opening quarter of the twenty-first century. The Lions forfeit 0.6 of a point. Judged in this context, the currency crisis may increase the forfeiture a bit—but only a bit. For Hong Kong, of course, reversion poses an additional complication.

Crises elevate the consciousness of scholars and practitioners alike and thereby stimulate thinking in many directions. The Asian situation fosters one line of thought that runs straight to the International Monetary Fund, questioning the organization's conduct as events unfolded.

In a provocative editorial the *Wall Street Journal* (1998) claims that the IMF precipitated the crisis by urging Thailand to devalue when a domestically oriented initiative might have been preferable. Soon, the opinion continues, the IMF stability program became an engine of instability. In the same vein Feldstein (1998a, pp. 22–24, 26, 30; 1998b) raises several criticisms, one being that the IMF undermined the confidence among international creditors by characterizing the threatened nations as incompetent and unsound. Similarly, it insisted upon severe changes in the institutional and economic structures of the countries, and it pressured for excessively restrictive monetary and fiscal policies resulting in higher interest rates and taxes. That such conditions struck ailing nations as onerous is exemplified, adds Feldstein, by the reluctance of Malaysia to summon the IMF cavalry. Jayasankaran (1997, p. 82) concurs in a note whose subtitle, "Malaysia's Worst Fear: A Visit to the IMF," leaves little to the imagination.

But in a spirited defense of strategy, Fischer (1998b), as first deputy managing director of the IMF, responds that the institution's rescue operations were quite appropriate. Bolstering that defense, Camdessus (1998), as IMF managing director, explains the heavy hand of the IMF's conditionality by pointing out that distressed countries often delay in seeking outside help until their situations are too far advanced for treatment by economic aspirin. In those eleventh-hour circumstances, economic surgery is both necessary and appropriate.

Manifestly, the conduct of the IMF in Asia's crisis is a matter of controversy. That controversy, however, tugs on purse strings as it affects the sentiment of Capitol Hill toward post-crisis money requests by the IMF (Raum, 1998). To be sure, the *Wall Street Journal* (1998) is ready with a "no" vote.[13]

Moving in another direction, thinking born of the Asian incident turns to the matter of capital controls. Loosely suggested by Klein (1997, p. 16), though forcefully championed by Krugman (1998c), controls would aim to combat the sudden loss of confidence associated with financial collapses of the Asian type. This form of external heterodoxy, rooted in Keynesian dogma (Cassidy, 1998, pp. 198, 201, 205), stands in marked contrast to the orthodoxy of untrammeled markets and has more than a passing acquaintance with the internal heterodoxy of incomes policy advocated by the Post Keynesians to deal with anticipations. Incomes policy, defined as action designed to provide direct economic incentives to moderate wage and price decisions, seeks to curb inflationary expectations, to break the back of inflationary psychology, and in the end to check the movement of product prices. In corollary fashion, external heterodoxy might strive to temper the psychological swings of international speculators and in the end to check the movement of currency prices; that is, exchange rates. To Krugman (1998c), they would give troubled countries "some economic breathing room."

Not everyone sees merit in external heterodoxy, however. Summarizing both sides of that controversy, Corsetti et al. (1998b, pp.

23–25) identify various arguments made against the strategy: It treats the symptoms rather than the disease, it lends itself to political misuse, it has a poor performance record, and by operating through anticipations, it even may hasten rather than forestall a crisis. Such arguments have a familiar ring as they resemble the criticisms leveled against internal heterodoxy in other forums.

Besides gravitating toward the question of IMF policy and the matter of capital controls, thinking prompted by the crisis proceeds in the direction of further research. At least two lines of additional inquiry might be fruitful. The first involves intensifying the development of an index that might be used to predict future currency catastrophes. A Currency Crisis Index, or CCI for short, might begin with the series identified in Table 8.1; specifically, currency overvaluation, export growth, and trade balance. It also might encompass the extent of foreign debt, the maturity structure of that debt, and the liquidity position of the financial system. Other measures identified by Klein (1997, p. 10) also could be included in the CCI. Just as a country may have a composite index of leading indicators to help predict internal output cycles, it might have a CCI to help predict external currency cycles. The external index even might be made reliable to the point at which it does not "accurately" predict nine of the last six cycles.

The second line of inquiry regards ICOM. As modeled in the previous section, that index ranks country against country. Alternatively, it could be redesigned to focus on industry sectors across countries in the fashion of the productivity analysis for Malaysia by the National Productivity Corporation (1997, pp. 21–22). It also could be tailored to handle individual industries across countries or even individual industries within a given country. In that latter construction the major industries of, say, a Tiger or a Lion might be identified and then ranked in terms of their international competitiveness. Of course, the collection of series behind the index might be reselected as the measure becomes more microeconomic in nature.

When reevaluating the component series of ICOM either in its global country-versus-country format or in a more disaggregated industry-versus-industry form, there may be good reason to consider including information from new survey work. Competitiveness concepts such as quality of product and promptness of delivery are difficult to quantify with data from standard sources. That difficulty could be overcome by specially prepared surveys circulated to appropriate representatives of the government and business communities. Besides, survey data would give ICOM a character of its own; ICOM would become unique.

Like CCI, ICOM has a forecasting dimension. Therefore, it can be used as more than an indicator of international competitiveness. It can be used as a policy guide for countries that are eager to maintain or to expand their presence in the world market. And in the wake of the currency crisis, that endeavor may assume special urgency.

A miracle is an extraordinary event involving divine intervention. Although the growth experience of the maturing nations in the Asia Pacific Region may have lacked divinity and hence may have failed to be miraculous in a literal sense, it definitely was not a myth. It was a reality based on fundamentals: on capital quantity, capital quality, labor quantity, labor quality, international trade, and total factor productivity. Not every determinant exerted the same influence. But together they drove growth, and for some creatures they drove it at a ferocious pace. Asserting that such performance was a fiction founded on bad debts and worthless checks misses facts of an elementary sort.

In economics, extraordinary events can occur without divine intervention. Economic growth in the Asia Pacific Region represents one of those events. That fact, as Sherlock Holmes might say, is "elementary."

APPENDICES

Appendix A

FROM VINTAGES TO AGGREGATES

DESCRIBED RESPECTIVELY IN EQUATIONS (3.19) and (3.20), the aggregate production function and the aggregate stock of efficient capital can be derived from their vintage counterparts. For convenience, the notation established in Section 3.4 continues to hold.

All embodied progress is capital altering; more specifically, capital augmenting. Furthermore, the vintage production function exhibits capital-generalized constant returns that leave, under the Cobb-Douglas,

$$Y_{vt} = \zeta \left(e^{\mu v} K_{vt} \right)^{\alpha} \left(E_t^{\theta} L_{vt} \right)^{1-\alpha}, \qquad (A.1)$$

equation (3.16). By the equi-marginal-product rule, labor is assigned to machines in a way that equates its marginal product across vintages. Thus $\partial Y_{vt}/\partial L_{vt} = N_t$, where N_t is the common marginal product at time t. Since it is the same for each vintage, it has no vintage subscript. Elaborating $\partial Y_{vt}/\partial L_{vt}$ from function (A.1) yields

$$(1-\alpha)\zeta \left(e\mu^{-mu} K_{vt} \right)^{\alpha} \left(E_t^{\theta} L_{vt} \right)^{-\alpha} E_t^{\theta} = N_t, \qquad (A.2)$$

which may be solved for L_{vt} to make

$$L_{vt} = \left(1-\alpha\right)^{1/\alpha} \zeta^{1/\alpha} N_t^{-1/\alpha} E_t^{\theta(1-\alpha)/\alpha} \left(e^{\mu v} K_{vt}\right). \tag{A.3}$$

By equation (3.18) aggregate labor sums labor units employed on all existing machinery; namely, vintages t through t-T. So

$$L_t = \int_{t-T}^{t} L_{vt} dv. \tag{A.4}$$

Substituting result (A.3) into statement (A.4) and factoring out the magnitudes that are independent of the vintage index generate

$$L_t = \left(1-\alpha\right)^{1/\alpha} \zeta^{1/\alpha} N_t^{-1/\alpha} E_t^{\theta(1-\alpha)/\alpha} \int_{t-T}^{t} \left(e^{\mu v} K_{vt}\right) dv. \tag{A.5}$$

The integral in this relation is the aggregate stock of efficient capital J_t:

$$J_t = \int_{t-T}^{t} e^{\mu v} K_{vt} dv, \tag{A.6}$$

equation (3.20). From this definition, relation (A.5) collapses to

$$L_t = \left(1-\alpha\right)^{1/\alpha} \zeta^{1/\alpha} N_t^{-1/\alpha} E_t^{\theta(1-\alpha)/\alpha} J_t. \tag{A.7}$$

Aggregate output, as description (3.17) tells, adds output across vintages; that is,

$$Y_t = \int_{t-T}^{t} Y_{vt} dv. \tag{A.8}$$

Inserting formula (A.1) into sum (A.8) gives

$$Y_t = \int_{t-T}^{t} \zeta\left(e^{\mu v} K_{vt}\right)^{\alpha} \left(E_t^{\theta} L_{vt}\right)^{1-\alpha} dv. \tag{A.9}$$

Then inserting labor equation (A.3) into outcome (A.9) and collecting like items leads to

$$Y_t = \left(1-\alpha\right)^{(1-\alpha)/\alpha} \zeta^{1/\alpha} J_t E_t^{\theta(1-\alpha)/\alpha} N_t^{-(1-\alpha)/\alpha}. \tag{A.10}$$

Specification (A.10) is almost an aggregate production function inasmuch as it relates aggregate output to aggregate inputs. Nonetheless, it misses being a conventional formulation because it contains N_t, the uniform marginal product of labor. That element, however, can be made to disappear.

Equation (A.7) may be rearranged to read

$$N_t = \left(1-\alpha\right) \zeta J_t^{\alpha} E^{\theta(1-\alpha)} L_t^{-\alpha}, \tag{A.11}$$

which may be folded into expression (A.10) to leave after consolidation

$$Y_t = \zeta J_t^{\alpha} \left(E_t^{\theta} L_t\right)^{1-\alpha}, \tag{A.12}$$

the aggregate production function (3.19). Function (A.12) duplicates function (A.1) but replaces the vintage measures with aggregate magnitudes: vintage output Y_{vt} is replaced by aggregate output Y_t; vintage efficient capital $e^{\mu v} K_{vt}$, by aggregate efficient capital J_t; and vintage labor L_{vt}, by aggregate labor L_t.

EFFICIENT CAPITAL: FROM LEVEL TO RATE

IN DERIVING THE GROWTH RATE of efficient capital as represented in equation (3.40) from the level of efficient capital as described in equation (3.21), it is prudent to recall the general formula for differentiating a definite integral (Gapinski, 1992a, p. 291):

$$\frac{d}{dc}\int_{p(c)}^{q(c)} n(z,c)dz = \int_{p(c)}^{q(c)} \frac{\partial}{\partial c}n(z,c)dz + n(q,c)\frac{dq}{dc} - n(p,c)\frac{dp}{dc},$$
(B.1)

where the notation is understood to apply only to the exercise at hand. Put loosely into words, theorem (B.1) says that the derivative of a definite integral equals the integral of the derivative combined with weighted derivatives of the upper and lower limits.

Equation (3.21) has

$$J_t = \int_{t-T}^{t} e^{\mu v} I_v e^{-\delta(t-v)}dv,$$
(B.2)

which immediately becomes

$$J_t = e^{-\delta t}\int_{t-T}^{t} I_v e^{(\mu+\delta)v}dv.$$
(B.3)

From the product rule of differentiation, the time derivative of J_t is

$$\frac{dJ_t}{dt} = (-\delta)e^{-\delta t}\int_{t-T}^{t} I_v e^{(\mu+\delta)v}dv + e^{-\delta t}\frac{d}{dt}\int_{t-T}^{t} I_v e^{(\mu+\delta)v}dv \tag{B.4}$$

or from premise (B.3)

$$\frac{dJ_t}{dt} = -\delta J_t + e^{-\delta t}\frac{d}{dt}\int_{t-T}^{t} I_v e^{(\mu+\delta)v}dv. \tag{B.5}$$

Evaluating the derivative of the integral in equation (B.5) calls upon theorem (B.1). More to the point,

$$\frac{d}{dt}\int_{t-T}^{t} I_v e^{(\mu+\delta)v}dv = 0 + I_t e^{(\mu+\delta)t}(1) - I_{t-T}e^{(\mu+\delta)(t-T)}(1), \tag{B.6}$$

whose right-hand terms are listed sequentially in accordance with the theorem. Consolidation leaves

$$\frac{d}{dt}\int_{t-T}^{t} I_v e^{(\mu+\delta)v}dv = I_t e^{(\mu+\delta)t}\left[1 - \left(I_{t-T}/I_t\right)e^{-(\mu+\delta)T}\right]. \tag{B.7}$$

From result (B.7), statement (B.5) becomes

$$\frac{dJ_t}{dt} = -\delta J_t + I_t e^{\mu t}\lambda_t, \tag{B.8}$$

λ_t denoting the bracketed expression on the right side of step (B.7).

Dividing equation (B.8) by J_t and rearranging components leads to

$$\frac{dJ_t}{dt}/J_t = \lambda_t I_t / \bar{J}_t - \delta, \tag{B.9}$$

for $\bar{J}_t = e^{-\mu t}J_t$. With $I_t = sY_t$ and with $\pi_t = \bar{J}/Y_t$, relation (B.9) reduces to

$$\hat{J} = s\lambda / \pi - \delta \tag{B.10}$$

absent time subscripts. This equation, whose symbol $\hat{J}$ stands for the capital growth rate $(dJ_t/dt)/J_t$, substantiates equation (3.40). In the special case in which capital is infinitely lived, λ reduces to unity, simplifying statements (B.9) and (B.10) respectively to

$$\hat{J} = I / \bar{J} - \delta, \tag{B.11}$$

$$\hat{J} = s / \pi - \delta, \tag{B.12}$$

time subscripts withheld.

NOTES

CHAPTER 1

1. Words such as *country, nation,* and *sovereignty* are used in the loose sense of being synonymous with *economy.* Strict legal interpretations may not apply.

2. Authorities on country taxonomies include—besides K. C. Ho—De Long and Summers (1992a, p. 96), Clark and Kim (1995b, p. 6), and U. S. Central Intelligence Agency (1995, p. 483). In describing ASEAN, the Central Intelligence Agency adds Brunei to the list by Ho, bringing that roster to six countries.

3. A picture capturing Victoria Harbour, the Extension, and Hong Kong Island appears on the cover of this volume. It was shot by the author only days before reversion.

4. Included among the observers preferring a divine interpretation are the World Bank (1993, pp. 1, 8, 26) and Western (1996a, p. 3).

5. Y. Wu (1997, pp. 12–13) confirms the spirit of these results by establishing that China, over the years 1981–95, had its real GDP grow at an average annual rate of 10. 3 percent. The period 1961–90 for China in Table 1. 2 actually pertains to the abbreviation 1979–90.

6. Data for the real wage drill are published by the International Labour Organization, the International Monetary Fund, and the Republic of China in the corresponding references listed in Tables 1. 2 and 1. 3.

7. The Phillips curves in Figure 1. 3 are sketched from data reported by the Asian Development Bank, the International Labour Organization, the International Monetary Fund, and the Republic of China in the corresponding references credited in Tables 1. 2 and 1. 3. The inflation

rate pertains to the implicit price deflator for GDP. Although the curves have not been derived by a formal econometric method, they are suggestive nonetheless. It may be worth noting that 1980 for Korea is treated as an outlier and therefore does not affect the rendering for the 1976–81 period.

Data preparation for the Phillips curves shown in Figure 1. 3 and for those displayed later in Figure 6. 1 was facilitated by Jennifer Platania, who deserves a tip of the bowler for a job well done.

CHAPTER 2

1. Authorities for this record of events are Kerr (1965, pp. 26, 37, 384), Clubb (1978, pp. 24–29, 36–44, 58–61, 103–04, 113–14, 122–31, 136–37, 144–50, 202–97), Grolier (1993), Soled (1995, pp. 4, 7–8, 12, 34–54, 66, 70–72, 85–94, 108–09, 307, 310–11, 324, 335, 338, 362), and R. T. Phillips (1996, pp. 3, 7–14, 119–29, 145–50, 207, 241–50, 254–57).

2. This section of the Panda story appeals to information reported in the following China–specific references: Riskin (1987, pp. 284–90, 316–17, 325–26, 341–49), Salisbury (1989, pp. 3–4, 11, 43–64, 160–61), Hay et al. (1994, pp. 3–13, 228, 321–35, 362–65), Soled (1995, pp. 112–17, 160–73, 196), R. T. Phillips (1996, pp. 255, 270–74), Eckholm (1998, p. A8), Faison (1998, p. A9), and *St. Petersburg Times* (1998, p. 8A).

3. The following Taiwan account comes from material prepared by Kerr (1965, pp. 61, 78, 310, 356–63, 371–77, 381–97); Gold (1986, pp. 44–55, 90–95, 97–99, 142); Hwang (1991, p. 43); Lai et al. (1991, pp. 13–56, 80–121, 141–60); Clough (1993, pp. 146–47); Grolier (1993); U. S. Central Intelligence Agency (1995); Hsiao and Hsiao (1996, pp. 215–30); and Leng (1996, pp. 23–27, 37–54).

4. Authorities on Korea consist of Sohn et al. (1982, pp. 259–66, 329–32); Lee (1984, pp. 283–90, 313–14, 338–45, 373–81); Hoare and Pares (1988, pp. 30–90, 221–23); Grolier (1993); Kim (1995, pp. 220–25, 235–36); and the *World Almanac and Book of Facts, 1995*.

CHAPTER 3

1. Further exposition of the dimensions of progress can be found in Gapinski (1992a, pp. 252–57; 1997b, pp. 600–02).

2. Indices B_t and C_t may be expressed more generally as $B_t = B_O e^{bt}$ and $C_t = C_O e^{ct}$ for arbitrary constants B_O and C_O. The text equates both constants to unity.

3. Inputs besides physical capital could act as vehicles of progress. Labor, for instance, might embody technology, and vintages might be established by the recency of formal education.

4. Fuller exposition of the celebrated beginnings of modern growth theory can be found in Gapinski (1992a, pp. 257–73).

5. The later growth paradigm by Domar (1946) has features akin to those of the Harrod system, and as a result the literature frequently speaks of a Harrod-Domar model. Nonetheless, the two conceptions are different if only in orientation.

6. Additional discussion of the theoretical extensions is given by Hamberg (1971, pp. 211–35) and Gapinski (1992a, pp. 273–76, 287–90, 296–302).

7. Further review of new growth precedents appears in Romer (1994, pp. 13–17) and Jones (1998, pp. 151–52).

8. Drandakis and Phelps (1966, pp. 833–34) obtain the same results. For present purposes restrictions on the elasticity of substitution are ignored.

9. By integration, rate $\hat{\zeta}$ in expression (3. 25) implies that the ζ coefficient in function (3. 19) equals $C e^{(\hat{\zeta}_F F)t}$ for an arbitrary constant C. Behind this link between $\hat{\zeta}$ and the neat exponential form of ζ is the proviso that F be constant. The constancy condition on F can be relaxed by including additional determinants of $\hat{\zeta}$ in relation (3. 25).

10. Basing labor productivity growth shares on the weighted magnitude $\hat{z}$ is preferable to grounding it in the unweighted value $\hat{y}$. Under the $\hat{y}$ standard, the third term in equation (3. 26)—namely, $\alpha(\hat{J} - \hat{L})$—implies that the share due to efficient capital $\alpha \hat{J}/\hat{y}$ may have to exceed 100 percent to compensate for the *negative* contribution from labor quantity: $-\alpha \hat{L}/\hat{y}$. In addition, the $\hat{y}$ standard leaves unsettled how labor quantity growth $\hat{L}$ should be assigned to capital quantity and quality growth in calculating shares. To elaborate, the third term in equation (3. 26) becomes $\alpha(\hat{J}_K + \hat{J}_\mu - \hat{L})$ from decomposition (3. 28), but the $\hat{y}$ norm leaves ambiguous the way that $\hat{L}$ might be split between $\hat{J}_K$ and $\hat{J}_\mu$. Neither anomaly arises with $\hat{z}$ as the yardstick.

CHAPTER 4

1. Summers and Heston (1991, p. 347) suggest that even if capital series had been included, they would not have been of a sort appropriate for

present purposes. That is, they would not have been corrected for embodiment in the spirit of equation (3. 21).

2. In point of fact, partitioning adheres to rules established in earlier work, and consequently there is one (albeit only one) exception to this taxonomy: Malaysia finds itself in Partition 1. Year 1980 provides the benchmark, as it lies at the heart of the data and omits none of the 120 countries being studied. Nevertheless, identical partitioning results from averages taken across all years, although the threshold levels change.

3. Lest prose create confusion, it is advisable to note explicitly that the nine maturing countries are Hong Kong, Korea, Singapore, Taiwan, Indonesia, Malaysia, Thailand, Papua New Guinea, and the Philippines. The four mature nations are Australia, Japan, New Zealand, and the United States.

4. The rate of change in the convergence index is the exponential rate ψ in the expression $CI_t = CI_o\, e^{\psi t}$. It is estimated over the period 1961–90 by ordinary least squares from the logarithmic transformation $1n\, CI_t = 1n\, CI_o + \psi t$. When described in percentage terms, the rate becomes 100ψ.

CHAPTER 5

1. Whether liberty or authoritarianism propels economic growth is a popular question in the literature. Krugman (1994, pp. 62, 65, 76), Swee and Low (1996, p. 2), and Western (1996b, p. 1) attest to its popularity.

2. Values for the structural variables y_o, m, and c together with the partition number can be given sequentially for the 13 Asia Pacific nations. In particular, Hong Kong has $y_o = 4,105$, $m = 0.\,0185$, and $c = 2.\,0$, and its partition number is 1. Korea has 2,244, 0. 0450, 5. 0, 1; Singapore, 5,171, 0. 0175, 5. 0, 1; and Taiwan, 2,339, 0. 0155, 4. 9, 1. Similarly, Indonesia shows 1,605, 0. 1170, 5. 3, 3; Malaysia, 3,461, 0. 0415, 4. 0, 1; and Thailand, 1,582, 0. 0655, 4. 0, 3. Moreover, Papua New Guinea lists 2,074, 0. 1040, 2. 0, 3; and the Philippines, 1,768, 0. 0600, 4. 5, 3. In like fashion, Australia posts 16,296, 0. 0140, 1. 0, 1; Japan, 2,707, 0. 0120, 1. 0, 1; New Zealand, 17,294, 0. 0155, 1. 0, 1; and the United States, 20,152, 0. 0165, 1. 0, 1.

3. A revealing example regarding changes comes from Gapinski (1992b, pp. 2–7; 1993b, pp. 300–03), who uses annual time-series data other

than the PWT magnitudes to estimate an output schedule rooted in the logic of Lucas (1973, p. 327). Fitted to ten OECD countries separately, the schedule produces R^2 values averaging above 0. 980 when postulated in level form but only 0. 281 when posited in change form.

4. Dividing the share of efficient (or total) capital into its quantity and quality components occurs by respective horizontal and vertical movements across the δ and μ parameter map in Figure 4. 2. In computing the quantity share, the procedure begins with homogeneous-shay capital to capture the investment part I_v of quantity and then moves horizontally by increasing δ to capture the depreciation part. From that point it travels north by raising μ to compute the quality share.

5. Analogous maneuvering of the labor productivity shares produces the same results.

6. A more detailed account of Young's findings for Hong Kong and Singapore is left for Chapter 6.

7. This attempt at reconciling results was prompted by Ishaq Nadiri of New York University in his commentary on a paper entitled "Economic Growth in the Asian-Pacific Region," which the current author presented at the Taipei International Conference on Efficiency and Productivity Growth held at Academia Sinica in Taipei, Taiwan, during June of 1997.

CHAPTER 6

1. Data on output growth and labor productivity growth come from Summers and Heston (1993). As regards the real wage calculation, data on the nominal wage in manufacturing come from the *Yearbook of Labour Statistics* published by the International Labour Organization; those on price relate to the deflator for gross domestic product reported in the *International Financial Statistics Yearbook* of the International Monetary Fund. That same deflator is used for the inflation rates in Figure 6. 1. The unemployment rates there are taken from the *Yearbook of Labour Statistics,* and the two-digit numbers in the scatter plots designate years. Curves should be interpreted as rough sketches inasmuch as they are not based on formal analysis. Still, they are consistent with the scatters, and they are suggestive.

2. An informative review of the issues and evidence on TFP in Asia is given by Dowling and Summers (1997).

3. Authorities for the aforementioned historical matters are Endacott and Hinton (1968, pp. 14–32), Endacott (1973, pp. 14–25, 91–93, 109–11, 260–63), Grolier (1993), and Roberti (1994, pp. 43–44). The Palmerston quote is provided by Endacott (1973, p. 18).

4. Happenings connected with the Joint Declaration or with the Basic Law are discussed by Grolier (1993), Roberti (1994, pp. 42, 87, 112–26, 287–92), and Sheng (1997).

5. Examples of the mixed emotions over reversion can be found in Roberti (1994, pp. 125, 133–34, 315–18, 322), Kahn (1997), Sheng (1997), and Stockwin (1997).

6. The effects of reversion on the growth prospects for Hong Kong have been widely discussed. Gapinski and Western (1997) offer an analysis that forms a basis for the next chapter.

7. The foregoing Singapore story draws on the accounts by Backhouse (1972, pp. 8–10, 37–72), Milne and Mauzy (1990, pp. 1–12, 42–76, 86), U. S. Central Intelligence Agency (1995, pp. 379–80), and Turner et al. (1996, pp. 185–87, 239–41, 448–53).

8. The long reach of the Singapore government's visible hand is described by Krause (1988, pp. S53-S54, S62), Milne and Mauzy (1990, pp. 8, 10–12, 63), Young (1992, pp. 15, 23), and Turner et al. (1996, p. 465). Raffles on laissez faire is noted by Milne and Mauzy (1990, p. 43), and positive noninterventionism is discussed by Chiu and Lui (1995, pp. 85–86, 100–03).

9. The elasticity estimates needed to calculate the marginal products of efficient capital from the Cobb-Douglas are obtained through the regression analysis described earlier. Series M_m is computed as the mean of the marginal products of the nine capital types. To calculate the real rate of interest r, the nominal rate is taken to be the six–month time deposit rate published by the Asian Development Bank in *Key Indicators of Developing Asian and Pacific Countries*. The inflation rate is based on the gross domestic product deflator tabulated by the International Monetary Fund in the *International Financial Statistics Yearbook*.

CHAPTER 7

1. Examples of the differing sentiments about reversion can be found in Roberti (1994, pp. 125, 133–34, 315–18, 322), Kahn (1997), Sheng

(1997), and Stockwin (1997). The slogan is attributed to Tung Chee Hwa shortly before he became chief executive of the new Hong Kong. It is found in Tung (1997, p. 49) and cited in Kahn (1997, p. All).

2. Authorities on the deterioration or improvement of the economic situation under reversion include Brauchli (1997, pp. A1, A12), Brauchli and Greenberger (1997, p. A10), Edwards (1997, p. 34), Patten (1997, p. A14), Stein (1997, p. A10), Thatcher (1997, p. A14), and Tung (1997, pp. 48–49).

3. The interviews were conducted by the author along Nathan Road and in the Star Ferry Terminal on Kowloon at the end of June 1997.

4. One analogy with Manhattan is made by Mihaljek et al. (1998, p. 67). Thanks go to Wonhyung Lee for locating the Mihaljek reference and others identified in this section and the next.

CHAPTER 8

1. The exchange between Mahathir and Soros is reported by the *Far Eastern Economic Review* (1998, p. 156) and by Roubini (1998, p. 2).

2. Throughout the analysis James Cobbe and William Laird, colleagues at Florida State University, served as interested and willing mentors while Melik Boudemagh, Wonhyung Lee, and Richard Nay supplied pertinent details along the way. Each merits a hearty round of applause. Applause likewise goes to Peter Kenyon and Harry Bloch at Curtin University of Technology for providing the chance to develop ICOM, the subject of Section 8. 4. It should be noted, however, that the ICOM endeavor was truly a team effort. Noelle Doss offered valuable input on the construction of the index, and her energy together with her knowledge of data banks kept the work moving on a tight schedule. Helen Cabalu, Michael Dockery, and especially Sandra Hopkins volunteered instructive thoughts as well. David Western, a mate of long standing, ran important parallel work and adroitly prepared those results. The ICOM project spanned the globe, and thanks necessarily assume global proportions. Still, blame for errors made at home or overseas rests entirely with the author.

3. Material in this section stems from rather diverse sources. Information on the exchange rates originates from the Asian Development Bank compilation *Key Indicators of Developing Asian and Pacific Countries* and from the PACIFIC Exchange Rate Service (1998); that on interest rates, from OECD (1998, pp. 104–05, 142, 147). Main authorities on

events and dates consist of chronologies by the Associated Press (1998), Duffy (1998, pp. 66–67), OECD (1998, p. 10), Roubini (1998), and Wong (1998). Newspaper accounts include those by Solomon and Goad (1997), Dorgan and Lin (1998), Landler (1998), Mydans (1998a), and Torchia (1998). Also helpful is the Korea Institute for International Economic Policy (1998, pp. 1–5). Additional references appear in the text.

4. The source for Figure 8. 1 and its twin, Figure 8. 2, is Professor Werner Antweiler, University of British Columbia, Vancouver BC, Canada. Copyright © 1998. The images are used by permission.

5. Hong Kong stock prices, by contrast, veered markedly. For instance, the Hang Seng index dropped 23. 3 percent from 13,601. 0 to 10,426.3 over a four-day period in October of 1997.

6. *Moral hazard,* a phrase that is humorously elucidated by Safire (1998), can be traced to the insurance industry of yore and may be defined as distortions brought about by implicit insurance against risk. Under that interpretation it is closely allied with the notion of soft budget constraint considered earlier.

7. A formal model behind this proposition appears in Chang and Velasco (1998b, pp. 6–15). There inequality (2. 14) conveys the central message.

8. Rather independent support for the synthesis view can be found in the account offered by the White House. U. S. President (1999, pp. 237–49) gives that account.

9. The 9.9 percentage-point drop in labor productivity growth for Korea in 1998 is easily consistent with the estimate by OECD (1998, p. 106) of Korea's output growth for that year. The estimate, as the present text observes, equals –0.2 percent, implying a figure of –2.8 percent for labor productivity growth when labor quantity change is taken into account from Table 4.2. Recognizing from the same display the baseline productivity growth to be 6.3 percent leaves growth under crisis at 9.1 points below base. Moreover, starting the exercise from the –1.7 percent estimate by the Korea Institute of Finance (1997, p. 1) for 1998 output growth puts the decline from base at 10.6 points. Thus the 9.9 statistic in Table 8. 2 not only meshes with the estimates by the two outfits, but also it lies between them.

10. The 11 series in ICOM stand against the hundreds behind an international competitiveness index published by the World Economic Forum (1995). Nonetheless, a test involving a preliminary version of ICOM generated a pattern of country rankings roughly the same as

the one produced by the large index. Gapinski (1998, pp. 1–5) reports on that test.

11. ICOM presumes that a high value for a component series signals high competitiveness while a low value signifies low competitiveness. Nevertheless, two series by nature tell the opposite story: high is bad whereas low is good. Those two components are Series 4, exchange rate volatility, and Series 10, the CPI inflation rate. Therefore, they are reversed, prior to any other calculation, by the negative exponential function. That is, $s_{4j} = exp \, (-s_{4j})$, and $s_{10j} = exp \, (-s_{10j}/100)$.

12. This conclusion proves to be rather robust as it holds for alternative weight patterns. ICOM actually was run under four different weight structures, three besides the one considered here; yet regardless of which structure operated, ICOM always positioned Korea, Thailand, and Indonesia at the bottom of the competitiveness scale for 1998 and 1999.

13. More discussion of the controversy surrounding IMF actions in the crisis is provided by Cassidy (1998, pp. 204, 205, 207), Corsetti et al. (1998b, pp. 15–21), Fischer (1998a, pp. 4–5), and Sanger (1998).

BIBLIOGRAPHY

Abramovitz, Moses. 1956. "Resource and Output Trends in the United States since 1870." *American Economic Review* 46 (May): 5–23.

Amano, Akihiro. 1967. "Induced Bias in Technological Progress and Economic Growth." *Economic Studies Quarterly* 17 (March): 1–17.

Asian Development Bank. Economic and Development Resource Center. *Key Indicators of Developing Asian and Pacific Countries.* Manila: Oxford University Press for the Asian Development Bank, various issues.

Associated Press. 1998. "Major Events in the Past Year." *USA Today,* 2 July, p. 3B.

Australian National University. 1998. "The International Economic Data Bank." Computer materials, Australian National University, Canberra, August.

Backhouse, Sally. 1972. *Singapore.* The Island Series. Newton Abbot, Devon: David and Charles.

Bahk, Byong-Hyong, and Gort, Michael. 1993. "Decomposing Learning by Doing in New Plants." *Journal of Political Economy* 101 (August): 561–83.

Barro, Robert J. 1991. "Economic Growth in a Cross Section of Countries." *Quarterly Journal of Economics* 106 (May): 407–43.

———. 1992. "Human Capital and Economic Growth." In *Policies for Long-Run Economic Growth,* pp. 199–216. Edited by the Federal Reserve Bank of Kansas City. Kansas City, MO: Federal Reserve Bank of Kansas City.

———. 1994. "Economic Growth and Convergence." Occasional Papers of the International Center for Economic Growth, No. 46. San Francisco: Institute for Contemporary Studies.

Barro, Robert J., and Lee, Jong-Wha. 1993. "Appendix Tables to 'International Comparisons of Educational Attainment.'" Mimeograph, Harvard University, Korea University, and National Bureau of Economic Research, July.

Barro, Robert J., and Sala-i-Martin, Xavier. 1992. "Convergence." *Journal of Political Economy* 100 (April): 223–51.

Barro, Robert J., and Wolf, Holger C. 1989. "Data Appendix for 'Economic Growth in a Cross Section of Countries.'" Computer materials, Harvard University and Massachusetts Institute of Technology, November.

Bloch, Harry, and Kenyon, Peter. 1998. "The Meaning and Measurement of International Competitiveness." Mimeograph, Curtin University of Technology, August.

Brauchli, Marcus W. 1997. "Homecoming: In Many Ways, Return of Hong Kong to China Has Already Happened." *Wall Street Journal,* 9 June, pp. A1, A12.

Brauchli, Marcus W., and Greenberger, Robert S. 1997. "As Britain Steps Aside in Hong Kong, U.S. Steps In as Chief Western Voice." *Wall Street Journal,* 2 July, p. A10.

Camdessus, Michel. 1998. ["Response to Questions on 'IMF Reforms and the World Economy.'"] Presentation for the World Affairs Council of Philadelphia, Philadelphia, November.

Cassidy, John. 1998. "The New World Disorder." *New Yorker,* 26 October and 2 November, pp. 198–207.

Centre for Economic Policy Research. 1998. "Asia Falling." *European Economic Perspectives,* no. 17 (March): 1–2.

Chang, Roberto, and Velasco, Andrés. 1998a. "The Asian Liquidity Crisis." Working Paper 98–11, Federal Reserve Bank of Atlanta, July.

———. 1998b. "Financial Crises in Emerging Markets: A Canonical Model." Working Paper 98–10, Federal Reserve Bank of Atlanta, July.

Chang, Winston W. 1993. "Commentary on 'Increasing the Saving Rate: An Analysis of the Transition Path.'" In *The Economics of Saving,* pp. 253–61. Edited by James H. Gapinski. Boston: Kluwer Academic Publishers.

Chen, Edward K. Y. 1977. "Factor Inputs, Total Factor Productivity, and Economic Growth: The Asian Case." *Developing Economies* 15 (June): 121–43.

Chiu, Stephen W. K., and Lui Tai-lok. 1995. "Hong Kong: Unorganized Industrialism." In *Asian NIEs and the Global Economy: Industrial Restructuring and Corporate Strategy in the 1990s,* pp. 85–112. Edited by Gordon L. Clark and Won Bae Kim. Baltimore: Johns Hopkins University Press.

Clark, Gordon L., and Kim, Won Bae. 1995a. "Asian NIEs in Transition." In *Asian NIEs and the Global Economy: Industrial Restructuring and*

Corporate Strategy in the 1990s, pp. 252–78. Edited by Gordon L. Clark and Won Bae Kim. Baltimore: Johns Hopkins University Press.

———. 1995b. "Introduction." In *Asian NIEs and the Global Economy: Industrial Restructuring and Corporate Strategy in the 1990s*, pp. 3–21. Edited by Gordon L. Clark and Won Bae Kim. Baltimore: Johns Hopkins University Press.

Clough, Ralph N. 1993. *Reaching Across the Taiwan Strait: People-to-People Diplomacy*. Boulder: Westview Press.

Clubb, O. Edmund. 1978. *Twentieth Century China*. 3rd ed. New York: Columbia University Press.

Conlisk, John. 1993. "Commentary on 'Increasing the Saving Rate: An Analysis of the Transition Path.'" In *The Economics of Saving*, pp. 262–78. Edited by James H. Gapinski. Boston: Kluwer Academic Publishers.

Corsetti, Giancarlo; Pesenti, Paolo; and Roubini, Nouriel. 1998a. "What Caused the Asian Currency and Financial Crisis?" Mimeograph, Yale University, Princeton University, and New York University, March.

———. 1998b. "What Caused the Asian Currency and Financial Crisis? Part II: The Policy Debate." Mimeograph, Yale University, Federal Reserve Bank of New York, and New York University, September.

De Long, J. Bradford, and Summers, Lawrence H. 1991. "Equipment Investment and Economic Growth." *Quarterly Journal of Economics* 106 (May): 445–502.

———. 1992a. "Macroeconomic Policy and Long-Run Growth." In *Policies for Long-Run Economic Growth*, pp. 93–128. Edited by the Federal Reserve Bank of Kansas City. Kansas City, MO: Federal Reserve Bank of Kansas City.

———. 1992b. "Equipment Investment and Economic Growth: How Strong the Nexus?" *Brookings Papers on Economic Activity*, no. 2: 157–211.

Denison, Edward F. 1967. *Why Growth Rates Differ: Postwar Experience in Nine Western Countries*. Washington: Brookings Institution.

Dollar, David, and Wolff, Edward N. 1994. "Capital Intensity and TFP Convergence by Industry in Manufacturing, 1963–1985." In *Convergence of Productivity: Cross-National Studies and Historical Evidence*, pp. 197–224. Edited by William J. Baumol, Richard R. Nelson, and Edward N. Wolff. New York: Oxford University Press.

Domar, Evsey D. 1946. "Capital Expansion, Rate of Growth, and Employment." *Econometrica* 14 (April): 137–47.

Dorgan, Michael, and Lin, Jennifer. 1998. "Pressure On for Suharto to Step Down." Knight Ridder Washington Bureau. *Tallahassee Democrat,* 19 May, pp. 1A, 5A.

Dornbusch, Rudiger. 1993. *Stabilization, Debt, and Reform: Policy Analysis for Developing Countries.* Englewood Cliffs, NJ: Prentice-Hall.

Dornbusch, Rudiger; Fischer, Stanley; and Startz, Richard. 1998. *Macroeconomics.* 7th ed. Boston: McGraw-Hill Companies.

Dosi, Giovanni; Freeman, Christopher; Fabiani, Silvia; and Aversi, Roberta. 1994. "The Diversity of Development Patterns: Catching Up, Forging Ahead and Falling Behind." In *Economic Growth and the Structure of Long-Term Development,* pp. 132–67. Edited by Luigi L. Pasinetti and Robert M. Solow. New York: St. Martin's Press.

Dowling, Malcolm, and Summers, Peter M. 1997. "Total Factor Productivity and Economic Growth—Issues for Asia." Mimeograph, University of Melbourne, September.

Drandakis, E. M., and Phelps, E. S. 1966. "A Model of Induced Invention, Growth and Distribution." *Economic Journal* 76 (December): 823–40.

Duffy, Brian. 1998. "Market Chaos Goes Global: The Troubles Spread to Latin America and Wall Street." *U.S. News and World Report,* 14 September, pp. 64–68.

Eckholm, Erik. 1998. "For Beijing, the Primary Need Is Recognition as a Major Player." *New York Times,* 25 June, p. A8.

Economist. 1995. "The Miracle of the Sausage-Makers." 9 December, pp. 33–34.

Edwards, Mike. 1997. "Hong Kong: Countdown to China." *National Geographic,* March, pp. 32–39.

Endacott, G. B. 1973. *A History of Hong Kong.* 2nd ed. Hong Kong: Oxford University Press.

Endacott, G. B., and Hinton, A. 1968. *Fragrant Harbour: A Short History of Hong Kong.* Hong Kong: Oxford University Press.

Faison, Seth. 1998. "Ex-Chinese Leader Confronts Beijing on 1989 Massacre." *New York Times,* 25 June, pp. A1, A9.

Far Eastern Economic Review. 1998. "Malaysia." In *Asia 1998 Yearbook: A Review of the Events of 1997,* pp. 156–60. Edited by Michael Westlake. Hong Kong: Review Publishing Company.

Feldstein, Martin. 1998a. "Refocusing the IMF." *Foreign Affairs* 77 (March/April): 20–33.

———. 1998b. "Focus on Crisis Management." *Wall Street Journal,* 6 October, p. A22.

Fischer, Stanley. 1998a. "The Asian Crisis and the Changing Role of the IMF." *Finance and Development* 35 (June): 2–5.

————. 1998b. "In Defense of the IMF: Specialized Tools for a Specialized Task." *Foreign Affairs* 77 (July/August): 103–06.

Fisher, Franklin M. 1965. "Embodied Technical Change and the Existence of an Aggregate Capital Stock." *Review of Economic Studies* 32 (October): 263–88.

Gapinski, James H. 1992a. *Macroeconomic Theory: Statics, Dynamics and Policy.* New York: McGraw-Hill.

————. 1992b. "Output, Expectations, and Surprises." Mimeograph, Florida State University, June.

————. 1993a. *The Economic Structure and Failure of Yugoslavia.* Westport, CT: Praeger Publishers.

————. 1993b. "Price Expectations, Adjustment Time, and Policy Effectiveness." *Australian Economic Papers* 32 (December): 299–310.

————. 1996. "Heterogeneous Capital, Economic Growth, and Economic Development." *Journal of Macroeconomics* 18 (Fall): 561–86.

————. 1997a. "Acceleration Principle." In *Business Cycles and Depressions: An Encyclopedia,* pp. 4–6. Edited by David Glasner. New York: Garland Publishing.

————. 1997b. "Technological Change." In *An Encyclopedia of Keynesian Economics,* pp. 600–04. Edited by Thomas Cate. Cheltenham, UK: Edward Elgar Publishing.

————. 1997c. "Economic Growth in the Asia Pacific Region." *Asia Pacific Journal of Economics and Business* 1 (June): 68–91.

————. 1997d. "The Growth of Tigers, Elephants, and Other Metaphorical Creatures under Heterogeneous Capital." *Southern Economic Journal* 64 (July): 147–66.

————. 1998. "Developing ICOM: An Index of International Competitiveness." Mimeograph, Florida State University and Curtin University of Technology, September.

Gapinski, James H.; Škegro, Borislav; and Zuehlke, Thomas W. 1989. *Modeling the Economic Performance of Yugoslavia.* New York: Praeger Publishers.

Gapinski, James H., and Western, David L. 1997. "A Tiger in the Land of the Panda: Growth Prospects for Hong Kong under Reversion to China." Mimeograph, Florida State University and Curtin University of Technology, July.

Gerschenkron, Alexander. 1952. "Economic Backwardness in Historical Perspective." In *The Progress of Underdeveloped Areas,* pp. 3–29. Edited by Bert F. Hoselitz. Chicago: University of Chicago Press.

————. 1962. *Economic Backwardness in Historical Perspective: A Book of Essays.* Cambridge, MA: Harvard University Press.

Gold, Thomas B. 1986. *State and Society in the Taiwan Miracle*. Armonk, NY: M. E. Sharpe.

Green, Richard D., and Doll, John P. 1974. "Dummy Variables and Seasonality—A Curio." *American Statistician* 28 (May): 60–62.

Griliches, Zvi. 1963. "The Sources of Measured Productivity Growth: United States Agriculture, 1940–60." *Journal of Political Economy* 71 (August): 331–46.

———. 1967. "Production Functions in Manufacturing: Some Preliminary Results." In *The Theory and Empirical Analysis of Production*, pp. 275–322. Edited by Murray Brown. New York: Columbia University Press for the National Bureau of Economic Research.

———. 1996. "The Discovery of the Residual: A Historical Note." *Journal of Economic Literature* 34 (September): 1324–30.

Grolier, Inc. 1993. *The New Grolier Multimedia Encyclopedia*. Release 6.

Gwartney, James D., and Lawson, Robert A. 1997. *Economic Freedom of the World: 1997 Annual Report*. Vancouver: The Fraser Institute.

Hamberg, Daniel. 1971. *Models of Economic Growth*. New York: Harper and Row, Publishers.

Harrod, R. F. 1939. "An Essay in Dynamic Theory." *Economic Journal* 49 (March): 14–33.

Hay, Donald; Morris, Derek; Liu, Guy; and Yao, Shujie. 1994. *Economic Reform and State-Owned Enterprises in China, 1979–1987*. Oxford: Clarendon Press.

Hicks, J. R. 1937. "Mr. Keynes and the 'Classics'; A Suggested Interpretation." *Econometrica* 5 (April): 147–59.

Ho, K. C. 1995. "Singapore: Maneuvering in the Middle League." In *Asian NIEs and the Global Economy: Industrial Restructuring and Corporate Strategy in the 1990s*, pp. 113–42. Edited by Gordon L. Clark and Won Bae Kim. Baltimore: Johns Hopkins University Press.

Ho, Lok-Sang. 1998. "The Economy of Hong Kong as a Special Administrative Region of China." *Asian Affairs* 24 (Winter): 227–35.

Hoare, James, and Pares, Susan. 1988. *Korea: An Introduction*. London: Kegan Paul International.

Hopkins, Sandra, and Cabalu, Helen. 1993. "International Competitiveness: A Critical Review of the Concept." Discussion Paper Series 93.05, Institute for Research into International Competitiveness, Curtin University of Technology, October.

Hsiao, Frank S. T., and Hsiao, Mei-Chu W. 1996. "Taiwanese Economic Development and Foreign Trade." In *Comparative Asian Economies*, pp. 211–302. Edited by John Y. T. Kuark. Contemporary Studies in

Economic and Financial Analysis, Volume 77, Part B. Greenwich, CT: JAI Press.

Hsiung, James C. 1998. "Hong Kong as a Nonsovereign International Actor." *Asian Affairs* 24 (Winter): 237–44.

Hwang, Y. Dolly. 1991. *The Rise of a New World Economic Power: Postwar Taiwan.* New York: Greenwood Press.

International Labour Organization. International Labour Office. *Yearbook of Labour Statistics.* Geneva: International Labour Organization, various issues.

International Monetary Fund. *International Financial Statistics.* Washington: International Monetary Fund, various issues.

———. *International Financial Statistics Yearbook.* Washington: International Monetary Fund, various issues.

Jayasankaran, S. 1997. "Anything but That: Malaysia's Worst Fear: A Visit to the IMF." *Far Eastern Economic Review,* 4 December, pp. 82–84.

Johansen, Leif. 1959. "Substitution Versus Fixed Production Coefficients in the Theory of Economic Growth: A Synthesis." *Econometrica* 27 (April): 157–76.

Jones, Charles I. 1998. *Introduction to Economic Growth.* New York: W. W. Norton and Company.

Jorgenson, D. W., and Griliches, Z. 1967. "The Explanation of Productivity Change." *Review of Economic Studies* 34 (July): 249–83.

Kahn, Joseph. 1997. "The Motherland: On Verge of Turnover to China, Hong Kong Taps into Patriotism." *Wall Street Journal,* 23 May, pp. A1, A11.

Kaldor, Nicholas. 1956. "Alternative Theories of Distribution." *Review of Economic Studies* 23 (March): 83–100.

———. 1961. "Capital Accumulation and Economic Growth." In *The Theory of Capital,* pp. 177–222. Edited by F. A. Lutz and D. C. Hague. London: Macmillan and Company.

Kennedy, Charles. 1964. "Induced Bias in Innovation and the Theory of Distribution." *Economic Journal* 74 (September): 541–47.

Kerr, George H. 1965. *Formosa Betrayed.* Boston: Houghton Mifflin Company.

Keynes, John Maynard. 1936. *The General Theory of Employment, Interest, and Money.* New York: Harcourt, Brace and World.

Kim, Jong-Il, and Lau, Lawrence J. 1994. "The Sources of Economic Growth of the East Asian Newly Industrialized Countries." *Journal of the Japanese and International Economies* 8 (September): 235–71.

Kim, Young Jeh. 1995. "Toward a Unified Korea in the 1990's." In *Toward a Unified Korea: Social, Economic, Political, and Cultural Impacts of the Reunification of North and South Korea,* pp. 220–39. Edited by Yun Kim and Eui Hang Shin. Columbia, SC: Center for Asian Studies at the University of South Carolina.

Kiyoshi, Itō. 1998. "China and Hong Kong Are Headed Toward Collapse." *Japan Echo* 25 (June): 38–42.

Klein, L. R. 1997. "Money and Financial Markets in Asian Economies: A Challenge to Asian Industrialization." Mimeograph, University of Pennsylvania, November.

Korea Institute of Finance. 1997. "Korean Economic and Financial Outlook: Economic Growth." Internet materials, http://www.kif.re.kr/forecast2_7.html.

Korea Institute for International Economic Policy. 1998. *Korea in Transition: Reforms Today, Rewards Tomorrow.* Seoul: Korea Institute for International Economic Policy.

Kornai, János. 1986. "The Soft Budget Constraint." *Kyklos* 39 (1986): 3–30.

Krause, Lawrence B. 1988. "Hong Kong and Singapore: Twins or Kissing Cousins?" *Economic Development and Cultural Change* 36 (April, Supplement): S45-S66.

Krugman, Paul. 1992. "Comment [on 'A Tale of Two Cities.']" In *NBER Macroeconomics Annual 1992,* pp. 54–56. Edited by Olivier Jean Blanchard and Stanley Fischer. Cambridge, MA: MIT Press for the National Bureau of Economic Research.

———. 1994. "The Myth of Asia's Miracle." *Foreign Affairs* 73 (November/December): 62–78.

———. 1998a. "What Happened to Asia?" Mimeograph, Massachusetts Institute of Technology, January.

———. 1998b. "Will Asia Bounce Back?" Speech for Credit Suisse First Boston, Hong Kong, March.

———. 1998c. "Malaysia's Opportunity?" *Far Eastern Economic Review,* 17 September, p. 32.

Kulick, Elliott, and Wilson, Dick. 1992. *Thailand's Turn: Profile of a New Dragon.* New York: St. Martin's Press.

Lai, Tse-Han; Myers, Ramon H.; and Wou, Wei. 1991. *A Tragic Beginning: The Taiwan Uprising of February 28, 1947.* Stanford: Stanford University Press.

Landler, Mark. 1998. "Protests in Indonesia Turn Deadly as Police Open Fire on Students." New York Times News Service. *Tallahassee Democrat,* 13 May, p. 8A.

Lee, Ki-baik. 1984. *A New History of Korea*. Seoul: Ilchokak, Publishers.

Leng, Tse-Kang. 1996. *The Taiwan-China Connection: Democracy and Development Across the Taiwan Straits*. Boulder: Westview Press.

Levine, Ross, and Renelt, David. 1992. "A Sensitivity Analysis of Cross-Country Growth Regressions." *American Economic Review* 82 (September): 942–63.

Lewis, Kenneth A., and Seidman, Laurence S. 1991. "The Quantitative Consequences of Raising the U.S. Saving Rate." *Review of Economics and Statistics* 73 (August): 471–79.

Li, Wei. 1997. "The Impact of Economic Reform on the Performance of Chinese State Enterprises, 1980–1989." *Journal of Political Economy* 105 (October): 1080–1106.

Lin, T. B., and Chou, W. L. 1996. "Country Report: Hong-Kong." Mimeograph, Chinese University of Hong Kong, 13 March.

Lovell, C. A. Knox, and Tang, Yih Pin. 1997. "An Alternative Tale of Two Cities." Mimeograph, University of Georgia, August.

Lucas, Robert E., Jr. 1973. "Some International Evidence on Output-Inflation Tradeoffs." *American Economic Review* 63 (June): 326–34.

———. 1988. "On the Mechanics of Economic Development." *Journal of Monetary Economics* 22 (July): 3–42.

McDermott, Darren, and Wessel, David. 1997. "Southeast Asian Banks Contribute to a Bust in the Economic Boom." *Wall Street Journal*, 6 October, pp. A1, A15.

Maddison, Angus. 1987. "Growth and Slowdown in Advanced Capitalist Economies: Techniques of Quantitative Assessment." *Journal of Economic Literature* 25 (June): 649–98.

Manzur, Meher. 1996. "International Competitiveness: Do We Have a Good Measure?" Discussion Paper Series 96.10, Institute for Research into International Competitiveness, Curtin University of Technology, November.

Mihaljek, Dubravko; Husain, Aasim; and Cerra, Valerie. 1998. "People's Republic of China—Hong Kong Special Administrative Region: Recent Economic Developments." Country Report No. 98/41, International Monetary Fund, April.

Milne, R. S., and Mauzy, Diane K. 1990. *Singapore: The Legacy of Lee Kuan Yew*. Boulder: Westview Press.

Mydans, Seth. 1998a. "Suharto Steps Down after 32 Years in Power: Vice President of Indonesia Is Successor." *New York Times*, 21 May, pp. A1, A8.

————. 1998b. "Top Opposition Leader in Malaysia Is Jailed in Sex Case." *New York Times,* 21 September, p. A3.

National Productivity Corporation. 1997. *Productivity Report 1996.* Petaling Jaya, Malaysia: National Productivity Corporation, April.

Nordhaus, William D. 1994. "Final Thoughts." In *Economic Growth and the Structure of Long-Term Development,* pp. 373–75. Edited by Luigi L. Pasinetti and Robert M. Solow. New York: St. Martin's Press.

Organization for Economic Cooperation and Development. *Main Economic Indicators.* Paris: Organization for Economic Cooperation and Development, various issues.

————. 1996. *OECD Economic Outlook.* Paris: Organization for Economic Cooperation and Development, December.

————. 1998. *OECD Economic Outlook.* Paris: Organization for Economic Cooperation and Development, June.

PACIFIC Exchange Rate Service. 1998. ["Daily Exchange Rates per U.S. Dollar."] Internet materials, http://pacific.commerce.ubc.ca/cgi-bin/xrget, July.

Pasinetti, Luigi L. 1994. "The Structure of Long-Term Development: Concluding Comments." In *Economic Growth and the Structure of Long-Term Development,* pp. 353–62. Edited by Luigi L. Pasinetti and Robert M. Solow. New York: St. Martin's Press.

Patten, Christopher. 1997. "How to Keep Hong Kong Rich." *Wall Street Journal,* 21 May, p. A14.

People's Republic of China. *China Statistical Yearbook.* Beijing: State Statistical Bureau, various issues.

Phelps, Edmund S. 1963. "Substitution, Fixed Proportions, Growth and Distribution." *International Economic Review* 4 (September): 265–88.

Phillips, A. W. 1958. "The Relation Between Unemployment and the Rate of Change of Money Wage Rates in the United Kingdom, 1861–1957." *Economica,* new series, 25 (November): 283–99.

Phillips, Richard T. 1996. *China since 1911.* New York: St. Martin's Press.

Project LINK. 1996. "World Outlook: Countries and Regions." Mimeograph, University of Toronto, University of Pennsylvania, and United Nations, 25 March.

————. 1998. "World Outlook: Countries and Regions." Mimeograph, University of Toronto, University of Pennsylvania, and United Nations, 14 September.

Radelet, Steven, and Sachs, Jeffrey. 1997. "Asia's Reemergence." *Foreign Affairs* 76 (November/December): 44–59.

Raum, Tom. 1998. "House Throws Out $18 Billion IMF Request." Associated Press. *Tallahassee Democrat,* 18 September, p. 3A.

Republic of China. *Statistical Yearbook of the Republic of China.* Taipei: Directorate-General of Budget, Accounting and Statistics, Executive Yuan, various issues.

Riskin, Carl. 1987. *China's Political Economy: The Quest for Development since 1949.* Oxford: Oxford University Press.

Roberti, Mark. 1994. *The Fall of Hong Kong: China's Triumph and Britain's Betrayal.* New York: John Wiley and Sons.

Rockwood, Charles E. 1979. "The Antiinflation Value of Direct Controls." In *Essays in Post-Keynesian Inflation,* pp. 161–77. Edited by James H. Gapinski and Charles E. Rockwood. Cambridge, MA: Ballinger Publishing Company.

Romer, Paul M. 1986. "Increasing Returns and Long-Run Growth." *Journal of Political Economy* 94 (October): 1002–37.

———. 1990. "Endogenous Technological Change." *Journal of Political Economy* 98 (October, Part 2): S71-S102.

———. 1994. "The Origins of Endogenous Growth." *Journal of Economic Perspectives* 8 (Winter): 3–22.

Roubini, Nouriel. 1998. "Chronology of the Asian Currency Crisis and Its Global Contagion." Mimeograph, New York University, September.

Safire, William. 1998. "Moral Hazard." *New York Times Magazine,* 20 December, pp. 30, 32.

St. Petersburg Times. 1998. "Chinese Greet Clinton in Tiananmen; Deals Made." 27 June, pp. 1A, 8A.

Sala-i-Martin, Xavier X. 1997. "I Just Ran Two Million Regressions." *American Economic Review* 87 (May): 178–83.

Salisbury, Harrison E. 1989. *Tiananmen Diary: Thirteen Days in June.* Boston: Little, Brown and Company.

Salter, W. E. G. 1960. *Productivity and Technical Change.* London: Cambridge University Press.

Sanger, David E. 1998. "U.S. and I.M.F. Made Asia Crisis Worse, World Bank Finds." *New York Times,* 3 December, http://www.nytimes.com/library/world/global/120398world-bank-review.html, pp. 1–3.

Sato, K. 1966. "On the Adjustment Time in Neo-classical Growth Models." *Review of Economic Studies* 33 (July): 263–68.

Sheng, Andrew. 1997. "Hong Kong Will Remain a Free Market after 1997." *Transition* 8 (April): 1–3.

Siebert, Horst. 1992. "Why Has Potential Growth Declined? The Case of Germany." In *Policies for Long-Run Economic Growth,* pp. 41–55.

Edited by the Federal Reserve Bank of Kansas City. Kansas City, MO: Federal Reserve Bank of Kansas City.

Sinai, Allen, and Stokes, Houston H. 1972. "Real Money Balances: An Omitted Variable from the Production Function?" *Review of Economics and Statistics* 54 (August): 290–96.

Sohn, Pow-key; Kim, Chol-choon; and Hong, Yi-sup. 1982. *The History of Korea.* Seoul: Korean National Commission for UNESCO.

Soled, Debra E., ed. 1995. *China: A Nation in Transition.* Expanded Reference Edition. Washington: Congressional Quarterly.

Solomon, Jay, and Goad, G. Pierre. 1997. "Recession Is Forecast for Indonesia Next Year: Moratorium May Be Needed on Commercial Debt to Stabilize the Rupiah." *Wall Street Journal,* 16 December, p. A15.

Solow, Robert M. 1956. "A Contribution to the Theory of Economic Growth." *Quarterly Journal of Economics* 70 (February): 65–94.

———. 1957. "Technical Change and the Aggregate Production Function." *Review of Economics and Statistics* 39 (August): 312–20.

———. 1960. "Investment and Technical Progress." In *Mathematical Methods in the Social Sciences, 1959,* pp. 89–104. Edited by K. J. Arrow, S. Karlin, and P. Suppes. Stanford: Stanford University Press.

———. 1988. "Growth Theory and After." *American Economic Review* 78 (June): 307–17.

———. 1994. "Concluding Comments." In *Economic Growth and the Structure of Long-Term Development,* pp. 376–79. Edited by Luigi L. Pasinetti and Robert M. Solow. New York: St. Martin's Press.

Stein, Peter. 1997. "Hong Kong Business and Labor Unions, United under U.K. Rule, Now Face Rifts." *Wall Street Journal,* 2 July, p. A10.

Stockwin, Harvey. 1997. "Uniform Mourning for Deng: A Politically Stable China?" *Jakarta Post,* 24 February, p. 5.

Summers, Robert, and Heston, Alan. 1988. "A New Set of International Comparisons of Real Product and Price Level Estimates for 130 Countries, 1950–1985." *Review of Income and Wealth* 34 (March): 1–25.

———. 1991. "The Penn World Table (Mark 5): An Expanded Set of International Comparisons, 1950–1988." *Quarterly Journal of Economics* 106 (May): 327–68.

———. 1993. ["The Penn World Table: Mark 5.5."] Computer materials, National Bureau of Economic Research, Cambridge, MA, 15 June.

Sung, Yun-Wing, and Wong, Kar-yiu. 1998. "Growth of Hong Kong Before and After Its Reversion to China: The China Factor." Mimeograph, Chinese University of Hong Kong and University of Washington, April.

Swee, Goh Keng, and Low, Linda. 1996. "Beyond 'Miracles' and Total Factor Productivity: The Singapore Experience." *ASEAN Economic Bulletin* 13 (July): 1–13.

Tang, Shu-hung. 1995. "The Economy." In *From Colony to SAR: Hong Kong's Challenges Ahead,* pp. 117–50. Edited by Joseph Y. S. Cheng and Sonny S. H. Lo. Hong Kong: Chinese University Press.

Thatcher, Margaret. 1997. "No Regrets." *Wall Street Journal,* 27 June, p. A14.

Torchia, Christopher. 1998. "With New President, Indonesians Are Feeling Freedom to Speak Their Minds." Associated Press. *Tallahassee Democrat,* 27 May, pp. 1A, 7A.

Tung, Chee Hwa. 1997. "Masters of Our Own House." *Newsweek,* special commemorative edition, May-June, pp. 48–49.

Turner, Peter; Taylor, Chris; and Finlay, Hugh. 1996. *Malaysia, Singapore and Brunei: A Lonely Planet Travel Survival Kit.* Hawthorn, Victoria: Lonely Planet Publications, November.

United Nations. Department for Economic and Social Information and Policy Analysis, Statistics Division. 1996. *Statistical Yearbook.* New York: United Nations.

United Nations Educational, Scientific and Cultural Organization. 1997. *UNESCO Statistical Yearbook 1997.* Paris: United Nations Educational, Scientific and Cultural Organization.

United States Central Intelligence Agency. 1995. *The World Factbook 1995.* Washington: United States Central Intelligence Agency.

United States Department of Commerce. Bureau of Economic Analysis. 1993. *Fixed Reproducible Tangible Wealth in the United States, 1925–89.* Washington: United States Government Printing Office, January.

United States President. 1998. *Economic Report of the President.* Washington: United States Government Printing Office.

———. 1999. *Economic Report of the President.* Washington: United States Government Printing Office.

Wall Street Journal. 1998. "The IMF Crisis." 15 April, p. A22.

Western, D. L. 1996a. *The East Asian Miracle: A View from the South.* Perth, Western Australia: San Casa Publishers.

———. 1996b. "The Reality of Asia's Miracle." Mimeograph, Curtin University of Technology, September.

———. 1998a. "Where to Go from Crisis." *Far Eastern Economic Review,* 30 April, p. 31.

————. 1998b. "Causes of the Thai Bubble: Internal or External?" Mimeograph, Curtin University of Technology, June.

Wolff, Edward N. 1991. "Capital Formation and Productivity Convergence over the Long Term." *American Economic Review* 81 (June): 565–79.

Wong, Kar-yiu, ed. 1998. "The Asian Crisis: What Has Happened and Why?" Mimeograph, University of Washington, September.

World Almanac and Book of Facts, 1995. 1994. Mahwah, NJ: St. Martin's Press for the Funk and Wagnalls Corporation.

World Bank. 1993. *The East Asian Miracle: Economic Growth and Public Policy.* New York: Oxford University Press.

World Economic Forum. 1995. *The World Competitiveness Report 1995.* Lausanne, Switzerland: International Institute for Management Development, September.

Wu, Changqi. 1997. "Hong Kong and Greater China: An Economic Perspective." In *Hong Kong under Chinese Rule: The Economic and Political Implications of Reversion,* pp. 114–32. Edited by Warren I. Cohen and Li Zhao. Cambridge, UK: Cambridge University Press.

Wu, Yanrui. 1997. "Productivity Growth, Catch-Up and Convergence in China's Reforming Economy." Paper presented at the Taipei International Conference on Efficiency and Productivity Growth, Taipei, Taiwan, June.

Yoshimine, Koichi. 1998. "Currency Crashes in East Asia: An Empirical Study." Mimeograph, Florida State University, April.

Young, Alwyn. 1992. "A Tale of Two Cities: Factor Accumulation and Technical Change in Hong Kong and Singapore." In *NBER Macroeconomics Annual 1992,* pp. 13–54. Edited by Olivier Jean Blanchard and Stanley Fischer. Cambridge, MA: MIT Press for the National Bureau of Economic Research.

————. 1995. "The Tyranny of Numbers: Confronting the Statistical Realities of the East Asian Growth Experience." *Quarterly Journal of Economics* 110 (August): 641–80.

INDEX